Maria Louisa Charlesworth

England's Yeomen

From Life in the Nineteenth Century

Maria Louisa Charlesworth

England's Yeomen
From Life in the Nineteenth Century

ISBN/EAN: 9783744713627

Printed in Europe, USA, Canada, Australia, Japan

Cover: Foto ©ninafisch / pixelio.de

More available books at **www.hansebooks.com**

ENGLAND'S YEOMEN

BY

MARIA LOUISA CHARLESWORTH

ENGLAND'S YEOMEN:

From Life

IN THE NINETEENTH CENTURY.

BY
MARIA LOUISA CHARLESWORTH,
AUTHOR OF
"MINISTERING CHILDREN;" "THE MINISTRY OF LIFE;" ETC., ETC., ETC.

NEW YORK:
ROBERT CARTER & BROTHERS,
No. 530 BROADWAY.
1864.

PREFACE.

AGRICULTURE has long been one of the fairest features of old England's island life. The open pastures of her farms stretch boldly to her ocean waves, while scattered over hill and valley stand the farm homesteads, each in the midst of its well-cultivated acres, brightening all the fertile land with thoughts of plenty and of peace. The following Tale draws back the curtain from the inner life of one such English farm, that its light may shine to the glory of God, and the blessing of those willing to learn by bright example. He whose inner and outward life it is the chief object of this Tale to portray, said to the writer, unexpectedly to all, at a time when self was lost in Christ, and earth almost in heaven, "If you think that any words of mine can be of any help in strengthening others, use them as if they were your own." This permission being confirmed by his family, the facts of his hallowed life are given. It was a life that in a peculiar way furnishes a personal test, because its advantages were few compared to those enjoyed by numbers who, content to walk by a lower standard, yet think to reach an end as safe, if not as happy. The reader may be reminded that if his individual experience does not furnish like examples of the power of vital Christianity, it is hardly a reason for doubting the existence of such delineations. The divine grace is not weakened by which the saints of the Old and New Testaments walked with God. Of those who doubt the like efficacy of divine grace now, we may ask "Where is the Lord God of Elijah?" "We speak that we do know, and testify that we have seen, to the praise of the glory of His grace, who hath made us accepted in Christ Jesus."

St. Mildred's, Bread Street,
November, 1860.

ENGLAND'S YEOMEN.

CHAPTER I.

"COME, and close the shutters, girl, and light the candle, do! There's more time lost than gained already; 'tis a true saying, 'One loiterer makes many idle men.'"

A stout young woman, of some eight and twenty years of age, came in answer to the call; but before darkening the long wide lattice-window, she opened the farm-kitchen door, and looked into the darkness.

"There now, Christina, girl, shut up," said the venerable woman who had spoken before. "If them away don't look homeward, the looks are but lost ye send after them."

Christiana came in, shut the door, and put up the shutter. It was plain that she stood in that venerable woman's confidence, and, rosy milkmaid as she was, she looked a woman who might be trusted. She lighted a candle, and set it on the little round table, covered with green baize, which stood by the old woman's chair, who, laying down the long stocking she had been knitting in the twilight, drew a needleful of white cotton from the ready-cut skein that hung round her neck, and reaching up a garment from the basket beside her, began to fell down a seam.

"Where's your mistress, Christina?"

"She did but now step out at the back door to listen," Christiana replied.

"Poor soul!" said the old woman to herself, mournfully, "one wandering heart makes another. There's never a fault upon earth but it casts its dark shadow somewhere."

Christiana's mistress came in, and, taking her work, sat down by her mother-in-law's table. She was an active woman of forty, but her countenance more painfully marked by care than was the beautiful face of the old woman of fourscore who sat beside her.

"Where are the lads, daughter?"

"I am sure I don't know, mother. I told them I would not have them out this evening."

"Then send Sam to find them; it will go ill with them one day if they be let to break from the word of their mother."

That mother was silent.

"Christina," said the grandmother, "tell Sam to look after the lads, and bid them come in to their mother."

The eldest son was at home, and came in, but the two younger had strayed off, and were not very easily found.

"I can't think why your father's not home, Ben!"

"Oh, father's never early now," replied the son. "When he once gets from home, one friend and another over-persuades him to step in for the evening, with them; but he'll be back here by night-time, for certain."

"I wish they were *friends*," said the mother, in a tone of sad bitterness; "I can tell him I don't reckon them that."

"Well, mother, 'tisn't easy for father to tell: he thinks well of all the world; he looks only at what lies outside, and that's often pleasant enough."

"Ah!" sighed Esther Northwood, the grandmother, "'tis hard to find a true block in these days; 'tis all plastering they're come to; smooth enough when they've spread it, but of no use, except to make a fair face outside."

"You and I know a true stone, grandmother," said Benjamin, "if ever there was one! And 'tis a wonder that some who pretend to think highly of it don't try to conform themselves to it."

This allusion to some person unnamed, shut up the conversation. The evening drew on; Sam Grist brought home the truant boys, the grandmother folded up her work, Christiana and Sam Grist came in to the family kitchen, Benjamin, the eldest son, lifted the large old Bible from his grandmother's round table to that under the window, and read the evening prayers in his father's place. The serene face of the old woman brightened as she listened: the chapter was Peter's deliverance by the hand of the angel out of prison; but her daughter-in-law's sad heart was absent, the angel light shone not on her, for the words passed by her unobserved. The husband was home before the clock had struck ten, but all the household then were sleeping, except the heavy-hearted wife, Sam Grist, who waited to take his master's horse, and Christiana, who never slept when her mistress was moving.

Time passed on at the farm with few changes, and those not important, until one autumn day brought a visit from the farmer's eldest brother; he was a widower, and had no child; he rented a farm thirty miles distant, and came over occasionally; on this autumn visit he expressed a wish that his eldest nephew should come and make a home with him, and stand second on his farm. He hoped he might then secure the rental of it for him after his own death; he felt the work heavy, and his situation lonely, since the death of his wife. The offer was a good one and kindly made, it could not be refused; but though a good offer, it did not make glad. The father was sorry to part with a son who was his chief stay in the business of his farm; yet ashamed to say so, because he knew that he was in full vigor himself, and his younger sons growing up into serviceable age; so he thanked his brother, and consented. The uncle returned to his farm, and Benjamin was to follow in a fortnight. The father felt dull; he saw the troubled look on the face of his wife; he knew in his heart that the son was better to her than the husband; felt vexed that it should be so; yet he did not care to make the effort of cheering her, but took his horse, and with a coward spirit rode away from the trial, which had he then turned to meet, he might have won back, as a conqueror, his true place in his home. The two boys got away as soon as the farm-tea was over; they were vexed that Ben was going, as it was likely they should have less fun and more work; and no one to stand for them when they got into scrapes. Benjamin stayed within; and his grandmother worked on with that calm steadfast aspect which seemed the only stay left on earth. He did not look at his mother, for he knew she was fretting; he never could bear to see his mother fret, from a boy; he had done all he could to comfort and cheer her; this was the first time that he had been the cause of her tears, and the fact that they were falling for him, made him feel at a loss.

"You see, mother, the distance is not so wonderful long, after all, but what I can often be home."

It was the tender voice of her son, and the poor mother sobbed. The ruddy face of the youth turned white; he went out unnerved; hid away beneath the barn-eaves, he wept the tears of a noble manhood that owned a father's authority, while it broke down at the sob of its mother.

"Master Ben, I say Master Ben," said a voice from behind him, "don't take on so heavy! 'tis the best chance could have fallen for you to get a stand in your uncle's farm housen: he's a man who looks afore him, and holds right on his way; he'll soon see he's got the right sort in you, and what's more he'll set store by it too."

"Oh Sam, my poor mother! 'twas her fretting broke me down; if I were to hear it again, I should be off in an hour, and not so much as say good-bye to a swallow."

"Why you see it fell on her so quick; she, quite unforethinking; and then master turning out because he couldn't stand it. It all goes against her like: but you take a bit of a turn, and not get in, I should say, much afore prayers, and by that, I'm right certain there'll be them words of comfort put to her that she'll not stand against, for my old mistress can speak them all the same as an angel!"

So spoke the faithful servant Sam Grist to the young master he loved like a child. Sam Grist had first come to the farm as yard boy and dairy boy to the mistress, Esther Northwood, before she gave up the house-work to her daughter-in-law. He had his difficulties now in his place, but Sam never thought a rough word from his master, or an act of hard usage, any reason for uprooting himself from the house of his service; he lived on, like the tree of the homestead that bends under the blast, and then rises again, only more firmly rooted than before. And he had his reward.

Benjamin Northwood took Sam Grist's advice, and soon left the farm fields behind him, and stood in the glow of the September sunset on the open common, where the shepherd of the next farm was watching his flock as they grazed the short herbage, before he led them home to their fold for the night. He was an old man, bent with labor: but though his eyes were **seldom** lifted higher than his sheep, his inward sight was ever looking up into heaven, and seeing, like Stephen, the glory of the Lord. The shepherd's dog saw the young farmer, and bounded to meet him. Benjamin Northwood **patted** the dog, who leaped up to caress him; that dog was **a** favorite with one who to Benjamin Northwood was even **more**. than his mother. **The** old shepherd looked round; he had guessed who the friend was, a friend always welcome to him. The young farmer joined **him, and** for awhile both stood silent.

"Well, shepherd, my fate's settled; I'm off in a fortnight to bide with my uncle."

"Oh, be you, **sir?** the poor dog will be sorry; if no one don't miss you, he will! But 'tis a good chance, I suppose?"

"Well, so far as business goes, it is *forward*, but I reckon it *backward* more ways than one!"

"No no, master, not so; we must go the way the Almighty's providence leads, and trust Him with the fears and the hopes left behind we."

"Is your mistress at home, shepherd?"

"Yes, sir, I don't **know** but she be."

"And **Miss Margery?**"

"Yes, sir, I did see her a-gathering her white lily leaves as I passed by, not an hour agone."

"I shall call in and tell your mistress how 'tis settled, I think; good-night."

"Good-night, sir. God bless ye!"

The wold farmhouse stood sheltered in the undulations of the ground, shaded by the only trees that grew thereabouts; its garden lay bright in the sunset, but Margery was not gathering her lily leaves. Benjamin Northwood found the farmer in his front kitchen. Margery, too, was there, steeping her white lily leaves in brandy, and corking them up in small bottles, to heal any wound of knife, or hatchet, or sickle. After some talk of the crops and the weather, Benjamin said he was going to live away with his uncle. The farmer replied he hoped it might prove for the better: no one else said a word.

Benjamin waited awhile, then rose, and shaking hands with the farmer, said, "I wish you good-night, Mr. Penforth. Good-evening, Miss Margery." Margery replied, "Good-evening, Mr. Northwood;" but did not offer her hand, though he had called to say he was going; it was not her custom to do so with any one—yet Benjamin felt hurt. "It is true enough," he said to himself, "I have never seen the world yet: there may be many a one fully equal to Margery, and not standing so high that no one can approach to say a word, but what it is her mind they should say. Where you can't see a chance to be heard, I say 'tis best to forget."

When her son had left the farm-kitchen, his mother wept bitterly on for a time; then her mother-in-law said, "Ah, daughter, we can never so much as lay the dust under our feet with our tears; how then shall they soften the sharp stones that we tread on? better look up to Him who trod the rough way for us, and He will brave up our hearts to follow on after Him."

"Oh, but it looks all so terrible dark!"

"Yes, my poor child, but don't ye know all our comforts on earth are but glimmering candles at best; and there comes a cold mist, and they all burn so dim that we see only the darkness around: 'tis best that we get the Lord's candle to shine on our way, of the which David says, 'He shall lighten my darkness'—'tis the nature of His heavenly light that it shines out the brighter for all the dark that gathers round it below—look up, child, sure enough it is shining for thee!"

That night, when the mother knelt by her bed, she said, in her prayer, "Lighten my darkness, I beseech Thee, O Lord, for the love of thine only Son, our Saviour Jesus Christ."

When the fortnight was ended, Benjamin Northwood drove away with his father to his new home. When he shook hands with Christiana, he said, "Be good to my mother!" no fear but she would, for she had been her mistress's shadow from a girl,—always after her, let her be where she would. Her parents had given her the name of the pilgrim saint, in the hope that she would be like her: they had brought her up accordingly, and now her faithful spirit requited all the care that her parents and mistress had bestowed upon her; and the house of her service had become the home of her heart. Still the young farmer said, "Be good to my mother!"

CHAPTER II.

THE Forest Farm, so called because it was held under the Commissioners of Woods and Forests, had long been rented by the Northwoods. The eldest brother, now its tenant, was a skilful farmer; and Benjamin found his uncle's land under high cultivation. It was pleasant to the young man to stand second in authority over so good a farm. Mr. Northwood had always had his eye upon Benjamin, whose conduct had pleased him well, and he now adopted him as a son. It was not difficult to Benjamin to become as a son to his uncle; he had long made his mother his first care; he had kept at home to cheer her, when he might have found companions glad to welcome him elsewhere; he had thought of a hundred things to please her, and been always at hand for any little service she wanted: it had passed into a saying, "Ben can always find time for his mother!" thus it came naturally to him to render the same filial care to his uncle, whose age and infirmities made him feel all the value of such thoughtful attentions. The old man soon leaned on him in every thing, and Benjamin found himself the chief stay in the home of his uncle, as he had been before in that of his mother.

"I should think I might ride the roan horse across home for a day, uncle, before the days come in shorter?"

"Why, boy, you have been from it no time yet—only three weeks to-day!"

"No, sir; but I thought if I took them first by surprise, it would be apt to make the distance seem less to my mother."

"Yes, yes, boy, by all means; it will cheer up your mother,—and stay a night, if you think she will like it better."

The aged grandmother's words had not fallen to the ground, when the mother's heart was broken at a separate home being fixed for her son. "Sure enough it is shining for thee!" still rested on her thoughts; and, day and night, and many times in the day, she still prayed, "Lighten my darkness, O Lord, I beseech Thee, for the love of thine only Son." She knew something of the love of a son, and she often thought to herself that it was as comfortable a prayer as any she ever heard; it met the want of her heavy, darkened heart; and, though light had not broken in on it yet, it strengthened her up to bear on through the darkness, for the moment the troubled spirit really prays, that moment it ceases to sink.

From the time that she took to saying this short prayer, her grief never broke her down; her tears often fell, but they were more quiet and less bitter; and, when she parted from her son, she took leave of him as that mother should who knows there is a God over all, and believes that He will hear the prayer that is offered through His only Son.

Not many days after Benjamin had left, his mother was riding home from market, for in those days the farmers' wives rode their stout nags to market, carrying their butter, eggs, and poultry. She was crossing the wolds on her way home. Farmer Penforth's old shepherd was there, tending his flocks; he saw Mistress Northwood in the distance, and did what he had never done before, turned from his flock to meet her.

All the country round knew what a son Benjamin Northwood had been to his mother: people spoke of her trouble in the loss of him one to another, but the old shepherd spoke of it to his God; and he now stepped aside to meet her in his sympathy.

"Pray, mistress, did ye hear any tidings of the young master, to-day, in the town?"

"Yes, Benezer," (the old shepherd had been christened Ebenezer, for his mother said the signification of his name should be *praise*, but four syllables makes a long name, so the village people left out the E, and called him Benezer,) "Yes, Benezer; I got a letter at the post; the poor boy writes more words about me than himself."

"'Tis a main opening for him, mistress; all can see that who know how he's minded the commandment that God has blessed with a promise."

"Yes, Benezer, I hold no fears for him, but it's left his mother's heart wholly dark."

"Ah, mistress, the dark, or the light, turns on which way we look! 'Twas but now I was minding them words, 'They looked unto Him and were lightened, and their faces were not ashamed;' for you see, yesterday my master thought I'd done wrong in regard of the sheep, and I could not show him to the contrary of that, and things had fallen out wrong at home, and I felt wholly cast down; but I lifted up a prayer to Him that's always a caring for me, and He lightened down a smile, and the dark couldn't stand that! Oh! 'tis wonderful when we get our light clear down from Him that's above all the darkness; we've enough and to spare so to speak, and we don't want to go begging at any poor creature's door for the comfort they ben't minded to give us. We can wait their ill-convenience with patience, and take a pleasure in showing them the best of good will, till it please the Lord perhaps they come round again more right than before. Poor Job's heart was after that way; he knew where the light lay when he said, 'Where is God my maker, that giveth songs in the night?' He knew right well that there was One who could give a song in the darkness, and he had it too when he prayed for his friends who had interfered so with him in his trouble! And see how it turned out with him in the end! And sure there will come a cheerly morning for we, if we look above the darkness to Him who is Lord of the light."

Mrs. Northwood thought upon the good words she had heard. Sometimes she prayed for light, sometimes for "a song in the night;" her prayers were very short, but they were the earnest desires of her heart. A change came over her spirit, she felt humbled instead of angry at trouble, and ready to listen and be taught like a little child. And a hope began to spring in her heart of a comfort beyond any thing earthly, a hope of heavenly comfort, of sin forgiven and peace with God, for the love of His only Son.

One day all had gone wrong at the farm, and the poor mother's heart failed. Still she said in her tears, 'Lord, lighten my darkness, I beseech Thee, for the love of thine only Son.' Then she thought of Benezer, and how his discourse before had done her good. She did not say a word to any one, but she put on her bonnet and shawl, and stepped out on the wolds. She felt glad when she saw old Benezer leaning upon his staff in the distance, his flock feeding before him; and she wondered that she had known him so many years, and yet never heard what comfortable words he could speak to a troubled soul before. The old man saw her coming, and turning his face to welcome her, said, "Good-day, mistress."

"I came out to speak a word to you, Benezer, for it seems to me the darkest day yet since Ben left."

The old man looked at her with a smile, and replied, "Oh, never fear, it won't bide so dark long. I met the GOOD SHEPHERD this way in the morning, so 'tis plain he is thinking of we!"

"Did you?" asked Mrs. Northwood in surprise.

"Yes, I got into terrible trouble with the lambs, as I was feeding them alone on a small bit of clover. There was thirteen of them I was afraid would be dead altogether. I couldn't help shedding tears in my trouble, and I prayed the Good Shepherd to lend me His help, and sure enough I found he was there, ready to save; so the smile came pretty quick on the tear. And though your trouble may be different, 'tis all one to He. He do lighten them that look to Him! let the trouble come which way it will."

Mistress Northwood went home with the feeling that the "GOOD SHEPHERD was near," and could help; yet she thought in her heart that no one but Ben could put the crooked things straight in her home. And when she turned in at the farmyard, Ben stood at the door looking out for his mother, come home on his unexpected visit. Then the mother felt what a true word it was—"They looked unto him and were lightened." And she longed to step back and tell Benezer what comfort she had found, for surely the GOOD SHEPHERD had sent her son home to her that day."

Benjamin was struck with the expression on the face of his mother; it seemed to him that she had caught a look from his grandmother; he did not know what it was or how it came, but it made his home visit happy, and cheered up his leaving again.

Time passed on, and Benjamin reached his twenty-first birthday; he returned home for a week's visit, and his mother invited a party of their friends to celebrate her son's coming of age. Farmer Penforth and his wife, and Margary, were of the number. Benjamin had seen more of the world, but he had seen **no** one like Margery, and he had found out that no one unlike her could ever seem right to his mind. And truly Margery was no common woman. In person she **was** tall and strong, with large full features, a dark penetrating eye, and lips that looked **as if** they never spoke a **word** that was not absolute. **Though** her manner **was reserved and** cold, yet she had long been one of Benjamin Northwood's best friends, for she was wise above her years, her principles were unyielding, and she always spoke her mind, truth standing first of all things in her youthful esteem. And, though her words and tone were apt to be severe, her heart was as kind as it **was firm.** Whatever opinion or feeling Benjamin heard her express became a law to him; the three earthly guardians of his life **had been** his saintly grandmother, his filial obedience to his mother, and his reverence for Margery. Margery stood high in the opinion of all the neighbors. The elder people seemed to consider something wanting in the honor due to them if Margery were not present at their festivals; the younger always wished to ask her, yet when she came often felt her presence a restraint. None were quite indifferent **to** her censure, and all valued her praise. She had a high morality, a natural dignity of character, strong integrity, and self-respect. Yet these qualities alone could not give her a heavenly life; they are earthly, and could not themselves raise her spirit or her influence higher than earth. But we cannot tell what Margery even then held in the secret of her silent soul, for she never told its deepest feelings to any one. To the distant observer Margery stood firm and strong, like some white marble rock, on which a sunbeam might play, or a bird light in passing; rather than like the sheltering tree where the wild bird builds her nest, and the timid squirrel makes his wintry home, and the tired wanderer seeks refreshment and rest. And yet, while it is true that to see Margery was to remember her, it is equally true that to know her was to respect her, and to live with her was to love her.

It certainly would not have been easy for Benjamin to find another, in natural character, equal to Margery. And, instead of forgetting her, each month of his absence had but made him think more highly of her character and worth.

He had not spoken to any one on this subject; he had thought that even if Margery answered kindly, which he very much doubted, his uncle might be hurt at his making an engagement, therefore he had kept his strong feelings to himself, and said nothing. But, now his longer visit at home, and all the sense of manhood that came upon him when his twenty-first birthday was kept, proved too strong for his resolution, and he thought that at least he would speak to his grandmother. She was always the first person he had consulted from his childhood, because there was a stay in her clear firm words that he felt he could trust to. The day following his birthday, when alone in the farm-kitchen with his grandmother, after watching, or seeming to watch, her quiet stitches for some time, he said—

"I suppose, grandmother, now I am of age, I shall have to think about getting married some day?"

"Ah, lad, take time and thought in the forecasting of that; 'tis hard work to pull against the noose when your foot is fast in it!"

"That's what I have done, I'm sure I couldn't say for how long; but it always turns up the same name,—and that's Margery!"

This sudden declaration was made not without effort, and the aged grandmother heard it with evident feeling; she looked up, took off her spectacles, and laid them down on the table, a rare sign of fixed attention and interest; she said nothing, but silence was now out of the question, so her grandson went on.

"I don't believe there is a young fellow all the country round with better prospects than I have to look to; but Margery stands so right up and high! Sometimes I have thought I would get father to tell her my prospects before I said a word; but then, dear me, in a minute I think that would be the death of it."

"You may rest certain, lad, Margery's never the woman to think on the store before she thought on the man."

"Then, grandmother, if I could get some one to speak

a word up for me? These two years I've been living away now, and 'tis like Margery may not know how steady I've kept. I have never so much as showed once at a hunt, unless my uncle had a horse for the gentry to buy, since I heard her say it was 'worse than idleness in them that were born to lay the land like a garden, to race over it and not leave it fit to be seen!' And she was right enough; for you'll see a gentleman often take the headland all round the field, on a horse that would scarcely cut up a blade, and make his servant ride after him; while the farmers, with a rough colt for a hunter, will ride over the best land ever planted, until you are ashamed to look at it after them, with no game in chase neither. Margery might well say 'such farmers were not worthy the plough!' If she did but know it, there's not a man the country round can lay a furrow to mine! I wish enough the gentry would get the young farmers to plough before them, instead of to hunt after them, then there would be some trying for skill in the land."

"Take my advice, lad, never use another's tongue when the work belongs to your own. You have made up your mind; tell your parents what you are after taking in hand, they could wish you no better; then put it plain to Margery, and God prosper your way!"

"But, grandmother, if Margery says No!"

"Well, lad, if she says it, it must stand; her first will be last. But 'tis written in the Book, 'A prudent wife is from the Lord.' There's none can doubt that Margery is prudent enow; ask her then of Him who has the right in His hand, and very like, when you come to it with Margery, she will not stand against you."

As Benjamin turned away, he said, "You can try that way too, for me, grandmother."

Suspense now seemed impossible to him: that evening he once more crossed the wolds, and found Margery in the garden alone. He thought she stood cold and high as ever, while he told her his heart; but when she spoke he heard the deep feeling in her tone as she said, "You can say what you like to my parents, Mr. Northwood; for my part, I shall never stand against trusting the man that has been such a son to his mother!"

That evening the parents on both farms were glad, and the aged grandmother thanked God; and the old shepherd, and Sam Grist, and Christiana said it was a good hope for many; and truly generations then unborn were to be made glad in the blessing that fell on the home of those young hearts that evening made one.

CHAPTER III.

BENJAMIN'S uncle was not in any way displeased when he heard of his nephew's engagement; he knew Margery by report, and the old man said it pleased him well that one who was worthy should stand in the place of his poor wife, and be mistress where she had ruled so long. He told Benjamin that he should never be the one to hinder such a prospect, for he was ready at any time to receive Margery as a daughter. And this kind feeling would probably have hastened the marriage, but a sickness fell suddenly on the old man; he was tended by his nephew, who waited on him like a son; but after a few days' illness he died, and Benjamin was left alone in the farm. The young man was allowed to continue in his uncle's place; but when this was decided, many other things had to be looked into and settled before he could claim the hand of Margery as his bride. He made frequent visits home; they were visits of only one night, because business pressed for a time; but he always made the way longer by riding round to the wold farm in coming and returning. By degrees all his farm difficulties were settled; one day, on returning home, after having had a long talk with his father, whom he met on the home farm, and with his mother in her dairy, he came in as usual to look for his grandmother, whom he generally found seated in her oaken chair in the kitchen, with her busy needle in her hand, or reading from the large Bible which always lay on the round table before her. On this day she was sitting there as usual, in the calm of her venerable age. Her grandson accosted her by saying—

"Well, grandmother, Tuesday's the day!"

The old woman understood, and looking up at her grandson, she said fervently, "The Lord that made heaven and earth, give thee blessing out of Zion!"

"Amen!" he said, softly; then sitting down beside her, he asked, "To be sure you will come to our wedding cheer, grandmother? Margery charged me to say, she hoped enough that you would, she always has taken wonderful count of you."

"Ah, lad, no! you may tell Margery she has my blessing, when she stands up as your bride, afore any one living, but I've done with earth's feasting; 'tis all very well for them it belongs to, but not for one who, like me, has only to wait by the doors till it may please God I enter into the marriage supper of the Lamb!" Then, after a moment's pause, she asked, "Who's to taste of your cheer?"

"Who, grandmother? Why, all the friends that can come; and Margery will have nothing but what's made in the house. She says she will have none of their new-fashioned ways of running off to a shop, as if wedding folks had no senses left them to do for themselves."

"Have ye thought on the poor?"

"Well, grandmother, I'll answer for it Margery has. I am sure, next to you, there's no one has stood such a friend to the poor. All the labourers say they would rather by far lose the doctor than her, she has such a hand for binding up wounds; and there's hardly a woman in the parish, I've heard them say, who has not, some time or other, been the better for her care."

"But, lad, have you thought on the poor? 'Twill be no use for you to stand on Margery's footing, when you have to answer for yourself to Him who has bid you remember them."

"I hope I've not been bad to them, grandmother; but I don't know that I've thought of them now."

"Then hear what it says in the Book; it gathers all together there plain enough, where 'tis written, 'Eat the fat, drink the sweet, and send portions for them for whom nothing is prepared.'"

"Well, I never heard that before!"

"Ah, lad, how should ye? When ye take more delight in turning up a straight furrow out of the earth of which ye were made, than in looking after a line of that Word that was given to new-create ye for heaven."

"I don't slight it neither, grandmother. I've bought a family Bible for Margery; I know she would never set foot in the house unless I laid in a Bible. And I had not forgot it neither; but one scarce ever sees it away from home here, except on Sunday at church, and by that it gets out of one's thoughts."

"Ah!" sighed the old woman, "would to God that Bibles were plentiful all over the land, that each babe might be born to one, and call it its own."

"Well, grandmother, I mean to get a book of family prayers, and do as we do at night-times at home. I know Margery's mind lies that way. And I'll ask mother for a suppering up here for our people. Christiana will see after that."

On "Tuesday," at the home of the bride, the wedding guests assembled. To the home of the bridegroom came the poor; the long tables were set in the back kitchen for the labourers on the farm, and their wives and such aged people as the venerable Esther Northwood had a special respect for. The beef and plum puddings appeared and disappeared; and the time came for all to drink the health of the bridegroom and the bride. Then Christiana hastened to tell her aged mistress that the time was come for her to make her appearance, as the one representative of the family. The venerable woman rose up, and, supported by her staff, entered the back kitchen. She wore that day her gown of best black stuff, her high white mobbed cap, and her full kerchief— excelling in whiteness. She had no skein of cotton over her shoulders that day, nor was even the sheath of her knitting pin by her side, for that day was a Sabbath to her.

The men rose and bowed low when she entered, the women rose and curtsied; and she said, in her kindly tone, "Good welcome, and good cheer to ye all!" Then the man who had stood king of the reapers that summer, first lifted up the brimming mug of brown ale and said, "Good health to ye, mistress!" Those were days when the aged were reverenced, so the king of the reapers first spoke of the mistress whom he had served when a boy, saying, "Good health to ye, mistress, and thanks for our suppering; and good health, and long life, and God's blessing on the bridegroom and the bride!" Then all the men lifted their mugs and repeated, "Good health to ye, mistress; and good health and long life, and God's blessing on the bridegroom and the bride;" and then, having drunk, each gave his mug to his wife, the women being silent because their husbands had spoken for them.

The venerable mistress stood before them, leaning both hands on her staff, and replied, "Thank ye! thank ye all!" Then looking round on the faces before her, most of which she had known from their childhood, she said solemnly, "There's a Bridegroom a coming for ye! Are ye all making ready? The call may come at an hour when ye think not; are ye ready to go out and meet Him? Have ye all washen your robes and made them white in His blood? Is your light shining ready? Look into your hearts, 'tis in them the oil must lie that's to make your light shine. Look each one to his own heart! Do ye love the Lord who died for ye? Do ye fear to sin against Him? Do ye try to please Him? Yo know what I say; I've told ye before. Now I charge ye, stand ready that ye may all enter in to the marriage supper above, before the door of mercy be shut; for if once that be shut before ye are safe in, be ye sure ye will never see it turn again on its hinges to open for ye! Pray God ye be all found ready! And be sure ye think on the young ones that stand wedded to-day, and give them a prayer on your knees to the God of mercy to-night. Let your women and the old folks come in to me, when ye go. God bless ye!"

She left them with the traces of feeling on each face.

After a while the wives of the labourers and the old people came in and gathered round her as she sat in her oaken chair in the kitchen, and she gave to each one some garment made by her hand, and kept in store for this day. And as she gave them she spoke a good word with each. While Christiana stood at the door, and as she afterwards confessed, "kind of hurried them out," for she said it seemed to her that her mistress must be almost already in heaven, to hear her speak to each one as she did.

When the poor people were gone, the aged mistress said, "Now, Christina, you get up a little of that old elder wine, and make a sip of toast to put in it, and heat it up, and I'll have a cup of it, and you and Sam have one too, and we'll drink to the health of the bridegroom and bride, and then I'll go to my bed, and get an hour or two's rest before the young folk come home, for I can't stand any more." The old woman herself read the chapter that night, with only Sam Grist and Christiana; it was early for evening prayers, but whenever she was left alone she always had them early, for she said, when the thing could be ordered so, she did not want to wait for a head heavy for sleep before she turned attention to that. This evening she could not read long, so she chose the first parable from the twenty-fifth of St. Matthew, and because her tired eyes could not see the small print of the book of prayer, she folded her hands on the open Bible and made her own supplication, in which Sam Grist and Christiana both joined with true feeling. Then the old woman went to her rest, and the Angel of Mercy watched over her.

Many bridal gifts had been presented to Margery, and not a few to Benjamin. Farmer Penforth had given a flock of sheep to his son-in-law, and his own father had enriched him with young kine and colts; poultry and household gifts had also been given. The whole array was started very early by Benjamin on the morning of the wedding day, that they might reach his distant farm on the evening of the next day, when he hoped to return with his bride. The day after the wedding a family breakfast was given, and at this the aged grandmother was present. Then followed the farewell—it could not fail to be touching when such a son and such a daughter took leave of both father and mother. Not one word did Margery speak. To have tried at that first and final "Good-bye" to all the home of her youth would have broken her down. Her lips trembled, yet she tried to keep firm, for all around were in tears. She took her leave last of the venerable grandmother, and stood before her a moment as if she expected that a blessing would fall from her lips. Esther Northwood breathed it forth on her "children," as she called them; and, at the sound of that heavenly blessing, Margery's restrained feeling flowed freely. The farewell was over. She saw nothing around her, not even the old shepherd, who had left his sheep with a keeper, and stood watching beside the garden wall to see his young mistress go off. Benjamin saw the old man as he passed out, gave him the farewell look of a friend, and heard his "God bless ye!" As Margery stepped up into the gig, she dropped a rose that Benjamin had gathered for her that morning from the garden borders of her home; she had placed it in her bosom—the first and last time she was seen to wear a flower—but unused to such additions to her dress she had not fastened it in, and it fell, unobserved by any one except the old shepherd. Benjamin drove off much faster than usual, for he said he never felt more afraid in his life lest Margery should say she could not go, so unused was he to see her calm strength broken down with the heart's deep emotion. While all were watching the gig fast disappearing in the distance, the old man came forward and picked up the flower, and taking it home to his wife he made her stitch it fast in the band of his broad-brimmed shepherd's hat, saying, " I will wear it there till I see the face of my young mistress again."

A long drive at last brought them to the summit of a hill, and Margery saw her new home lie before her, all its rich fields and woods, its homestead and farm stacks. She heard the bleating of the flock, that had been sent by her father from the wolds round her home, and with the sound came that sense of the severed tie of a life, that the heart has to summon its best strength to withstand. Benjamin took his bride into his home, but then had to leave her there alone a little time, while he hastened before dusk to see the cattle safe for the night, after their two days of travel. Phœbe—the same servant who had lived with the old master—had made all things in cheerful readiness within. But Margery stood alone at the lattice window of her chamber, for her strong heart was full of mingling emotions. She looked to the left of the farm, back on the road that had brought her so far from her home; to the right where, over long meadows rich with foliage, the sun was sinking in glory; on the valley before her, the brook that glided through it tinged with the sunset, the little bridge over it, guarded at either end by a tree that stood like a sentinel, the open passage of the brook for carriages and cattle, with its rough stepping-stones, the steep verdant slope that rose beyond it to the high road above, and the old church tower. How fair lay the scene in that calm evening hour! almost too calm for Margery at that moment. Oh, could the years to come have then opened in vision before her!—The feet of childhood treading the green turf, of youth, of manhood, all her own! The knees low bent in prayer, the study of the Holy Word, the voices raised in praise, the music of her home, the feet of the poor that from far and near would cross her threshold stone, the many of every age and station that would ascend her home's green hill and look in love upon it, could Margery but have seen in that calm evening hour the bright, the blessed throng, it might, it almost *must*, have broken the silent spell around her heart, and poured it forth in magnifying praise!

CHAPTER IV.

THE Rectory of the village to which Benjamin took his bride was in the gift of a college, and being a valuable benefice, it was generally accepted by one of the senior fellows. "Multitude of years should teach wisdom," but yet "great men are not always wise, neither do the aged (always) understand judgment." Those who through the greater part of their life have been shut out from the active struggle of the world, separated from the ties of a family and household, and from all the social influences that a parochial ministry gathers around them, may well find it difficult to be "nursing fathers" to their people—difficult to dwell amongst them "as a nurse that cherisheth her children." Yet it is sometimes found that the heart has kept its sympathies ready for the call, and the senior fellow of a college has left its walls to become the friend of the poor man, the instructor of babes, and the teacher of the ignorant. And so it was when Margery first came to her home. She looked with joy upon the aged clergyman who entered her dwelling, the day after her arrival, to bid her welcome as mistress of the Forest Farm. His venerable aspect, the grace of his courtesy, and the benignity of his countenance, made Margery say, as he left, that it was the best sight she had seen yet! On Sunday, when the bell tolled for service, the people came flocking from every cottage and farm, in their clean and bright Sabbath garments; but the prettiest sight of all was to see them in groups crossing the Rectory pasture. The green pasture lay stretched like a lawn beyond the Rectory garden, in full view of its windows; a stream ran all down it, in whose banks the kingfisher built his nest of small bones, soft as down; and fine trees grew around it—the pastor's trees, therefore no feller rose up against them; and one little path lay across it, leading straight from the village to the old church on the hill. It was a sight dear to the pastor to see fathers, mothers, and children slowly crossing the path through the green pasture to worship their God; he would put on his robes for the service, and with his staff in his hand and his daughter beside him he walked up with them to the sanctuary. They passed silently on, but many a child stole a look up at his face, sure to win some kindly notice in return.

There were no Sunday schools in those days as now, to make all the land glad in its Sabbath morning rest, with the feet of little children on every side treading lightly and quickly on their way to the Sunday school, whispering to themselves the holy texts or the hymn that if repeated perfectly would win a smile from the teacher. This sunshine of Sabbath schools had not then lightened the land; but the children of each parish stood up before the desk and were catechized by the clergyman. In those days, when this world's work did not press so heavily as it does now, attention on Sunday did not grow weary so quickly, the poor liked to listen to the questions asked by the clergyman, and to hear their children answer; and the parents and children both learned together. But the Bible was then a rare book; it cost, for the most part, gold to buy it, and it was only here and there a poor man or woman could read. All looked to their clergyman for teaching: if his heart were dark, then ignorance and sin grew around; but if the clergyman were a burning and a shining light in the midst of his people, then it was as with John Baptist in the wilderness, "many for a season rejoiced in that light;" as did Benjamin and Margery when they entered on their home at the Forest Farm.

The farm fields and woods lay scattered over hill and valley; it was a beautiful landscape then, abounding in wood; the parish took its name from the magnificent trees that grew in it, and three fair woods crowned the hills upon Benjamin's farm. Benjamin had a true heart for nature, and a tree was a more beautiful object to him than it is wont to be in the eyes of a farmer. The stream that flowed through the valley, in which the farmhouse then stood, turned its course abruptly to the left, and murmured on through deep banks to the level ground of the valley again. These deep banks of the stream looked bare and unclothed to the young farmer's eye, so now that he stood master of the farm, he planted young trees, with his own hand, the whole length of the steep bank— oak, ash, and elm; and there they still stand untouched in their beauty, save now and then when a strong wind brings a noble tree down to the ground; they rustle still in the breeze of the summer, with the green turf below them, leading the eye along their line of varied foliage to the gold, the rose and purple of the sunset sky.

The farmhouse had long been falling into decay, and the following spring Benjamin made preparations for building a new one.

"I suppose we can't do better than build on the same ground again?" said Benjamin to Margery.

"To be sure you won't go and build again on the hill-side, when its top lies all open before you?"

"But the out-buildings, you see, must stand on for a time, and to be up there above them I'm afraid won't be handy."

"Let them stand while they can," replied Margery, "I'll answer for it, it won't be for long; and 'tis better for you to look down on your farm than up to it, I am sure, any day."

So the site for the new farmhouse was chosen on the very summit of the hill, where it looked over the fair valley and the green and wooded hills beyond it. The rooms were built higher and larger than was usual in farmhouses at that time, and wherever it was possible, Margery would

have a window. She needed no philosopher to teach her
the value of both air and light; she drew her inferences
from nature, and these inferences were as unyielding as
nature's own facts. "Let the light and air come and go,"
said Margery, "as it pleases Heaven that they should, and
don't think to be better off for stifling up in the darkness." The new garden was laid out down the slope of
the green hill; one straight gravel walk like an arrow
reached on to the end, kept level as far as possible, then
broken by small wooden steps; grass-plats lay on either
side in front of the house. Beyond were arbors, and
arched ways of twisted laurel and seringa with honeysuckle intertwined; and below these grew the flowers in
small beds, so arranged that it was impossible to go over
all the little paths in between them without treading over
some of the little walks twice. In them white lilies grew
up in abundance—great peonies also looked imposing in
such extremely small beds; winter cherries, sweet pinks
and carnations, and large bright polyanthuses, grew beside
still gayer anemonies. Margery said, "Plant the flowers
and have done with it; what's the use of hunting up the
new things that can live but a year, when you may have
all the old ones that do better for standing?" Beyond
the flowers grew a large supply of both vegetables and
fruit; and it was Margery's refinement to have rose-trees
planted down on either side the straight walk between
the vegetables and fruit, that when you went on to gather
fruit you might have the flowers still beside you. Beyond

lay a fish-pond, dug out in a curious device; and farther still, the green orchard stretched down to the stream. Such was the new home of Margery. There came one trouble to Margery in building the house higher, and this was leaving the roof-tree in its solitude below. It could not overcome her wish for the hill-top, still she said she felt sore loth to forsake it; it was a fine tree, with widespreading branches, and when all the buildings were gone, that household tree looked so desolate to Margery's eye that she sometimes was ready to wish that they had never moved the homestead away from its side.

On market days Margery rode her good horse to the town. Her saddle, almost without pummel, was of white cloth embroidered, strong and well made, to last on to after generations, as household things did in those days.

This first spring, while the house was building, Margery went for two days to her home on the wolds. Benjamin drove her over, but he could not be long absent himself from the workmen. She felt more impatience, than she perhaps had ever felt before, as she first saw those familiar wolds break on her view; but when she had seen the dear faces of her parents again, and made them promise to come over when the new house was built, her staid heart was satisfied, and she told her husband she had more than half-a-mind to go back that same day with him. But he objected to this, said his own mother would be hurt, and his grandmother disappointed, if she left without seeing them: so he returned home without her:

and towards evening Margery crossed the wolds to look for Benezer, on her way to her father-in-law's farm. The old man hastened to meet her; "dearly glad" he said he was "to see her on them wolds again." His first question was for the flock he had picked out for her farm, and how the young lambs had thriven; and he told her how at nighttimes when he left his flocks folded, and prayed the GOOD SHEPHERD to keep them under His care, he always thought of the poor sheep he had sent off with her! Margery told Benezer she must have him come over and see her husband's farm some day, which he would find altogether a different situation to the home farm on the wolds. Benezer said if he could any way see clear how to order safe for the sheep, he should think much of the opportunity of coming. Then taking his broad-brimmed and weather-worn hat from his head, with a smile he said to Margery, "Do ye look here, my dear child; that poor weltered flower was none other than the brave rose ye dropped when ye lifted your last step from the ground that had nurtured ye up to a woman. I did see it fall, and I did make free, for there was none else did see; they all stood so busy a straining their eyes after ye, so that poor flower did seem like a token dropped there for me. And I've misered it up in my old hat ever since, and been thinking how it is written in the Book, 'The flower fadeth, but the word of our God endureth for ever.' I pray God ye be nourished with the sincere milk of His word, that ye may live in His presence for ever!" Margery was touched, and the more so because she had been vexed, on that day, when she found that she had dropped the flower. Now she saw it had been kept with a more sacred care than even if it had been in her keeping.

All her greetings were kind on her father-in-law's farm, and the aged grandmother's face beamed on her with maternal affection; but the mother sore longed that her son could have been over too. And Margery's true heart was traveling after her husband, and her secret thought was that the next whole day of his absence would certainly be the longest she had ever spent in her life. But it did not prove so, for she was up with the dawn in her own mother's dairy, her firm cold hand making the butter that all the country round used to praise; then busy seeing to a few little comforts for her parents that she thought they had neglected. She had promised to go up with them to drink tea with her mother-in-law; and as they were starting, most unexpectedly her husband drove in. He said that to the best of his knowledge he had ordered things pretty straight for one day, so he thought he saw an opportunity to come. "The best thing you could do," said his mother-in-law, "for I can tell you, when you left yesterday, Margery lost more looks after her husband than ever she did for her lover; so 'tis likely a good bit of time will be saved her to-morrow, that would have been lost looking out after you!" Mrs. Penforth thought it necessary to speak out for her daughter; but Benjamin had got quite beyond any need of words of assurance from Margery, "The heart of her husband did safely trust in her."

That evening was a brighter scene at Benjamin's paternal home than had ever been there before; for a gleam of that light, that will shine on brighter for ever, is better than all the glare of this world, which the night of sorrow or of death must turn into a darkness that nothing can lighten again. Benjamin thought his mother's face looked happier than he had ever seen it; he secretly hoped that things were more comfortable for her in her home; he did not know that she had found a comfort whose source was not on earth, and could not therefore be dried up by any barrenness here.

Farmer Northwood still spent his evenings too often away, things were not better in that respect than before: his two younger sons took ill advantage of their father's absence, and breaking from the word of their mother, they entered into companionships that did them no good. Yet the "evil day" of adversity came not yet, time was still given them to amend their ways—but they would not. It often happened now, that when the hour came for evening prayer, the sons as well as the father were absent: then their mother, with their venerable grandmother, and Sam Grist, and Christiana, comforted themselves alone in the Word of their God. One evening they had been reading the fifth chapter of the Romans, "Tribulation worketh patience, and patience experience, and experience hope;" and as the mother sat alone with her mother-in-law, watching beside the wood ashes for the return of her husband and sons, she said, "I be afraid I ben't off the first step of that ladder yet, I be often so impatient still!"

"Ah, child, 'tis not all of one heavenly grace, but a glimmer of each, that shines out in the heart God has lightened! ye know right well ye be more patient now than ye once could attain to; and don't ye know ye have had many an answer to prayer, dropping down very often on the same time that ye asked, and what can that be but "EXPERIENCE?" Didn't ye find Him ye looked to was near ye, ready listening for you? That's EXPERIENCE! what thing else should it be? And for "HOPE," don't ye know ye are always looking out on the promises, that have left the door open behind them of the holy heaven that they came from? and what can that be but HOPE?— Like the bow in the cloud that says the water floods shall not drown ye, because your God will be with ye. Troubles roll on amain, and darken over sometimes, but heavenly PATIENCE, and EXPERIENCE, and HOPE, they shine out again, and will shine on for ever, till the day that makes perfect. Don't ye go disowning these good gifts of Heaven, as if ye couldn't see them in the darkness of earth; but bless the Hand that they come from, and be ever asking for more, and be ye sure they'll shine on brighter, till there be no darkness left."

CHAPTER V.

THE venerable clergyman stood at the old font, and Margery brought her first-born child to devote him to God. When he took the infant from her arms it was as if he received it with a spiritual father's love. Solemnly and tenderly he went through the service of that sacrament, which can be received only once in a lifetime. It seemed not much to him to devote the short time that service required to earnest feeling and prayer for the child, whom it started on a never-ending existence, and whose future weal or woe must have an awful connection with its infant dedication to God. Margery deeply felt that sacramental service; it was the first wish of her heart that her children should be given to their God—she was well aware there was no other place of safety than the arms of that Saviour to whom she hastened to bring them: her heart was silent in words, but it was steadfast in action, and "whereunto she had attained, she walked by that rule." It was ever one of the moments she felt most in life, when her infant was received and baptized in that GREAT NAME, so awful, yet so blessed!—that NAME which rules heaven, earth, and hell, the threefold name of FATHER, SON, and HOLY GHOST—and signed with the sign of the cross, the token of redemption from the power of Satan and of sin, and the object to be ever kept in view in life and in death. It was with a spirit not unmindful of the blessing that Margery bore her infant home, to celebrate amongst its relatives and friends the day of its consecration to God.

On these occasions visits were received from the paternal farms, and there were fresh rejoicings at the birth of each child. Benjamin always read at evening prayers on that day, Psalm cxxvii.: "Lo, children are an heritage of the Lord. Happy is the man that hath his quiver full of them." He read it not as if he thought this "happiness" depended on how much money might be waiting for each child in the bank, he had no money there for himself; but he read it as one who believed it depended on the blessing of the God who gave them, and "Who feedeth the young ravens who call upon Him." And of Benjamin's children the Psalm proved true to its last words, "They shall not be ashamed when they speak with their enemies in the gate."

Benjamin's mother had returned home after the baptism of her third grandchild, full of thankfulness to see her children happy, and blessed in all their worldly concerns. And when she next saw the old shepherd on the wolds, she stopped to tell him of the prosperity she found at the Forest Farm.

"Yes, I've left another grandson there, as fine a babe as you ever looked on, Benezer; they have named him Stephen."

"The Almighty bless him!" said Benezer; "and be pleased to keep him, for ever, as the apple of His eye."

"That I believe He will! It's wonderful the comfort that has all followed on since I made such a sorrow when my poor Ben went away."

"Ah, yes, mistress, that always come of looking HIGHER. Sure as ever we keep down our eyes upon earth there'll be trouble, some way or other, spring up to meet them; and 'tis none the less certain when we keep them above, there'll be many a dear comfort to look down from heaven to enlighten them."

"Well, Benezer, I can't tell you how it hurts me sometimes to think I never had the heart to look that way till 'twas all darkened here. It seems so hard-hearted never to give a look up to Him that's above till, as you may say, I had no comfort left."

"Ah, mistress, it may well surprise we, but it don't surprise He; Him be so used to it! He met our hard heart face to face, when He came down to die. I've often thought how close 'twas put when they must choose He or a murderer, and they turned their faces from He, and cried out for Barabbas; He remembers that day, and sure enough we don't let He forget, for 'tis what we be after, the best of us sometimes, looking any way but to He. If Him were not God of PATIENCE 'twould be all over with we, not once, but aye, thousands of times, I'm right certain. But 'tis written, ' He waits to be gracious,' for He knows there's no other Hope for we; and, dear me, when He sees we be at last looking up He calls the whole blessed heaven to rejoice over we!"

"Oh, Benezer, I can't think upon it enough; 'tis the wonder of my life when I come to consider."

"Yes, 'tis just that He do say, 'Oh, that they would CONSIDER!' 'tis the last thing we come to; we go slaving and complaining, and worrying to death, when He be telling us only to look up to He and consider; and 'tis when we takes to that we find the world be soon under our feet."

Years passed away; and a day came when little Stephen, Margery's third child, was promised by his father that he should go over with him on a visit to his grandfather's farm, to see his great-grandmother. A little crippled tailor, an extremely small man, came from time to time to work at the farm, and now he sat on the kitchentable, his usual seat, in the bright southern window, making a little coat for Stephen, to be worn on his first visit to his great-grandmother's farm. It was Stephen's first little coat, and being made for so great an occasion he very often stood watching by the table, intent on its progress; and when little Spedly, the tailor, had sewed on the last button, Stephen could hardly be persuaded that the important moment was not come in which to start for his great-grandmother's farm. At length the day did arrive, and Stephen was dressed in his little coat by his mother; and, full of personal dignity on this his first visit out with his father, he listened to his mother's parting charge, "You are going to see your great-grandmother; she is the best woman in the world, and you must mind what she says to you."

It was a long drive, but the good horse did it well, and not the less willingly from a secret expectation of Sam Grist's hospitable entertainment at the end. Christiana was putting away her new cheeses in the cheese-room, when, on hearing the sound of wheels, she looked out through the lath windows, and saw her young master driving up with one of his children at his side. Christiana glided down the cheese-room ladder as if she touched not a step, and rushing into the family kitchen she exclaimed, "If there ben't a child come, I declare!" and leaving all other facts or probabilities to be guessed, she opened the door and ran out to the gate. The horse drew up at that moment, and Christiana, clasping little Stephen in her arms, dragged him out of the gig, and carried him in with vehement kisses. Now, Stephen had expected to make a very different entrance at his great-grandmother's home, and being entirely unused to such an outbreak of affection, he strongly resented it as a personal affront; he struggled, kicked, and on entering the kitchen succeeded in regaining his feet, then taking a distant attitude of defiance, he exclaimed, "Now meddle again, if you dare!" The father, entering at this moment, seeing Stephen standing aloof, his young face all displeasure, inquired, "What's the matter here?" To which Stephen, still keeping his post and distance of observation, replied, "She carried me, and kissed me!" The father laughed, and turning to his mother said, "I've brought you Margery's own son; he's his mother all over!" While Stephen, in his ruffled composure, continued to keep a cautious look out around him.

It was winter, and the aged grandmother now sat in the parlor as a warmer retreat from the cold. Stephen's father soon called him, and taking hold of his hand said, "Come and see your great-grandmother." Then, opening the black door of the parlor, they went in. There sat the venerable woman, feeble in her great age, seated in the same oaken chair, with the Bible on the round table beside her; her basket of garments for the poor at her feet, and her work in her hand.

"Ah, lad, I thought 'twas no tongue but thine," she said, as she took off her glasses, and, laying them down, looked with parental affection on Benjamin.

"I'm glad to hear well of you, grandmother; I've brought a great-grandson to see you." And he led Stephen up to her knee.

The old woman laid her hand on the head of the child, and said fervently, "God's blessing rest on him!" and then began to talk to his father, who seated himself in a chair, with Stephen between his knees. The child looked intently on the face of the old woman; it was his great-grandmother, of whom his parents spoke always with reverence, and of whom his mother had given him her parting charge. His father had often said to him, "Some day you shall see your great-grandmother," and this was her! Stephen looked, and wondered, and listened, until his father, rising to go, took his hand again to lead him away. Then the old woman said, in her strong, kind tone, "Will ye stay with your old grandmother, or do ye like best to go?"

"I'll stay," replied Stephen, with a tone of determined confidence.

"He's Margery's child, grandmother," said Stephen's father, "so it's pretty sure he'll take well to you." And he left Stephen standing beside his great-grandmother's chair. The old woman put on her spectacles again, and went on with her work in that quiet way that thoughtful children feel most at ease with. She inquired first for his mother, then asked at intervals for his sisters and brothers, then about the aged clergyman, and things on the farm; all the while working on, as was her habit to do. Stephen felt quickly at ease by her side, telling all he could think of in reply to her questions; and it soon became evident that a link was fast forming over the three-fourths of a century between them.

After the early farm tea, Stephen hastened to his retreat again on the stool by his great-grandmother's side, where he soon began the conversation. "We have an ass and a foal; the ass is brother's, but the foal is mine. I have named him Blackberry, and mother says I shall ride him when I go to school."

The old woman replied, "If ye ride on an ass ye must

be meek and gentle, like the Son of the Blessed. He rode on an ass, and a colt, the foal of an ass."

Stephen looked up in silence.

"Have ye never heard how the Lord Jesus, our Saviour, rode on a young ass, that had never been ridden before?"

"No," replied Stephen, with evident interest at the mention of a fact so like his own young expectations.

It was at the hour at which the old woman always opened her Bible, when she sat alone in the parlor, and with the tender heart of Heaven's love she would not turn from the child, but would interest and lead his young spirit along with her in the green pastures of the Divine Word. So she opened the Bible at the place where it tells of the Saviour's triumphant entry into Jerusalem,— engaging his interest in every particular of the wonderful history, leading him on from the facts his own young life made familiar, to those that must for ever engage the glorious assembly in heaven; until the soul of that infant of days faintly mirrored back the scene described by the pen of the Evangelist, the mystery which angels desire to look into.

But the black parlor-door opened, and Christiana came in to tell the child it was time for her to put him to bed.

"I am not coming with you," replied Stephen; "I am going to stay with this old lady to-night."

Christiana looked at her aged mistress, who said, "Let be, let be, I shall be early myself, and I'll see to the babe;

sure he'll prove one of them out of whose mouth is ordained praise!"

The next morning little Stephen rose when his great-grandmother was up, and kept close by her side.

"Go and tell 'em to bring in a batling and make up the fire," said his great-grandmother, as Stephen took his place on his stool by her chair.

"I can do that myself!" replied the child; and he ran out to the back-door, where Sam Grist saw him, and offered his services.

"If you'll show me the batlings I'll thank you," said Stephen.

"There they be, master; but I'll lend you a hand,—they be's heavy."

"No, thank you, let alone," replied Stephen, as much used as any little woodman to the work.

Sam Grist looked after the boy delighted: "'Tis the hope of the homestead!" he said to himself; and full surely Sam Grist found his prophecy true.

Standing sideways, with one foot over the fender, little Stephen made up his great-grandmother's fire, then rubbing the moss stains from his new little coat, he sat down again on his stool.

"Now, my child, 'tis the prime of the morning; are ye ready for the teaching of Heaven? Do ye want to hear the words that tell of the Son of the Blessed?"

"Yes," said Stephen; "tell again how He rode on that young ass."

"'Tis what He showed forth by that ye must think on, my child; how meek and gentle He was. Shall I read you how they led Him like a lamb to the slaughter, and how He stood like a sheep in the hands of the shearers and never opened His mouth?" So, again, from these familiar comparisons, well understood by the farm child, his saintly relative gently led him to look on the death of his Redeemer.

As the morning wore on, some of the poor people of the village came up the garden walk to the door of the farmhouse parlor, which opened into the garden, half wood and half glass. One after another Stephen let them in. They came to pour out their hearts to their venerable friend. She counselled them in difficulty, or warned them, or comforted them, as the case might be; to some she reached out a garment, and little Stephen looked on, and heard their parting blessing breathed on her.

"I will take you home with me to my mother," said Stephen when they were alone again; "there's plenty of room in our gig."

"Bless you, my child, but I am going up where no carriages of this earth can carry me."

"Where are you going?" asked Stephen.

"Up yonder, where that sunbeam glints down from the snow-cloud."

"How will you get there?" asked little Stephen, as he looked up to the bright opening in the heavy March sky.

"The Son of the Blessed lives up there," replied the old woman, "He who rode meek and lowly on an ass, He who was led as a lamb to the slaughter, and stood patient as a sheep afore her shearers! He lives up there, 'tis the house of His Father, and He has promised to come back again for all who love Him."

"I love Him!" said little Stephen; "will He take me back with you?"

"Ah, child, no, you must serve Him first here! Get His words in your heart, they are all written in the Bible, they'll learn you to please Him, and then one day He will come again for you."

"How can you get up there?" again Stephen asked, wondering.

"Oh, the Son of the Blessed will order all that! I have only to wait till He sends. Shall I read to you out of the book how, for one who loved Him greatly, He sent down a chariot and horses of fire?"

"Yes, read it now." And little Stephen and his great-grandmother soon forgot all else in Elijah's ascension.

After the early farm-dinner, Benjamin said to his boy, "Now, Stephen, say good-bye, we must be off in no time."

"No, thank you, father, I don't want to go back. I shall stay with this old lady, I like her right well."

Benjamin at first laughed, but when no persuasions could make the child move from his great-grandmother's chair, he grew angry, and put him by force in the gig;

but the boy in a moment climbed over the other side, and rushed back again to the old woman's chair. It might have seemed at that moment that all her teaching had been useless, but oftentimes the lessons that govern a lifetime yield no result in the moment of teaching. She had won the child's heart, and the first impulse of his young but strong will was not to leave her; her gentle words would have soon brought him back to obedience, but Benjamin was angry, and threatening Stephen severely, he tied him fast into the gig with a rope, while the boy sobbed out, "I don't care what you do to me, I will run back again as soon as ever I'm home." The aged grandmother wept for the child, his struggle had been much for her to bear. "'Tis a high will and strong spirit," she said; "but there's One that can break it in for His kingdom—O that He may!"

Benjamin was vexed that his boy should have entered and left his grandmother's home with a struggle. And little could the father then think what that visit had done! On the way back the poor child fell asleep, and when he awoke, his mother was chafing his cold limbs on her lap by the fire. She took off his little coat, and laid him down asleep in his bed; and the first sight of his mother the next morning brought obedience back again to his heart.

CHAPTER VI.

ONE day in each year was spent by Margery's children at the Rectory. A day never to be forgotten by them, lying always, through life, in that sweet sunshine of memory, in which some blessed days upon earth look as if they might almost have been spent in Eden. Margery dressed the children in their Sunday graments on that day; they went up the green hillside hand in hand, their fun quieted down and their merry shouts hushed in the thought of the great event now before them. They crossed the bridge of the old moat that surrounded the Rectory gardens, went in at the high gates, and were received at the door by Mr. Wyemark the footman, looking splendid to them in his livery. Mr. Wyemark would take up the youngest child in his arms, saying to the older ones, "Follow me, little dears," and in this order they proceeded to the study, where the venerable clergyman received them, seated in his arm-chair, with his long white hair on his shoulders, and the beautiful calm of his face beaming on them; the children came up to his knee, and he gave a kiss to each young brow, laid his hand on each head, and implored a blessing. The youngest child was lifted down from Mr.

Wyemark's kind arms to the pastor's knee, and the others stood around him; left alone with him while he taught them from his own heart the holy truths he most desired to have written upon theirs. They spent a long time in the study, but it never seemed long; then the eldest was sent to look for Mr. Wyemark, who, returning, conducted them in the same order to the parlor, where the clergyman's daughter received them with many pretty little devices around her to entertain children. They dined under charge of Mr. Wyemark, in a little side room, having small dishes of good food somewhat quaintly prepared for their greater entertainment. After dinner the boat was drawn out of the boathouse, and under the safe keeping of Mr. Wyemark, and Mr. Brown the coachman, they rowed many times round the deep clear moat, amongst the great water lilies that bloomed on its surface, peeping down for the fish that glided in and out from the green weed underneath. This was the only excursion ever made by Margery's children "on the water, and it was with very lingering steps that at last they left the boat, though it was to go with Mr. Brown to the stables to see his fine horses and the harness shining with silver; while Mr. Wyemark set their tea ready. After tea they were conducted in exactly the same order to take leave of the aged clergyman and his daughter. Mr. Wyemark always made an excuse to carry the youngest child a little way home, then with a kind kiss the tall old footman took leave, and the children hand in hand walked faster and faster, until it fairly came to a run, to get home and tell their mother what a day it had been!

On one of these occasions Mr. Wyemark presented Margery's eldest girl with a China rose-tree, planted in a pot. He had observed the child's great pleasure when he plucked her a rose from the Rectory tree, so in his kindness the old footman had planted a slip from the same tree, and watched over it until it grew and bore a rose; then he gave it to the little girl to take home for her own. The gift greatly delighted her; it was kept in the southern window of the kitchen until another sprig had been taken from it and trained into a little tree; then, in presence of all the family, one was planted on each side of the front doorway, to grow up and cover with fair blossoms that happy home of childhood.

Bright was the gleam that then lighted that English farm; on each young head it shone; there was no vacant place in all the circle of affection; the pastures with their flocks, the valleys with their **waving** grain, the woodcrowned hills, all glowed beneath it; on the pastor's home it rested, making it a centre of light and love to all around. No cloud of sorrow had yet darkened Margery's happy lot, and it seemed as if her children were to grow up around her in the same sunshine and prosperity. But it is not the calm seas that train the skill of the sailor, nor the time of peace that gives courage to the soldier; neither can prosperity discipline the heart of the Christian. Yet sorrow drew near gently to Margery; its first approaches only woke a deeper tenderness of feeling, as though sorrow itself were unwilling to darken so bright a home. But it is written, "Whom the Lord loveth He chasteneth, therefore despise not thou the chastening of the Lord, nor faint when thou art rebuked of Him."

Letters in those days were rare things in farmhouses, but one morning a letter came to Margery; a man on horseback had brought it over from her mother-in-law. It was sealed with black wax. Margery's hand trembled as she opened and read—

"MY DEAR CHILDREN:—God bless ye both, and the little ones. I hope this will find you all in good health, as it leaveth me, thank God. It hath pleased the Almighty to take your dear grandmother to Himself; none can truly say when; for she laid down to sleep in good health, and as comfortable as ever we saw her in her life, and being some deal feebler of late, Christiana did ofttimes take her up a cup of tea from our breakfast, before she did rise, and when she went up this morning the Almighty had taken her, for the dear soul was gone. I've fretted more than I ought, but God knoweth I've good cause, for the angel of our poor home is departed, and the shadow falleth darker that she's not by to lighten. So no more at present, only I shall hope to see Ben as soon as he can order any how to come; and if your wife could be here on the day of the funeral it would be a great stay to all, for

there's nothing but tears a-falling, turn which way you will. So this is all at this time from your
          Sorrowful Mother,
              Sarah Northwood."

Margery wept. It was the first time her children had seen their mother in tears, and they felt awed at her grief. After a while she said, "Children, God Almighty hath taken your great-grandmother to Himself. She followed close after Him here, and she is gone to be with Him for ever; but you will never see her again, until it please Him you go to Him where she is; but that won't be unless you follow on after Him as she did. Your poor father will be terribly cut up when he hears it, and you must pray God to comfort your grandmother."

Little Stephen cried first, and then all the children cried with him; his infant tears were true grief, for his great-grandmother had lived always in his young heart since the memorable visit he had paid to her with his father. But the expression of all his thoughts about her had been kept more silent than they otherwise would have been, by his constant recollection of the disgrace he fell into on leaving. He still hoped his mother did not know of the rope, for the sleeping child knew not that her hand had untied him. He answered all his mother's questions about his visit, but did not venture to say much himself, for fear it should bring down the dreaded reproof. But Stephen's offence on that occasion had not much troubled his mother, because it came from the child's love for one whom she thought well worthy of it. Margery always went straight to the root of an offence, and judged it chiefly by the feeling it sprang from. She sometimes punished severely what others thought a trifle, and would pass over what to them seemed a much greater outbreak; and when wondered at for so doing, would reply, "Can't you see 'twas an outbreak that did not rise up out of bad feeling? We must know when 'tis for good to pass over a transgression!" But the greater silence in which little Stephen had felt constrained to keep his thoughts of his great-grandmother did not make them less strong in his heart. And now he longed to ask whether those grand horses of fire, his great-grandmother had read to him of, came down to carry her up to the Son of the Blessed; and there was no one to tell him that holy angels, who kept their watch around her while here, had borne her meek spirit in their arms to the kingdom of heaven.

The boy had been led to the feet of the venerable woman, that her last work on earth might be to breathe an influence on him no after time could wear out. She had been beforehand with the world, and had won his early reverence and love for the Bible, and kind feeling for the poor. The promise was in her to be fulfilled, "Shewing mercy to thousands in them that love Me, and that keep my commandments."

One evening on Benjamin's return from the market,

seated at the long family table with his wife and children at tea, he said to Margery, "There is strange news to-day in the town."

Margery had an exceeding objection to news. Her husband said what he pleased and was always listened to by his wife, but no one else had any chance of getting half through with their discourse when the subject of it was news: Margery was sure to cut the tale short before the most important part was told, and even her husband never found her a very cordial listener to his news from the town. On his announcement this evening of strange news in the town, Margery only replied, "I should like to know whenever you hear *news* that's not **strange!** There's one puts something to the head and another to the tail, till the wonder would be if 'twere not a **strange** confusion in the end." So said Margery, never on any occasion found ready to "kiss the lips of unacquainted change."

"Tell us, father," said the eldest lad at the table.

"It won't please your mother, boy."

"Oh, I never trouble myself about news, one way or other," replied Margery, in a tone of indifference, with a touch of displeasure.

"Tell it, father," again said the boy.

"You won't understand it, child, but your mother will; they are going to put a tax upon window lights, and we shall soon have to shut up."

"They may talk as they like," replied Margery, "I

don't believe it. Put out the light indeed! I wonder they be not afraid to spread about such ill inventions of news!"

But for all Margery's disbelief, the news was too true. A notice soon arrived at the farm which turned the news into fact.

Poor Margery now must believe. "'Tis a day we've lived to see, sure enough!" she exclaimed. "It may well be said that money's the root of all evil, when it turns the light into darkness. Do they think, then, He who gave the light, gave it only for money?"

"They have settled it that have the power," said Benjamin, in his calmness; and 'tis no use our rising against it."

"No use our rising? why 'tis enough to raise the country! If they want taxes let us have them, but not on the free gifts of our Maker." But then, as if her loyal heart had taken alarm at giving consent to a national rebellion, she added, "You may rest sure 'tis none of your crown men have done it; they'd have too much respect for the King that's above, to go taxing the light He has given as free to the beggar as the prince: tis the doing of them that are always meddling with change!"

"'Tis *change*," replied Benjamin, "but 'tis become law, and we had best settle the windows while we've time to consider."

Poor Margery was in no state for quietly *considering*, so she only replied, "I settled once how the heaven's light could best be let in, and I'm not going after settling now how to shut it out. Let them that have ruled for the darkness settle that."

Margery was ironing, a few days after this conversation, in her large and light back kitchen, when the tax-gatherer arrived, and entered in at the front door. Benjamin was fortunately at home, and he presently stepped to Margery, shutting the back-kitchen door behind him.

"The tax-gatherer's come, so we must settle the lights."

"Settle that without me," replied Margery, "it shall never be said that I gave my voice to put out the light!" and there was a terrible sadness in her strong tone as she spoke.

Benjamin was vexed: he would gladly have saved every window for Margery's sake, but it was true there were more than were wanted; charges were heavy on all sides; and eight young children were already growing up around him. Yet he thought it hard to vex Margery; but she must know it could not be helped; so he took the tax-gatherer over the house to settle the windows alone.

When all was done, he returned and asked, "Could you give the man a morsel of food? he is quite ready now."

Margery's justice never lost itself in displeasure. She knew that the tax-gatherer was the servant, not the master of the tax, and therefore, though he had entered her home as the most unwelcome office-bearer in the world, she distinguished between the office and the man, and quickly loaded her hospitable hands with refreshments, which she carried to the kitchen, and spread out before him.

"'Tis a troublesome business I'm sent on," observed the man.

"That's their look out that sent you," replied Margery.

"So it is," he answered; "and after all it is only a question of money!"

Margery's cheek flushed at this avowed connection between money and light—two things that she believed ought never to have been put together; but she refrained from all comment, and returned to her ironing again.

The next morning early she was seen looking long out at the sunrise from the eastern window in the favorite guest-chamber, as if she knew that look must be the last. Margery said not a word when they blocked up one window in her large pleasant back kitchen, putting it all into gloom, obliging her ever after to work with the upper half of the cold northern door open for more light. She said not a word when they blocked up one window in her boys' chamber, one in each of the guest-chambers—the eastern window in one and the western in the other; she said not a word when they put out the only window of the upper chamber in the house, because it got a twilight from the casement on the stairs; but when they planted themselves ready with their mortar and bricks to block up the light little parlor's western window, Margery did speak, and said to her husband with a starting tear in her eye, "I do say I will not have that west window *bricked*. You have not had a child but it has spent the day of its baptism in that room, with its best friends about it, and the sun has gone down shining full on its young head in at that western window, and now if it must be darkened for money it shall only be *boarded*, and as sure as another babe has its baptism I'll have it righted for that day. I'll not have half the light that shone down on the others, shut out above one, and that only for money!" So the west parlor-window had only boards nailed against it, and at every fresh baptism these were taken down, on that day, and on that day only the setting sun lighted up the farm-parlor. Did that mother's silent heart on each baptismal day think of the time when the sun of her child's earthly life must go down? did she trust that it would set in glory? was it this feeling made her cling to the thought that the sun of that western sky should shine on each infant head? if so, in that same room that hope's fulfilment was abundantly given.

CHAPTER VII.

WHAT has thrown a sudden grief over every face in the village?—stopped the servants in their work, the children in their play, while Margery and her husbnad stand sorrow-stricken, looking from their farm-kitchen window up towards the old church tower and Rectory? and, as the tidings spread along, not a face in the village whose expression does not tell of unexpected sorrow. It can be but one event that so touches the parish—its pastor has fallen asleep, and will wake no more upon earth! Alas! then faded the gleam that from the village Rectory had fallen on the farm, and cottage, and field, and Margery's eyes never saw it rekindled again.

"I knew it was not for nothing that they put out the light," Margery said, in her strong tone of sadness, "I knew 'twas against some evil that was coming, and now 'tis come, and 'tis darkness indeed!"

A few weeks passed away, when, one day, a stranger arrived at the farm. He was a clergyman, had come from the college, and asked for the key of the church. Benjamin was absent, so Margery put on her bonnet, and went up the hill with him. Margery formed her own opinion of the man before they reached the hill-top—not a favorable one; still, when he had looked into the church, she asked him to return and take refreshment at the farm; for never guest, whether stranger or friend, crossed Margery's threshold, but met with hospitality there. Having finished his repast, he departed. Margery did not give one look to follow him, but she turned to her kitchen's southern window, and looked long up at the chancel of the church, where the friend of all hearts lay sleeping, and whose like, she could plainly see, it was not for them to hope to welcome again.

"I hear the new Rector's been over," was the first thing her husband said on his return; "is there any hope he's a right sort of man?"

"There's but little can be thought about him!" replied Margery, "he stood here and looked on the children, and all he had to say was, 'So many mouths, I wonder you can find bread to put in them!' 'Sir,' said I, 'I never knew the God above send mouths, but he sent the bread to put in them!' Not much use it will be for him to come teaching if he cannot reach a thought beyond DOUBT!"

Margery's decided character always formed a decided opinion, and she was rarely mistaken. Her judgments sometimes seemed hastily made, but they always turned on a principle. The clergyman might be supposed to have spoken without thought, but no thoughtlessness that questioned the providence of God met with any excuse from Margery. Trust in the God of providence, was as fixed a principle in her heart as trust in the God of nature. She prayed for bread to be given day by day; rising early, she labored for it; she was bountiful to the poor, but she never allowed the least thing to be wasted on indolence, extravagance, or finery; and so living, she doubted not that bread would be given. Whenever a doubt of God's care was thrown in her path, she instantly trod on it, trampled it out, and went on. And her strong trust was honored; the God of providence so did His marvellous works for Margery, that they ought to be had in remembrance.

The new Rector remained but a few months: the loneliness of the parish was unattractive to him; and he exchanged livings with another fellow of his college, who, having quarrelled, report said, with his town parishioners, was glad to take a village where no active opposition could hinder his course. No need for Margery to wait for words from his lips; one look was enough. He entered the Rectory, and gross darkness settled down on that beautiful dwelling, and spread its baneful influence around. But He whose name alone is Jehovah was still the Most High over all, and that His Name is near, His wondrous works declare.

And now the farm became more and more shut up to itself. Margery's was not a character to invite much intercourse with neighbors. The Rectory had led into association with other hearts and lives than their own, that now was closed; and the family life of the farm grew and flourished alone. The plants that blossom but slowly seem guarded, at least for the most part, with a sheath of firm fabric in their leaves. Such a sheath was Margery to her home, within whose strong fold its household life bloomed slowly, but in full beauty, when at length it expanded, blossom after blossom, until gathered to the skies.

Benjamin and Margery both stood firm in their authority as parents. The house was full of children, who never felt themselves in the way; their high spirits did not trouble their mother; she understood them, and let them flow on. They had been trained from their infancy to an instant obedience to her word, which kept her rule easier as the children grew older. They sometimes had disputes with each other, but neither parent would ever allow them to make any appeal to them. "Bring no quarrels to me," Margery would say, "I will not hear a complaint. I shall SEE who is wrong before the sun is gone down, so settle it the best way you can, or I shall know what to do. Neither Benjamin nor Margery would ever punish, nor even reprove anything in children or servants, except what they had themselves seen or known, apart from all report from the children. But then they were so observant, that if a child had been in the wrong, the day seldom passed without the parent seeing proof that it was so; and the certainty of this quick observation generally made the offender hasten to get right, lest the eye of his parent should read his wrong-doing. It strengthened the children in right efforts; it strengthened their family union; and it strengthened their moral principle; for if they complained of a servant or laborer, the mother was sure to say, "Don't come telling me what you have seen wrong; if you had been what you ought to be, the wrong would not have been done in your presence, that you know."

This principle of acting only on personal observation answered well on the farm; but then it was strengthened by the parental integrity that governed the house, and guarded by a watchful observation that nothing escaped. Benjamin and Margery had a very quick perception of wrong-doing, and could therefore safely leave all to their own observation; but this quick perception was the result of their own moral integrity; they had from their youth tried to do the thing that was right, and this gave them a quick eye to see when it was wrong. Obedience and truth were lessons learned by each child of Margery's, and most carefully their mother watched over their words. She knew well that if the mind frames the words, so also do the words frame the mind. Simple as words could be were the words of her children, but so pure and true, that, as life advanced, many a mind of intellect and refinement found refreshment in their society; the maternal care that dwelt always in the midst, had exerted an influence over them that proved a far richer gift than of silver and gold. Like all noble natures, there dwelt no suspicion in Margery, creating the evil it expected to find; watchful, but not suspicious, she maintained the dignity of true authority, which can always allow a freedom to others in proportion to its own conscious strength. Under such a training the bloom of youthful vigor, the open courage of truth, and the willing labor of diligent work, set their stamp on her children for life. Their love for their mother bore the aspect of reverence, but it was a loving reverence that not only obeyed, with rare exceptions, her slightest wish, but enshrined in their hearts every feeling of hers as a law for their life.

The school to which Benjamin sent his boys was a small grammar-school in a neighboring town; the town, though not large, had its antiquities and charities, of which this grammar-school was one. By the will of the excellent founder, the Psalms appointed for each day were always read by the boys: this regulation was welcome to little Stephen, because of the reverence and love he had so early felt for the Bible. Every boy in that school learned to write a fair hand, and some of Benjamin's sons excelled in beautiful penmanship; they learned to read distinctly, and were taught the first rules of arithmetic; and at this point the grammar-school considered its work was complete. It took some years to attain to this degree of education; and the town lying distant from the village, seven donkeys were kept on the farm. Each son of Benjamin claimed one of these donkeys as his own;

and though the lads were not all of an age to go to school at the same time, yet each boy had his donkey, and made it his business and pleasure to tend and train the animal with such skill and kindness that the whole seven were raised quite above the average of donkeys; and both in appearance and intelligence gave evidence of being so entirely well-bred, that all who saw them looked on them admiringly. Happily the true secret of successful training was well known; there was no unmanageable creature on that farm, save occasionally a bull, whose malpractices could not be mended. No cruelty or unkindness within doors or without broke the harmony of that happy farm. The boys, trained from infancy themselves with a justice that they knew would never fail, a firmness that never yielded, and a kindness that never spoiled, practised the same on the creatures around them. The donkeys must obey their young masters, but then the donkeys, from their birth as foals on the farm, were always treated with kindness, and never had an opportunity of getting up any dislike to authority which was reasonable, kind, and strong.

Stephen had called his young donkey Blackberry, from its very dark coat. When Stephen first went to school Blackberry was not ready for service, so he rode another donkey, and had, as he said, the regular breaking-in of Blackberry to his mind. When Stephen thought this breaking-in was accomplished, he rode Blackberry to school, and the sleek donkey excited great admiration.

At the evening mounting for the return home, there was a general gathering of the boys round the new handsome donkey, and many questions were put to its young master, who felt himself an important person on the occasion. "The stubborn in him is to come yet," said a boy; "there never was a donkey born and bred yet without it!"

"I can tell you then," said Stephen, "that 'tis not the born,' but the bad breaking gets the stubborn into beasts. My father's right when he says, 'Don't talk to me about stubborn! beasts are sensible enough, if you go the right way to work; 'tis you hav'n't got the sense how to manage them, that's the long and short of it all.'"

"Tell us how you brought him to," said a boy.

"Tell us how you went at it," said another.

"Well," answered Stephen, "I suppose there's a right and a wrong way, and the end will pretty soon show which way you've been after. 'Twas not reasonable to think that if he never knew the meaning of me till I got on his back he should be all right for minding me then; so I made much of him beforehand; there wasn't a place he would not follow me into, or try at it at any rate; and now as soon as ever he hears me come chirruping after him he's all as gay as a lark."

"Let's see how he'll start!" cried a boy, not without a secret mischievous intent. But Stephen lifted the rein, gave a whistle, and off went Blackberry as fleet as the wind, until Stephen caught up his brothers on the road.

There were keen eyes on Stephen and Blackberry, to

find out, if possible, some flaw in the well-trained donkey. All went on right, until one day, when the rain had made a water channel over the road, Blackberry came to a sudden halt at the runnel, and threw his young master over his head. A laugh rose from his brothers as Stephen got up from the mud; they rode on to school, and left Stephen alone with his donkey. And now it might for once have gone ill with poor Blackberry, and all Stephen's good training of his animal been lost in one act of unreasonable anger; but Stephen thought of his mother, and what she would be certain to say if he and Blackberry fell out on the way; her justice could never be cheated; and Stephen cared more for what she thought and said, than for all the boys in the kingdom put together. He felt it provoking that his brothers should have ridden through and Blackberry alone made a halt; provoking to have perhaps to go late into school and see the boys make a laugh, and ask if the stubborn had got the better after all; still he resolved he would keep master of himself if he could not of Blackberry, for he knew well enough, from all his home teaching, that to keep master over himself was the sure road to highest success in the end. So having at first in vain tried to lead Blackberry over the runnel, he now tied his handkerchief over Blackberry's eyes, but still the donkey would not go; he mounted and urged him, but not a step would he move. "Ho, ho, and so you won't be cheated?" said Stephen; "and not to blame neither; I would not be made to go blindfold where I would not go seeing!" Stephen looked round, the banks were too high to break over, and there was no friendly gate into which he could lead Blackberry by way of avoiding the road. So he turned Blackberry into the hedge, while he cut down small branches and strewed them thickly over the runnel; then, taking out the small cake of bread which he had for his dinner, he gave a piece to Blackberry before he took him out of the hedge, then cutting up the rest into narrow slices, he laid them down on the branches across the runnel. Blackberry stooped and ate up the first, stepped on after the second, and so on until fairly over; then Stephen sprang on his back. Once over the runnel, the donkey was willing to go as fast as his young master pleased, who felt twice master because he had also conquered himself in his own impulse of anger.

On returning, the sun had dried up the water, and the donkey was intent on reaching home. But Stephen felt that the point must be settled; so, after tea, he went to his mother. "Mother, it cost me the biggest half of my dinner to get Blackberry over a water runnel to-day; if I had a carrot, I think I could cure him of such fancies as that."

"Yes, child, half a dozen, if it be to save the stick upon Blackberry."

Stephen ran down the garden with his great pocketknife in his hand, and as he ran he said to himself, "Mother don't love the stick, though she knows right well how to use it!" The largest carrot was pulled, and peeled to look temptingly red; then Blackberry was led out to one of the many little streams to be found thereabout, to one as much as possible like the morning hindrance on the way to school. Stephen let fall a few slices beyond the water-run. At first he let Blackberry walk over to reach them, then, dropping more, he rode him across, and finally rode him up quickly to another water-run, throwing the bits of carrot over before him. Blackberry stopped, sidled a little, but went over, and the second time made no objection. Blackberry had had a great fancy for carrots from a foal; and, after a little practice in this way, on different occasions, water-runs and carrots became so agreeably associated in Blackberry's mind, that he never afterward felt a water run any hindrance in the way.

"There, mother, the carrot has got the better of that fancy. I'd have given my pocket-penny sooner than not have had a carrot!"

"I reckon, child, 'tis YOU have gained the victory, and in more ways than one. Go the right way to work, keep master over yourself, and ye may stand king to the creatures; but try the wrong way, and ye may be sure 'twill be the worse for ye some day!"

Priceless to her children was that mother's rare praise. And so the seven donkeys, each trained to perfection, proved a good beginning for lads under whose care, for half a century, the animal creation was to flourish and rejoice.

CHAPTER VIII.

THERE was a hero on the farm, by name Gruff, a mastiff of great strength and fierceness. Gruff seemed to consider his position fully equal in dignity and authority to any other that he saw around. Benjamin had a great value for the dog, who returned his master's friendship by strictest fidelity, without any demonstration of affection. Gruff had never made a friendship in his life; he did not appear to consider any one sufficiently his equal to be caressed as a friend. The most that any one could expect was to come and go unmolested,—the only exception to this negative friendship being in favor of his master; for, if Benjamin had been out, Gruff would in expression go so far as slightly to wag his tail on his master's return. When the children grew old enough to run about, many a charge was given, "Be sure you don't go near Gruff." Margery did not share in this fear; she said she "never yet knew the farm-dog that would harm the farm-child, and, for her part, she thought that they who stuck close to their business like Gruff, were the folk most to be trusted in a fair way after all." And it was not long before little Stephen was seen peeping out of Gruff's kennel, in which he had hid himself, and a slight wag was perceptible of Gruff's short tail, showing that he shared in the pleasure of the achievement. And very soon Gruff became the children's greatest friend. When they gathered round him he would stand up, hang his ears, drop his head, and remain in passive endurance of all their hugs and caresses. Gruff had not been unchained for years, his great ferocity being well known in the neighborhood. But the man who fed him one day lifted Stephen upon him, put his little sister behind him, in the fashion of a pillion, then unchaining Gruff led him off the farm, round by the roads, and so home again. Margery shook her head, and said, "You'll go too far for safety some day;" but the man often allowed Gruff to perform this heroic act of forbearance, and always declared that it did not signify who met Gruff on the road; the dogs said what they liked to him, creatures that he would at other times have destroyed at one gripe, snapped at him unnoticed; not even a beggar drew forth any displeasure; he carried the children, with the steadiest attention to their comfort, turned home when desired, and stood at his kennel until they were safely off, then looked up at them with the same slight wag of his tail, which seemed to say he felt satisfied at having given them the pleasure.

The children had other friends beyond the limits of the farm. One of these was Benedict, the village blacksmith; he was a man of great strength and skill, and a chief favorite with Stephen. If Stephen were missed, he was often to be found standing beside Benedict at his forge; and the observation of the child went beyond the red metal and fiery sparks of the blacksmith. He learned to distinguish good work in a trade so important to farmers, and made a friendship with Benedict which lasted through life. There were other old-fashioned tradesmen who lived round about the farm, men who took their stand on good work rather than on outward show. Of these, the principal were Jolly, the carpenter; and old Faithful, the harness-maker. This last old man's name was not Faithful, but the boys called him so, because he never broke a promise. He was too honest, men said, to grow rich in a village harness-maker's trade, and too industrious ever to come to poverty. The old man worked all day in his little shop, with shining leather and bright brass hanging round him, and on no one did his mild face beam more kindly than on his young friends from the farm. It was an object of interest to the boys to save money to buy one tool after another used by the old harness-maker, or Jolly, the carpenter. And they soon learned to puncture the holes in the harness, to polish and mend. Daniel and Philip took most to these neat arts, and were always ready for any job of carpentering or harness mending, that might be within their skill to accomplish. It was capital cheer to the boys when they could get as far as old Faithful's, the harness-maker; who lived in another village six miles from the farm, but who, though distant, was yet their chief friend, for the cheer was not less when they saw his little cart driving in at the farm-gate. Their mother well knew how such interest in childhood would help to keep them from evil in youth, and she silently encouraged all innocent pursuits. And the tradesmen made it a pleasure to teach their knowledge to boys so civil in manner, so pleasant in behavior, and quick to catch the right thing when put before them. Nor must little Spedly, the tailor, be forgotten in their circle of friends; he had no children, and he said he thought twice as much of them at the farm as he believed he could ever have done of his own! So many boys made much work for him, and he made much fun for them. His extremely small size and comic look was irresistible to the active, merry boys, who would often spring in unexpectedly, lift him up on their shoulders and carry him off, with his crutch left behind, to some safe place in the garden, from which return was impossible alone. Then the boys danced in their glee, and the small tailor pleaded with fun peeping out from his little keen eyes. "Oh, my coat sleeves! my day's work! 'twill be the end of all favors for me!"

"When mother counts your stitches you shall reign king of the needle, but till then you may just as well have a turn with us between!" "Count my stitches! if they be not too quick for a body to reckon I'll never stitch here again; but she knows when the sleeve is seamed for all you may say. Oh take pity, and I'll make soldiers of you some day!" "When mother scolds, tell her we've just been after helping you a bit, and see if she don't know what that means!" So the lads had their fun, and the small tailor his part in it, though it took some courage to feel safe in the wild freaks of the boys. But there was no one save his wife, that little Spedly the tailor loved like Margery's sons through his long after life.

There were other pleasures at the farm for its children beside work, and friendship, and fun; they all greatly loved music. Their father played well on the horn, and took a great delight in having his children instructed on the instrument that each one might like the best. Margery said she considered that if music and melody were so much followed in heaven, they ought to be tried at on earth; and she should always approve that each son of hers should perform on the instrument he might fancy best, and 'twas for him to see he did his part well upon it. No piano or harpsichord was introduced, because, though it was music greatly admired, it was not thought the right thing for a farm. It became an established custom, that one hour after tea should be given every evening to this family harmony. Some of Margery's sons had fine voices, which they interchanged with their instruments, bassoon and serpent, violin, French-horn, flageolet, and two flutes; their sisters sang with them in parts, and Elsie, dear Elsie, who had no gift of song, performed on the tambourine. They faithfully kept to the old English Psalm tunes, to which they sang the old version of the Psalms; varied with chants and anthems, and a few magnificent hymns, such as Luther's, and occasionally Handel's water-piece went off with a flourish of instruments at the end. And as the music swelled, and its harmony flowed through the open window in summer, the passers-by in the distant road stopped beneath the elm-trees to listen.

Then a wish was expressed in the parish that Benjamin's sons should lead the singing at church. Benjamin said he could never be against his sons doing their best in the worship of God. So the parishioners built a gallery for them; and Sunday after Sunday, from her large pew below, Margery saw her seven sons lead the praises of God in the sanctuary; while her daughters sat with her, and from their mother's side raised their voices, to join the chorus of their more distant brothers.

No household of twelve children could have seemed more ready for a hand to lead them on to the kingdom of heaven; but that hand was not yet given! Reverence and loyalty had grown with them from birth, they honored and obeyed their parents, respected their superiors in station, and showed kindness to all. Holy things were holy to them; with wit and fun abounding amongst them, the least mention of holy things brought a silence and awe over them all, from their childhood. They seemed to stand on the threshold of the kingdom of heaven, with none to show them the Door by which alone they could enter in. Some memory they carried with them of the early instruction of their venerable pastor, but he was laid in the chancel before Margery's youngest children were born; and their mother had need of more heavenly teaching herself to enable her clearly to understand, and freely to speak to her children of Him who has said, "I am the Way, the Truth, and the Life; no man cometh unto the Father but by Me."

"I tell you what, Sam," said Christiana, as she stepped into the back kitchen late one dark winter evening, "you will be very much to blame if you don't take in hand to do as you said. If I were you, I would have no words about it, but take the horse and the lantern at once, and make your way to our young master and tell him the truth. If one won't speak, another must, or worse trouble will come of it."

"I'm ready," said Sam; "I've never had two minds upon that. You can tell our master in the morning that you sent me off by night without disturbing of him."

"Yes, and make all the haste that ye can. I wish enough you were there, and our young master here!" Sam lighted the lantern and went out softly. His mistress was ill, and no one except the faithful servants seemed to lay it to heart. Sam Grist had sat up the first half of several nights, and Christiana the whole; the doctor said there was danger, still the master saw no reason for sending off for his son. Christiana and Sam Grist better knew the heart of their poor mistress; they had spoken many times of taking it upon themselves if no one else did, and now, when their old and young masters were sleeping, Sam Grist started off in the darkness, riding fast along the high road with the stable lantern beside him; and Christiana went back to keep watch by her mistress.

The night was long in tossings to and fro under the fever of sickness. Sometimes Christiana heard the prayer, "Lord, lighten our darkness, for the love of Thine only Son." Sometimes her poor mistress was talking to the old shepherd Benezer; then welcoming her aged mother-in-law with a tone of joy, as if she saw her again after her long years of absence. Sleep came towards morning, and on waking she said to Christiana, "Should you think that poor Ben has heard of my sickness?"

"I reckon he has by this time," replied Christiana, "and we shall for certain see him here before sunset." It was a word of earthly promise that soothed the earthly unrest, and the burning head lay in quieter thought on its pillow until sleep relieved it again.

When the master heard that Sam had gone off in the night, it seemed to awaken him to a sense of the probable end of this illness, and he took Christiana's place for some time that morning by the sick-bed of his wife; but she was wandering, looked at him vacantly, did not seem to know him; his own conscience reproached him, and he was glad to get away from the reproof that lay for him in the unconscious gaze of that silent face. He went out to his fields, and began to feel anxious lest the poor mother should die before the son came.

But Benjamin lost not a moment; leaving Sam Grist

behind to rest himself and his horse, he started at once for the sick-bed of his mother. The ear of death is quick to hear, and the dying mother looked up and said to Christiana, "'Tis the footfall of my poor Ben's own horse that I hear on the roadside! Oh! Christiana, he's come!"

Christiana looked out; he was not yet in view, but in two minutes more he stopped at the gate. He was soon in the room, kneeling down by the bed, and his tears flowing fast. The doctor had been; he said his patient was weaker, and sinking quickly, but all wandering left her mind at the sight of her son; that one dear calming stay of her troubled earthly life—the restful face of her boy—was before her in death. She could speak to him as she could to no other; he had shared her troubles, he could best share her joy.

"Ben, my poor Ben, don't fret for your mother; it's over now, past and gone, like the night gloom all lost in the morning!"

"Not over yet, mother; the Almighty may hear my prayer and yet spare your life."

"'Tisn't life I was minding, 'tis all of them troubles I mean. They seem so far behind me I've lost sight of them now; and there's only comfort, comfort, comfort. I see Him I've prayed to so often, and them as taught me to pray, and they all look down so cheerful on me as if they knew there was no trouble more. I don't know very well were I am, but 'tis all light as day; 'tis as your dear grandmother always said it would be, 'there's no darkness left,' and I don't know right well, but I think it must be what Benezer often spoke on, 'A song in the night.' This world's nothing now, Ben, and the sin that did trouble me is clean put out of the way. 'Tis the Almighty has done it, as I so often begged of Him that He would, for the love of His only Son our, Saviour Jesus Christ."

Then the weeping Christiana gave some wine to her mistress, who slept after taking it with her hand in her Benjamin's. She woke again, but spoke to no one, only they heard her still faintly saying at times, "For the love of thine only Son, our Saviour Jesus Christ." And when Sam Grist returned, his mistress was gone. How glad was his faithful heart that he had won that last drop of earthly comfort, to sweeten her cup of many sorrows that she now would drink of no more.

Benjamin returned home the next day, and brought Margery back with him to follow their dear mother to the grave, where they laid her to sleep beside the green turf that covered the dust of the angel mother-in-law she had listened to and loved.

CHAPTER IX.

"I WOULDN'T be the one," said Christiana, "to hide it from you, Sam; I've given my word to Farmer Day, and our banns are to be published on Sunday. I am sure he's full as good as I am, not to say better; and there's but few men, 'tis my belief, would have waited so patient when I could never set them a time."

"'Tis all ordered for the best," Sam Grist replied, "and I know right well that a blessing will follow you, let you go where you will, if it were only for the sake of our poor mistress that's gone!"

And Sam Grist turned away; the sudden tidings had affected him. He had shared the household place of service with Christiana from the time when they were both in their youth, and now, when Christiana was fifty, and Sam Grist over sixty, it seemed hard to lose her, and have to see a stranger in her place doing all the things wrong that Christiana had done right, and setting aside the good ways of the poor mistress that was gone. But Sam said to himself, "I can't blame her, I am sure; Farmer Day is worthy to have her; he's waited on these five years and more, and never troubled her one way or other, for he knew 'twas the love of her poor mistress that kept her denying of him. And I am sure there's no comfort left in doors, save to think the Almighty's angels have been here, and that lies but heavy when the place knows them no more. If I may but taste of their heavenly comfort 'tis all I look after now, for 'tis plain there'll be no stay here when Christina is gone."

Isaac Day rented a small farm in the parish; he had for many years been a widower, his children were married, and his small farm only wanted such a mistress as Christiana he thought would be, to make it as comfortable for him in his age as it had once been to him in youth. He had kept everything up both indoors and without to a pattern of neatness; yet Farmer Day and all around him looked perceptibly brighter at the prospect of his long-patient hope being near its fulfilment. Christiana had lost both her parents, and had no relations near, but every one in the parish felt a respect for her. Mrs. Penforth, Margery's mother, out of kind feeling to Benjamin's family, and esteem for Christiana as a most faithful servant, invited her to stay on the wold farm, and herself gave the wedding breakfast. Her master felt in some measure the debt that he owed her, and bestowed on her many things that had belonged to her mistress, which Christiana valued more than any new purchased gifts. And Benjamin said that the least he could do was to be at the wedding and give the faithful Christiana away. The day before the wedding he drove over to the wold farm, not in his gig, but in his light cart, with his two eldest girls beside him, and bridal gifts for Christiana most carefully packed in behind; his children sent their cosset lamb of that year, Margery one of her young calves of the summer before, with gifts of poultry and some household offerings beside. Farmer Day had been invited by Mrs. Penforth that evening to tea, and now she called him out to see Christiana's wedding gifts, the faithful Christiana having hastened out first at sight of her young master's children. Margery had trimmed their bonnets with white love, and put them on print frocks of soft grey, as they could not wear colors, for their dear grandmother's sake. Benjamin brought Christiana a white shawl for the wedding, having heard that though she had consented her gown should be lavender, she meant to wear the small black cloth shawl trimmed with crape that she had bought to mourn for her mistress. Benjamin told her that white garments must be nearer the mark for them that thought rightly of the place where his poor mother was gone; and when she saw his girls in their white tippets done up for the occasion, she could not but say that the thing seemed all settled for her that way. It was a pretty sight in the farmyard to see the children alighting, with all their anxiety about the gifts packed in behind. Benjamin in his black coat with the deep crape on his hat, notwithstanding all his thoughts about the white garments being nearer the mark; Mrs. Penforth bent on making the most of the occasion; Farmer Penforth catching the cosset lamb in his arms till the girls ran round to hold their pet safely, then looking on with his honest-hearted face and declaring that Benezer should match it as true as he could with a young lamb from his fold. And the girls looking up and saying, "Oh, grandfather, Benezer can never match Daisy! Mother says she never saw such a beauty; we should not have given it away to any one but Christiana!" And Christiana stood by with her womanly charms, looking brighter and more attractive than ever; and Farmer Day, in his high-topped boots and his Sunday coat, beside her, all his face one pleasant smile on the happy occasion. So Christiana was married, and many a peaceful year succeeded to the sorrows she had shared, which, having been borne by her for others, she was not called to go through for herself. Sam Grist remained in his place on the farm; it was not so desolate for him as it would have been for Christiana, because his work lay mostly out of doors, and all the animals on the farm were friends to him, his kind heart attaching to him every creature that he tended.

When little Stephen in his childhood read the Psalms month by month in the grammar-school, there were two verses that always arrested his thoughts, the 8th and 9th of the 118th Psalm, "It is better to trust in the Lord, than to put confidence in man. It is better to trust in the Lord, than to put confidence in princes." He always took more notice of these verses than of any others, and each month as he read them they fixed themselves deeper in his thoughtful mind. It was remarkable that the boy should so early choose, in the Divine Word, the principle that so strongly governed his mother's heart through life; it did not come to him in any conscious connexion with his mother, it made its own separate and powerful impression, yet it is probable that the seeing her rest every difficulty in her high trust in God, made him more thoughtful on the subject when it came before him in the striking language of the Psalm. So, while yet a child, Stephen chose those two verses for his own, and settled that he would always think upon them and mind them. And now his school days had been long over, and he had taken his place amongst the laborers on the farm; for Benjamin trained each of his sons, as they grew old enough, to regular work. He always said that "the best wealth to a farmer was his own practical knowledge; that he ought to stand as the best workman, before he had to stand as the master." And on this principle it was that he trained all his sons, and Margery her daughters. Stephen and his brothers were out at their work by five o'clock in the morning; they guided the plough, drove the harrow and roll; but the plough was their chief pleasure, because of the skill it required. Stephen often rose at midnight to go out with the wagon, to carry corn, which was chiefly threshed and sold in the winter. Mile after mile he trod the frosty roads beside his long team of horses with his whip in his hand, the stars shining clear and cold above him, and silence in the land all around. Then it was that he pondered many things, and often repeated the words that so strongly impressed him in childhood, "It is better to trust in the Lord than to put confidence in man; it is better to trust in the Lord than to put confidence in princes." He weighed their meaning well, and bound them to his heart as the law of his life.

The wind never blew strong over the farm without Margery giving a thought to the old household tree. She had felt more than she was prepared for when she saw it left alone on the hill-side, after sheltering the home from generation to generation. Yet the tree, though left exposed to the winds, had been anything but desolate, for it was the children's chief playfellow. Their favorite haunt was beneath its wide branches, and as soon as each boy felt the vigor of his limbs, his first achievements in using them were made on the old tree; they climbed it, peeped out from its green leaves, sang their sweet psalms in its old boughs, and loved the tree like a friend. The old tree looked down on their pastimes, waved over their young heads, and shed its rich leaves in autumn to come out again attired in green verdure in the spring. And the old tree had seen its children when they heeded it not—when their young hearts were all sorrow, and their tears falling fast; they had lost first an infant brother, and then a sister from amongst them, and two and two in their little dresses of black they had followed their parents, hand in hand, behind the lost brother and sister, under the tree's spreading branches, down the green hill, up to the old churchyard, to lay each departed little one in its grassy grave, to slumber there until the Saviour shall call it to awake and live for ever with Him. When the strong wind woke Margery at night, she always listened with a thought of the tree. And now one night came a storm, the wind caught the branches, and with a terrible crash down came the tree.

Not one little sleeper had been awakened by the storm or the crash of the old tree when it fell; and the younger children could hardly believe it was true, until they one and all stood around it, and saw it covering the hill-side with its great prostrate branches. They felt it a friend whose sheltering arms they had lost. Margery went not out with the children to look, and she said but little in reply to their words; she liked not the fall of the roof-tree! Her husband saw that it troubled her more than might have been expected; and when at length the old tree had been all cleared away, and its stump with much labor dug out, he went himself and chose a little sapling-ash from the wood, brought it home, and with his own hand planted it in the same spot where the old tree had stood.

"Mother, mother, come quick!" said little Edward, "father's now going to set in the new tree!"

"So he may," answered Margery, "I'm not coming to see."

"Oh mother, 'twill stand right where the old roof-tree stood."

"So it may, 'twill be no roof-tree to me!"

The child ran back to be in time for the planting, unable to understand why the mother should not care for the new tree; but Benjamin read his wife's heart in her words, when his child said, surprised, "Mother says 'twill be no roof-tree to her!" The young tree was planted, and grew, and to this day sheds its soft shadow on the green turf below. And though its fibrous roots interfere now with one land drain, and now another, for the springs on that hill-side are abundant, yet the laborers work and the tiles are replaced, that the ash tree may wave on undisturbed by the sons, because planted by the hand of their father.

It was soon after this, that fear of invasion in our country caused a general training to arms; and Benjamin found, by what he heard at the market town, that he must give a son to the militia. It was a startling proposal to bear home to the rural quiet of that lonely English farm, and his first thought was of Margery—how she would take to the tidings. But Margery was Roman matron enough to have yielded up her seven sons to their country's defence, and loyal-hearted enough to have made them each one a cavalier. However, on any questionable subject her husband always began cautiously, setting but small sail at first, until he saw which turn the wind was likely to take, knowing well by experience that it would sweep pretty strong whichever quarter it lay in.

"It seems," Benjamin said, "by what I can hear, that they will look for one of our boys to train in the militia."

"Better send one at once, then," replied Margery.

"I don't know that we need be beforehand," said Benjamin; "they are pretty sure not to look over our seven."

"But if you know the boy's wanted, that's enough," responded Margery; "are the lads to sit round the fire till the crown comes and orders them out? If a boy of ours be to go, let him be found standing ready."

Benjamin finally consulted Margery on which son should go.

"Why, the one that's most fit, and I should reckon that's Stephen; he's not quite so tall as Nathaniel or Daniel, but he's the strongest boy that we have, and as firm as any one of them in the thing he takes in hand. He'll never lay open his country's crown to an enemy; let him go, and God bless him!"

Stephen's high spirits rose to welcome the choice: his regimentals were first-rate, to do honor, not to him, but to the service in which he was to wear them: his helmet with its colored plume was heavy enough for the strong neck of an "Ironside;" and his sword of such a length as perhaps few, save a broad-shouldered yeoman, could wield: he had a scarlet cloak for night encampments; and he rode a black charger, named Starlight. He was already a first rate horseman, and Starlight had been trained in perfection by Stephen himself. It was great joy to all that the good horse was now not to be sold, because Stephen must have him, to fight for his country. The horse was a beautiful animal, and well off in the hands and the care of his rider. One white star on his forehead, one on his side, and another on its fore foot, won for him the appropriate name of Starlight. All the household assembled at the farm-gate to see Stephen and Starlight make their first start in the service of the crown. Reared in the heart of such peace as blessed that English farm, Starlight did not understand being mounted with the accoutrements of war; he pranced, turned about, and snorted. Stephen let him have his fancies, as he said, until he could settle his mind as to what was upon him; but as Starlight was rather longer than usual in reaching the right conclusion, Stephen made a remonstrance, "Come, sir! What, isn't your mind made up yet? I can tell you mine is, and the crown wants us both!" Of course this was final, and Starlight galloped off for the charge, as the best trained war-horse in the land might have done.

War on our own peaceful fields was in mercy averted. God's shield was extended over England, and saved her then from the dreadful strife of the battle-field. Had it been otherwise, and Stephen been called to the conflict, an early grave would have covered a hero, or his deeds as a soldier been his laurels through life. But Stephen was training by Heaven for the yet harder strife, in which no force but that of calm self-restraint, highest moral courage, and a firm hold of truth, could prevail. All these graces may ennoble, though they are not always the accompaniments of the warrior. True laurels are unfading, and will be verdant in heaven. Such many a soldier's have been, and such Stephen won; while his war accoutrements were finally laid up at the farm—untouched by the blood of a foeman, to repose there as the trophies of peace.

All looked prosperous now at the farm. Stephen and Starlight forgot the roll call and the marshal file, and the soldier's hand guided the plough. But an invader drew near whom no warlike array can appal; the angel of death entered Margery's home, not now to bear one of her bright children away, but to take the husband—the father. The warning was short, and the bereavement unlooked for; poor Margery stood a widow, alone in the midst of her fatherless children. Strong grief is a terrible thing, but there was no violent expression in Margery's hour of woe. She wept as she never wept before, but her deepest anguish lay buried in her silent heart. The light she had attained to still guided her spirit through the terrible gloom that had so suddenly darkened around her. "My poor children," she said, "God forbid we should murmur! It is the Lord, let the Almighty do what He will! He has promised He will care for the widow and the fatherless, and He won't be less good than His word!"

Alas! there was not one to draw near with words of

peace from the God of the widow, not one to help her to read sorrow's lesson aright, in the light of that love that shines from the cross of Him who bore our sorrows and carried our griefs; none to testify of Jesus—whose presence is light in our darkness, peace to the broken in heart, and the very balm of life in our bitterest cup. That strong matron, bowed with a sorrow the world could not lighten, on Sunday, in her deep weeds of widowhood, ascended the hill, amidst her eleven children, to worship God in the sanctuary—a sight that woke tenderness in the hearts and eyes of the peasants as they passed, but no pastor's benediction was breathed on the widow and the fatherless.

CHAPTER X.

WE have sometimes to learn in sorrow that God's ways are not our ways, nor His thoughts our thoughts; but faith finds its rest in the assurance that this is because they are HIGHER. "For as the heavens are higher than the earth, so are my ways higher than your ways, and my thoughts than your thoughts." "It is high as heaven, what canst thou know?" must silence our hearts when we would question and judge the mystery of God's divine providence. Margery questioned not nor murmured. Her eldest son occupied a separate farm in the same parish, but six sons and four daughters still filled the parental home when the bereavement came that deprived it of a husband and a father. Truly the roof-tree had fallen! and left with so large a family, and sons so young, Margery felt herself a widow indeed, and desolate. But she had long trained her heart to trust in God, and that trust upheld her now. In the first week of her widowhood she called her second son, Stephen, before her, and said to him, "My son, you must stand in your poor father's place; 'tis an unlooked-for call for you to meet the world alone, but 'tis come, and you must rise up and obey it. You know what belongs to it; hold on your way right forward, and the God of the widow and the fatherless will be with you."

In respectful silence, and with deep feeling, Stephen took his commission from the lips of his mother. It was a solemn call—in the first opening of manhood to step at once into an office so responsible! Was he ready for the call? High spirited, quick tempered, and full of lively humor, as he was, many an anxious foreboding might naturally arise in a widowed mother's heart; but if Margery felt them, she uttered them not. She had never lowered her children's filial obedience, by lowering her tone of expectation from them; each child felt from infancy, "My mother expects me to do my duty," and dreaded the shock of her surprise if he failed. This high tone of expectation and trust had done much in strengthening the moral character of her children; and now, though the occasion was greater than any that had met them before, Stephen felt that his mother expected him, in dependence on God, to fill the place left vacant by the death of his father. No one can watch the life of a heart that trusts in God, though it may be trusting only dimly and from afar, without finding how truly God does for those who ask of and trust in Him, exceeding abundantly above all that they asked or thought.

Heaven has its nurseries, schools, and cloisters upon earth, unseen by the world, in which its children are trained for their service. As surely as Philip was sent of God to the eunuch crossing the desert of Gaza, so surely was little Stephen led by the same divine providence to the feet of his great-grandmother, there to meet the influence that was to be his earliest preparation for the service of God on earth, and His glory in heaven. Margery little thought on that morning, that she was sending her boy to receive the first impression that was to prepare him to stand as the staff of her widowhood. Let no mother ever forget that the influence of a single day may tell for good or evil on her child's whole future life; remembering this, will she not keep ever above him the shield of her prayers?

At the side of his great-grandmother Stephen had learned a love for the Bible, that after-life only deepened; he had also learned to give the poor a home in the compassions of his soul. No human eye read his spirit's inner life; none saw him, after school-days had passed by, still bending in youthful reverence over the Word of God, no one knew how literally he meditated day and night in the law of the Lord—behind the plough by day, and by night beneath the stars when he led his team to the town. The call came and found him ready to meet it.

For a short time things held on their own way at the farm, in respectful memory to the departed master; but Stephen knew the day was near when he must speak to the men, and take his place over them. His deep feeling dreaded the time; he would follow out all his father's orders, carry on all his plans, make no sudden changes, as if he thought his judgment better than the one that was gone; but there was one thing Stephen felt he must do, and resolved that he would do, let the consequence be what it might. During the years in which the parish had now lain neglected in all ministerial care, swearing had increased amongst the men. Stephen heard it behind the plough, heard it from the stables, heard it even in the harvest-fields when they were full of the goodness of the Lord; it made his spirit burn with indignation. He reproved it, but still it went on; and as the ignorance around grew darker, this sin of cursing and swearing grew louder. And Stephen resolved that his first act as a master, should be with the strong hand of authority to put down the evil that testified a contempt of the Most High, which, refusing to be softened by His goodness, would not yield to man's voice of persuasion and reproof.

So when Stephen first gave his orders to the men as their master, he said in conclusion, "And now I have one word for you all. Whatever I plant the ground with, it shall not be with oaths; too many of them have dropped on it already, and I am determined there shall be no more. The first oath that I hear, if it be from the best workman on the farm, that day he shall go. 'Tis a sin that no excuse can stand up to plead for, 'tis a scorning of the Almighty, in whose hand your breath is; therefore think on the warning, for I can promise you that you will not have a second!" It was reverence that spoke from the firm lips of the youth now first taking his place as master on the farm of his birth; he spoke from a soul that obeyed the divine precept, "Thou shalt fear before that great and terrible name, the Lord thy God." Surely it is a scene to detain for a moment the thoughts of the reader. The youth on whom the care of a large and anxious business, a widowed mother, and nine brothers and sisters had suddenly fallen, first meeting the laborers as their master, and exalting above all things the name of his God. Young in years, with ignorance and ungodliness around, standing there alone, without the knowledge of a single friend upon earth to whom he could turn for counsel and support, knowing well from past experience that his position must be one of difficulty and trial, and yet boldly declaring, before he took one step on that farm as its master, that he would cast from it the best labor that it owned, if it must be kept with dishonor to the name of his God. When we think of how firmly he stood for the glory of God, it must condemn the half-heartedness of many, who have been aided with instruction and encouragement that Stephen never knew. The men heard, and felt that their young master had taken his resolve; no question had been raised of serving him better than they had served his father, it was a solemn requirement that on the land he tilled the name of the God of the whole earth should be honored; no longer urged by him as a duty, nor pleaded for as a wish, but given nobly forth as a command.

Authority over those fields was his own, and so far as that authority extended his God should not be dishonored. And well was that word fulfilled to Stephen, "Them that honor Me, I will honor." The men turned to their labor, and a feeling of sacredness invested the ground on which the foot of no swearer might return again to tread. And Stephen could say to a friend in after life, "Over the farm as I am all day long, it is eleven years since I have heard an oath uttered upon it." Those corn-covered valleys, as they shouted and sang, could witness that the land mourned no longer for cursing and swearing.

Stephen now left many things he had followed before; he no longer guided the plough from headland to headland, no longer rose at midnight to go out with the corn-wagon, and tread the roads in the silence of the calm country night, no longer took his part in breaking-in and training the horses; these and many such things he must now leave to others, but he left not the law of his God, on that he pondered more than ever. He still said to himself the words that arrested him in childhood, "It is better to trust in the Lord than to put confidence in man; it is better to trust in the Lord than to put confidence in princes." Then communing with himself, with a beautiful simplicity he would silently say, "'BETTER,' then why not do it? Why should any take up with the less when they are welcome to the greater—not to say the greatest? Why should I put my trust in man when I may trust in God? Better than in princes too! No doubt 'tis a great way from me up to them, and it must seem a wonderful stay to have a friend amongst them, yet it says, 'Better than in princes!' I'll try it then, for why should I turn to the less when I may have the greater?" From the Prayer-Book he had reverently and thoughtfully used from a boy, he chose out the prayer which he thought most met his need; it was the collect for the Tuesday in Whitsun week; he always called it "that prayer for a right judgment in all things." And this choice he never changed; whatever supplication in older years ascended from his soul, when he became conscious of other and deeper necessities than his earthly calling required, he still kept the prayer for a right judgment in all things always breathing from his heart; it was not the prayer of his retirement, but the prayer of his activity. Those anxious moments to be ascertained in the life of a farmer; when the grass is ripe and will injure by standing; when the hay has attained its highest sweetness, which will lessen by lying; when it is cool enough and may be stacked, or too hot and would fire; when the corn may wait on for fine weather, or had better be cut in faith that the weather will follow in due season; with the thousand calls for a decision, and the importance that rests on each one; in farms where rent and tithes, and rates and taxes, and labor must all be paid out of the produce, and that without delay; all the anxiety the corn-market brings, where prices rise and fall, and the wisest find themselves mistaken; no wonder Stephen felt the necessity of a better judgment than could be found in one weak erring mind, and so acted on the promise in Isaiah—"His God doth instruct him and teach him," and as he went about his long day's anxious business prayed in his heart, "Grant us by the same Spirit to have a right judgment in all things." Well might his mother lean on such a son as the staff of her widowhood, and never did that staff give way beneath her.

It was not long before Stephen was called to try the divine armor which he had secretly and in silence buckled on, and, as it often happens, this first test was a sharp one, putting both the armor and him who wore it fully to the proof. A tradesman in the next parish, sent in to the widow an unjust balance of accounts. Benjamin had had large dealings with the man, and they had always been fairly settled; but now the grass was green above the husband, and "the man of the world" thought to make the widow and the fatherless his prey. David prays, "Deliver my soul from men of the world" (Ps. xvii.), and all that are desolate and helpless have need to pray the same prayer. The tradesman sent in a settlement a hundred pounds short of the true one, probably thinking that late entries might not have been made before the father's sudden removal; but Benjamin did the work of the day in the day, and Stephen succeeded to books strictly balanced. The settlement was returned to the tradesman and the error stated; it came back again by a messenger to the farm; all alteration refused, the widow's claim set at nought, and his power to prove it defied. Margery was alone. She opened and read the letter from the man who had always been fairly dealt with, and who had often sat down at their hospitable board. Bitter to the heart's depths is the moment when the widow first feels the cruel hand of the oppressor, on the home that bereavement has left open to the footstep of wrong. Margery felt that her life's shield was gone, and, stunned and cold at the shock of this cruel defiance, she stood looking from the window on vacancy. She was still standing there when Stephen entered. She turned her face, and he saw his mother's countenance fixed and pale. She tried to speak, but her lips quivered and she could not. "Mother, what is it?" At the voice of her son the tears rose to her eyes; that firm, true-hearted voice, in which at times all the tenderness of his father's tones lay, it softened the stony feeling at her heart and gave a power of utterance. "Take, and read it," she said, and put the letter in his hand. Stephen read it all at a glance. What he then felt can be told only by the son who, full of reverence and filial devotion to a widowed mother, at whose side he has taken his dead father's place, sees his youthful protection set at nought by the world, sees the "man of the earth" make his first cruel venture upon her, and sees the first tear that oppression ever brought to her eye.

Had this wrong to his mother met Stephen anywhere else, it is probable that his quick temper would have been suddenly roused to some vehement expression of his just indignation; but his mother's presence had never from childhood been the place for an outburst of anger; self-restraint was habitual before her. This habit of filial reverence came in now to his moral rescue. Looking up at his mother, with a face in which deep emotion could always be read, if the occasion called it forth, he said, "Never trust me again, mother, if you don't hear a very different story from this before night-time!" then, putting the letter in his pocket, that it might never again meet the eyes of his mother, he left the house.

It was a moment of great extremity, but the promise to those who bind the divine law continually upon their heart is, "When thou goest, it shall lead thee." As Stephen turned anxiously and thoughtfully away, questioning with himself what he should do, the words on which he had meditated day and night rose up within his soul, "It is better to trust in the Lord than to put confidence in man; it is better to trust in the Lord than to put confidence in princes." "I will venture upon it, and stand or fall by that word!" said Stephen resolvedly, and said no more. His resolution was taken; but how much depended on the results! The hundred pounds in question—important as it was to them then—was perhaps the least anxiety that lay in it; it was the world's contest with the fatherless youth, who had to take his place as a buyer and a seller in the midst of it; if he failed in this his first contest, every unjust trader would have an inducement to try their worst upon him, and the home of his widowed mother might in the end fall before it. Yet, like the stripling David, when he refused the royal coat of mail, Stephen thought of no earthly defences, but set out alone, armed with nothing but the "sword of the Spirit," to contend with "the wrongful dealings of men." He passed the fields where his young corn was springing, and others where his brothers were guiding the plough, but his quick, observant eye heeded nothing that day. At length he reached the distant brow of the hill and looked down on the wide-spreading valley, a scene of loveliness now, but far richer then in its beauty, when the woods waved where the plough now cuts its straight furrow; too beautiful it looked to have a home for the oppressor. A mile further brought him to the village and the house of the tradesman. He had need of his chosen prayer, "Grant us by the same Spirit to have right judgment in all things, and evermore to rejoice in His holy comfort, through the merits of Jesus Christ, our Saviour."

"I have come down," Stephen said, "to settle the business in hand."

"By whose reckoning, yours or mine? that's the first question."

"Not by yours nor by mine," replied Stephen, "but by my poor father's own books. I shall stand by his figures, and not go from one of them; and you know, as well as any one, that he never set down a wrong one."

"I am not going to have any words about it, young man. I have sent you my reckoning, and, if you think you can disprove it by law, I advise you to try."

"I am not come here about the law," replied Stephen, "nor to wish you to think that my widowed mother has no better refuge than that! 'Tis true my poor father is dead, but there's a greater than he stands up in his place, and I tell you candidly I am come to you only from Him, and His Word is the message I bring, and that is a true Word, you know; for He has said, 'Cursed be he that perverteth the judgment of the fatherless and the widow!' You must choose—and you know right well that you must—between the just dues of the widow, and the curse of the Almighty, who will plead her cause. If you send me back to my mother with fair reckoning in my hand, there will be no evil follow from this falling out between us; but if you refuse her just claims, the Almighty is witness, and the curse He has threatened will surely know how to come."

The trader staggered beneath the strong calm words of the youth. Anger, threatening, revenge, he could have met with defiance; but this calm strength of truth he had no weapon to combat with. The fear of God, whose words the youth brought alone to the contest, fell upon the man, and he asked, "What's the reckoning you have set it at?"

Stephen held out the very paper that the trader had refused before, who, vexed at the sight, said, "I told your mother I should be ready to stand to my reckoning, and to no other."

"Let alone what you said to my mother," replied Stephen, "that's not the question now; 'tis what you mean to say to the Almighty, who stands now in my poor father's place, when his widow puts a just claim before you. There is not one item false; I can prove every one. Will you do the thing that is just by her? or do you say you will not?"

The trader answered not, but counted out the money to the full reckoning. Stephen signed the paper, put the money in his pocket, and turned to the trader, saying, "I leave you now with no strife between us." The hard-natured man was moved to feeling.

Stephen quitted the village, climbed the long hill, impatient until again he could stand before his mother. His sisters were setting the tea, and his mother seated in her arm-chair looking anxiously into the fire, when Stephen appeared at the door. That was a moment earth's conquerors might envy, when Stephen placed in his widowed mother's hand his lost father's own reckoning, paid in full, and heard her voice saying to him, "The God above has been with you, or you never could have carried it so." He who single-handed comes off conqueror in the strife with oppression, ascends a throne whose rights others are slow to invade. "He that handleth a matter wisely shall find good, and whoso trusteth in the Lord, happy is he." But Stephen told not then how his victory had been won:

he had in his soul reverence, trust, and obedience; but it is love that brings expression to the surface. The Hand that created and governs the world may well command the reverence, the trust, and the obedience of all men; but it is the Hand nailed to the cross for our sins, that alone can open in the soul the deep well-springs of the sinner's love; it is the sense of "much forgiven" that is alone followed by the "loveth much," and this Stephen as yet had not. But in his chamber kneeling that night, he could fervently say, "In Thee, O Lord, have I trusted; let me never be confounded."

CHAPTER XI.

STEPHEN told no one at that time of his contention with the trader, and Margery was always silent on matters of business; but silence has oftentimes more weight than words, and secret things are not kept concealed, "for a bird of the air shall carry the voice, and that which hath wings shall tell the matter." Stephen, at his entrance on business, was treated with respect and consideration beyond what could have been expected at his years; many from right feeling, but there were others who would have watched their occasion against him if he had not shown himself able to hold his own position. Stephen felt himself strengthened by the victory he had gained; but he who wins his way by "the sword of the Spirit" exalts not himself in that victory. Stephen was not elated, but felt as one who has gained a vantage-ground by leaning on the arm of a Friend. The chief comfort to him was, that from that day he could see that his mother left the care of the business with him, and trusted him as she trusted his father before him.

Some changes were now made in the home. Margery sent her third son, Nathaniel, to serve his time with a miller; her eldest was already established on a separate farm by himself; this left five sons at home—Stephen, Daniel, Edward, Philip, and the fair-haired little Matthew, who was the youngest of her thirteen children, and always called by his mother "the boy." There were four daughters—Margaret, Charlotte, Mary, and Elsie the youngest; little Nancy and her infant brother William lay sleeping in the green churchyard with their father. The eldest daughter, Margaret, had had years of ill-health, often unable to leave her bed, and when at length she grew better she had not the power to keep up with the activity around her; so she one day said, "Mother, I wish I had a little place by myself, where I could take my own time, and order all as I am best able to do it."

"Do you, child? then you shall try it, if I can any way make it out for you."

Margery's husband had rented two farms in one. On the opposite hill to the family home there stood an old whitewashed farmhouse, close to the church. It had a farmyard around it, and a high sunny garden, that ran along by the churchyard, separated only by a hedge. This farmyard was always well filled, and the stackyard the same, but the house was let. When Margaret expressed this wish, her mother felt it was reasonable, talked with Stephen, and arranged to give this farmhouse up to her; and it was settled that Stephen should make his home with Margaret, spending the day in his mother's house as before, but going up every evening to the household prayers, and for the night, to the church farm, as the whitewashed house was called. Stephen did not leave his sister on Sunday, but spent that day with her in the quiet retirement of the little farm-kitchen. So Margaret had her wish, and it answered well. She had her own little dairy of cows, her own poultry and bees, her own flower-garden, vegetables, and fruit—on which Stephen bestowed his skilful attention; she had also her own little maid, and everything in plain simple order for a farm; and she lived in sight of her mother's own home, with only the green turfy valley and rippling stream lying between them. She still sat by her mother on Sunday at church, and often went down to the family home to tea, walking back when Stephen was ready. She rose early in her little farm, almost as early as her mother, who never rose later than five o'clock; but she could now take things in her own quiet way, not confused by numbers, nor hurried and tired by seeing the energy around her that she did not possess. She grew silent, more silent by far than even her mother, who was never given to much speaking; but she lived with her own kind quiet thoughts, and never wanted much other company. In those days there were but few who thought of teaching the poor, but Margaret would call in her little yard-boy, and take patient trouble to instruct him: she would teach her young servant-girl, and speak words of good counsel to the man who lived as farm-servant in the house. She greatly loved her brother Stephen, and so her satisfied heart made its home and never wished for another.

Margery had always been famed for her bees; the flowers that flourished under her eye, and the large white lilies in particular, greatly encouraged the bees. The hive stood at hand near the house, and its small inhabitants were watched over with great interest by all. The little winged insects formed the same attachment to Stephen as their great neighbor Gruff, the farm dog, had done; they knew him so well, and were so entirely assured of his good intentions, that they never resented anything he might do. When they swarmed, he took them up in his uncovered hands, and lifted them into their new habitation, and they only buzzed a gentle acknowledgment; even on the dark autumn evening, when, year after year, several swarms of poor bees were destroyed with sulphur for their honey, (the good hives invented now were not known at the farm,) even on that destructive evening the poor bees flew round his head and remonstrated loudly, but never revenged themselves on him by giving him a sting. After Benjamin's death the farm bees began to fail, and Margery, who knew more about the habits of bees than any one at that time near or distant, said sorrowfully, "I knew it would be so; it always is when the head of a household is taken away. When your poor father died, if you had knocked by the door of each swarm, and told the bees your trouble, they would not have gone, but they never can stand it if they be forgotten at such times, and I don't blame them neither; and I can promise you it will be many a year before you get a good hive here again." And it happened as Margery said; even Stephen's care could not cherish the bees for many a year at the paternal home; but Margaret had a hive on her high sunny grass plat, and up there the bees made themselves happy, and flourished as a prosperous community.

While the farm brightened beneath the blessing of God, ignorance and evil grew darker and bolder around. "Oh my people, they that lead you cause you to err!" The Rectory, which should have been the centre of light, was a dark spot in the parish. And now the stiles on either side of the Rectory pasture were pulled down, and the hedge filled in with thorns, that the feet of the villagers might no longer tread there on their way to the church; that church was desolate, and none loved its gates; but Margery was still seen in her place, with her sons and daughters in theirs, for she had said from the first time of the present Rector's coming, that "no evil doer should turn her from her church; she had not lived so long without finding out that it held better teaching in the prayers, which none could alter, than in most of the preaching to be found otherwhere." But now a frightful act of the minister's towards the poor of the village roused a feeling in all, and sent a shudder through the farm. Margery's sons said to their mother that they "would go no more to hear the words of such a man; he might preach alone for all them, and most likely soon would; they were not going to play their psalmody for him; it was certain the less of such a man the better!" Their widowed mother let them pour out their just indignation, and then gave her high-toned command. "Now, lads, I'll hear no more of this; you will all go to church, every one of you. Do ye suppose 'tis the man ye go there to worship, or that ye sing your praises for him? And as to his words, he may preach his own darkness, but the reading and the praying are none of his, nor ever likely to be, by all I can see! You go and do your part; look to it that ye be found honoring the church of your God if no one else be, and be sure ye will have your reward."

It was well for Margery's sons that they forsook not the law of their mother; it was not their own village alone that was darkened; darkness lay on the land all around, and had the tie once been broken that bound them as a family in public worship, other disunions would soon have broken in, and each one have done that only which was right in his own eyes. But they forsook not the law of their mother, and it proved an ornament of grace unto their head and chains about their neck; and many a villager, who would no more have honored the Sabbath, still crossed the church's threshold, won by their sacred melody, and being there heard the divine teaching of words which, as Margery said, man could not alter, by which many a wanderer has been led into the paths that are pleasantness and peace.

Stephen was elected parish churchwarden at the death of his father, and this office sometimes brought him into a necessity of painful opposition to the minister, but nothing moved him from his course of right-doing; he held on his way, and always said, "We must do the day's work, and trust God with what may come of it to-morrow." But there came a morrow that brought results little expected by Stephen. **A letter** arrived **at the** farm. All knew the look of it in a moment; it came from London, and was directed, as they said, in "that large grand-looking writing that those particular letters always bore." It was from the Commissioners of Woods and Forests, and to the effect, that having been credibly informed that the widow had no steward or bailiff to carry on the business, and her sons under age, and therefore incapable of so large a **concern**, they thought it not likely that it could be continued in her hands; nothing had yet been determined against her, but this was to forewarn. **The** widow looked on her children in dismay, but there was no outbreak of feeling. Her voice was terribly calm, as she said, "I doubt there's **the** hand of an enemy in this, and that one not far from **our** own door, and our cause is a lost one unless the good God take it up." Stephen spoke not, and not one had any answer to make; all knew too well who their enemy **was.** It was not the trader who at first tried to wrong **them;** they could now venture any dealings with him, for an enemy conquered, as he had been, ofttimes becomes a sure friend. It was one who had aimed this cruel stroke unseen and in secret, and who could not therefore be met and contended with as a man. Stephen had thought himself well established in his poor father's place, but he knew that if any testimony were likely to be listened to against him, and believed unexamined, it would be the Rector's, who held his living of the college, and whose character was little known beyond his own neglected parish. He felt sure it must be from him that this evil report had gone up, but all proof was absent, and therefore he said not a word. A dull weight of oppression fell on all; each one looked around as if a sentence of separation were already written on the home that was the only spot they loved or knew on earth. In the evening Margery said to her son, "You must consider what you can best write in answer, for we have no friend to turn to to speak for us."

Stephen replied, "Well, mother, my mind is to wait till the morning."

The mother said no more, and Stephen had the calm night before him in which to ponder on a trouble so terrible and strange. As alone in the darkness of evening he crossed the green valley and ascended the hill, he thought to himself, "I am no hand at a letter when the thing lies plain before me; and now to write an answer to such great men, and that to speak up for myself, as if I thought highly of my great ability to manage the estate, that will never do for a moment. That's a true word, and well to be minded, 'Let another man praise thee and not thine own mouth; a stranger, and not thine own .ips.' But I don't know where to find another to do it; no gentry hereabout that I could ask to take it in hand: and if I could get any one to speak for me, that might look like setting up my good authority against theirs. Of course, they must think their friend's judgment better than my friend's, if I had one; and they would not thank me for telling them that their friend is wrong. Dear me, I can see pretty clear what won't do; but the thing is to get a light on what will!" So talking with himself, Stephen reached the church farm, said what he could to comfort poor Margaret, led the household worship, and then went to his chamber. There, on his little table, always lay his Bible and Church Prayer-Book; and he turned to the words he most wanted to express his difficulty and distress.

STEPHEN'S PRAYER.

"O Lord, we beseech Thee mercifully to receive the prayers of Thy people which call upon Thee; and grant that they may both perceive and know what things they ought to do, and also may have grace and power faithfully to fulfil the same, through Jesus Christ our Lord. Almighty God, who seest that we have no power of ourselves to help ourselves, keep us both outwardly in our bodies, and inwardly in our souls, that we may be defended from all adversaries that may happen to the body, and from all evil thoughts which may assault and hurt the soul, through Jesus Christ our Lord. Amen."

The prayer of faith has strong, swift wings, on which it bears the burden that is committed to it, from the heavy-laden spirit up to the throne of grace; therefore, the spirit that has prayed is lightened of the overwhelming load. Stephen lay down to sleep. As he rose in the morning, the trouble again stretched its dark shadow before him. Then these words passed through his recollection: "Seest thou a man diligent in his business, he shall stand before kings; he shall not stand before mean men." For a moment he thought on them; then exclaimed, in rejoicing energy, "I see it! it's laid out there for me as plain as words can be put. I am to go and stand afore them myself! Don't I know I have been diligent in business? Well, then, it says, 'he shall stand before kings; he shall not stand before mean men.' 'Tis pretty plain he must be a mean man who could turn against the widow in that secret way that no one should know by whom it was done, and by a tale that's not true; it takes me right out of his way, whoever he be, and says I shall stand before kings: that must be our great men up in London; for sure enough they stand kings over us. Now I've found it I'll follow it, let come what will!' So communed that youthful spirit with itself and the word of its God. Well Stephen proved the promise, "When thou goest it shall lead thee, when thou sleepest it shall keep thee, and when thou awakest it shall talk with thee." His resolve was taken, and when he had once resolved, no more questioning arose in his mind.

Margery's breakfast hour was six, sometimes earlier, never later. Stephen always went down to the family home before breakfast, and this day he did so as usual. His mother said nothing on the subject so heavily pressing; she knew the first hours of the morning were full of arrangements for the work of the day. Stephen also was silent; he set the men to their work, gave his brothers their directions as usual, looked once on the face of his mother, thought of all that must pass before he saw that honored face again, and then turned from his home. He went up to the church farm, put on his Sunday coat and high-topped boots, told his sister that he was going out on business, that she must not sit up for him at night, as he was pretty sure not to be home until the next day.

"What! sleep away from home?" inquired Margaret, with unbelieving surprise; "why, that's a thing that you never have done!"

"Never did, does not make never may!" replied Stephen; "you expect me when you see me, that's all I have to say." And he went out of the door.

Margaret looked after him; he did not turn across the valley for home; could he be going round by the drift? No, he held on the road, and yet "he was on foot; he could never mean to walk so far as sleeping out all the night! Perhaps a friend might be waiting somewhere near to convey him." This opened fresh wonder; but the milk had curdled ready for the press, and Margaret hastened to make her good cheese. Stephen walked by the distant field where the men were that day at work, and beckoning his brother Edward, whose young hand was skilfully guiding the plough, he said to him, "You run home to our mother, tell her that I am off by the coach for London; say that I am going to answer the letter, and that I cannot be home until to-morrow, but I hope by teatime she will see me back again." It would not be easy to describe the surprise these tidings caused at the farm. London lay to them in the distance almost like the ends of the earth, a place of wonder and mystery; it was a day's journey to reach it, and Stephen travelling by coach too, when none of them had ever travelled on the road, except behind a good horse of their own. "However will he tell how to order when he gets there?" said one. "Whatever can he say to such great men?" said another. Margery was silent; she felt it was a venture of strong trust in God; and what could she do if she mistrusted His mercy? While Stephen, hastening with active step along the field-path and highway, felt none of the wondering questionings that arose in his home. He walked the six miles to the wayside inn where the coach stopped to change horses, found an outside place vacant, and was soon on the road safe from all recall from his home.

That day and the next could not fail to be days of great suspense and anxiety at the farm. The widow's spirit was bowed down very low. The terrible threat of being turned from the home of her youth, the birthplace of her children, and the only place she knew that could **make a** home for them upon earth; and that by the cruel, unjust word of one who had no reason to bear her ill-will, for she had wronged no one. It was a bitter cup to have held to her lips; too bitter it seemed to her then sinking spirit to drink. And then Stephen's journey to London must be thought a great venture; what could he know of the ways of such great **men?** They might take it amiss that he stood up before them; besides, how could he tell how to find them? Such a strange great place as **London!** who could say that he would ever make **his way** safely out of it again?" But if Margery's thoughts were troubled, her lips were silent. When she could **not speak** well **of** God's ways, she **never** spoke **at all**; no murmur was ever heard to pass from **her lips.**

Stephen's sisters **set the long** cheerful tea table very early the next day. Margaret, **in her anxiety,** had come down for the evening; but they could not cheat the time, which wore on slowly enough. Their brothers were not within, and their mother did not watch from the window **where** her daughters **were** gathered, but sat **by** the large open chimney **in her** arm-chair, thoughtful **and sad.** "Poor lad," she said to herself; "no doubt the **London folk** have strange ways of their own, **such as he** little forethought; he never should have had my consent to run **into** the midst of them so unawares of what it might be. God **grant him** safe home again!"

The tall old kitchen clock struck out six from the corner where it stood; it was an hour past the tea-time, but no one thought of not waiting on, in expectation of Stephen's greatly longed for arrival.

Little fair-headed Matthew stood out by the drift-hedge.

"Matthew looks the wrong way," said Mary; "I can't think what he does there."

Then little Matthew started, turned round and ran in, saying breathlessly, "Philip threw up his cap, so I know he is coming!"

Then Philip leaped the drift-stile, and rushed in at the door; "Edward shouted from the oak boughs, at the top of barn field, so he must be coming now!"

Then the slight, swift-footed Edward came running in sight: the bright crimson that always flushed his young cheeks glowing red with his haste—"Daniel hurrahed from the stile on the top of Stony Croft, so 'tis certain he must be safe home in no time!" Then, having poured out his tidings, he ran back with those eager feet that no one but Daniel could outstrip in a race, to meet the brother whom his young heart so looked up to and loved.

A few minutes and Stephen came in sight, with Daniel beside him, and Edward all glee, hardly able to keep back his fast feet from hastening home again, yet sure to feel the propriety that Stephen should tell his own tale. The mother did not rise from her seat; she could not; deep emotion unnerved her. Now that she felt that Stephen was safe, the question rushed fearfully through her heart what his tidings might be. But as quickly as could be her son stood beside her, and said, "Thank God, my mother! none can turn you from your home. The gentlemen say they are satisfied, and of course that's enough!"

Words cannot give the touching home scene that followed. The dark cloud had parted and rolled away from above them, shining bright with the rainbow of hope, and glistening with the tears of deep feeling. But Stephen soon turned to the cheerful home table, saying, "I've not tasted food for these ten hours, and I think I'm hungry;" so he asked the blessing, and they all sat down together.

CHAPTER XII.

LITTLE MATTHEW looked up the long table more than once to see if he could venture to begin with his questions. There was more silence than might have been expected on such an occasion; but Margery's children always waited until they found what their mother might be going to say, and her emotion that evening was too deep for much speaking; so little Matthew took courage, and presently asked, "I say, brother, did you see the king?"

"No; that must be when you go," replied Stephen, "for the town is so large I did not even get a sight of the house where his majesty dwells. I thought for certain I should when I stood on London Bridge, but they said it was far enough off from there, so I had to think no more about that."

'What did you see then?" asked Matthew in great disappointment.

"Well, I saw them that stand very near to the king; for, I take it, most of our great men that I stood before are the members of the Parliament, and have places pretty near to his majesty."

"However did you get into their presence?" asked Daniel.

"Well, the thing was all ordered for me, and I had only to follow. Once up on the coach, there was no more trouble for me; the four horses knew their business, and drew me right into London. I made a small acknowledgment to the coachman, and showed him the address in the letter, and asked if he could put me in the way; and he made no more ado about it, but called up another coach that stood there waiting, as if on purpose for me, and tells the man to drive me to Temple Bar. So he makes his obedience and shuts me in by myself; and all the way we went I thought how singular it was I should happen of a spare coach there, with just nothing to do but to carry me where I wanted to go. What had happened I don't know, but the streets were so full as nothing could be like it that you could imagine. When we got to Temple Bar I asked the man how I could order to make my way back again to the inn where the coach put up for the night; and he said he had nothing better to do than to wait upon me. Well, thought I, I don't know, but it seems as if coming to London makes a great man of me. So I thanked him, and he showed me where he would stand ready against I came out. Then I made inquiry if the gentlemen were there, and the man who answered at the door said they were, but he said they were busy, and could not be seen. 'I am pretty sure of that,' said I, 'but if you tell them I am here they will do me the favor to see me, for 'tis on their business I am come. You will please to take in word so from me.' So I waited, and presently he came again and said the gentlemen were pleased to do me the favor to see me; so then I was all right, and after a time I went in and stood before them."

Here Stephen paused, as though his tale were concluded, and no further wonder remained to be told; but Elsie asked, "However could you order to approach them when you went in?"

"I made my obedience, and said, 'Your servant, gentlemen.' As far as I knew, that was all I could do."

"But," said Elsie, "however did you order what to say?"

"I order what to say! If I had taken in hand to order that, 'tis likely they would soon have put my fine speech into pretty disorder! No, I knew very well that all I had to do was to stand in their presence, and when I was there they would know what they pleased to say to me, and then I should know how to answer. So, when they saw me standing there, they put what questions they pleased, and I answered them all. Then they ordered me out of their presence for a time, after which they sent for me again. And one that to me seemed the head said, 'We are satisfied; your mother shall retain the farm, you may tell her so from us.' So I made my obedience, and thanked them, and there was an end."

So calmly had the farm youth carried through this heroic act for his home!

When the wonder of this visit again subsided a little, Stephen finished his tale. "When I came out again the two-horse coach stood there waiting, and took me back to the inn. I asked for some supper, and stayed there for the night. I was up by four o'clock in the morning, for I thought I should like to see London; but I never saw such a change, the streets were as silent as our own lanes round us here. I went down stairs and got out, and I soon found that was the time to see London, for I had it all to myself! I made my way to London Bridge, and the river and the buildings looked as beautiful and clear as anything could be; so I stood for an hour on the bridge and saw London, as well, I suppose, as ever any one did with so short a time to stay. And, certainly, I will allow 'twas a wonderful sight. I went back to the inn, but it was seven o'clock before I could get them to give me any breakfast. By eight o'clock we were on the coach, and starting off from the inn; and by that things were astir, and time indeed that they should be! I could have told our great men that we should make but poor farmers if we laid in bed as they seemed to do up in London! But one thing did astonish me; we talk of good driving here, where we have the road all to ourselves, but just go and see what it is up there! The dray horses, that are monsters to look at, and the driver, not speaking a word, but just walking ahead, and the horses turn in among the thick of the carriages, and follow, as true as can be, only by the turn of the whip!"

And so for that time Stephen finished his tale, but no wonder that it was often told again, and remembered amongst the heroics of the home. And well might Stephen say, as he often did in after-life, I shall always think much of that word spoken to Joshua, "This book of the law shall not depart out of thy mouth, but thou shalt meditate therein day and night, that thou mayest observe to do according to all that is written therein, *for then thou shalt make thy way prosperous, and then thou shalt have good success.*"

Stephen knew not at this time how to lighten the spiritual darkness that gathered around, but he did all he could for the moral good of the men. He would say, "I believe no one knows temptation like the poor man, and whenever you can, you must step between him and it. Not stand by to see him fall, and then blame him when you never put out a hand to uphold him." He always felt that the farmers' turnip-fields were a temptation to the men. Any one of the laborers who liked to come to him or his brothers, and ask for a basket of turnips to take home for supper was never denied. "Poor men," he would say, "'tis certain they will sometimes be looking out for themselves, so why not make a way for them to have a few without sin." He followed the same merciful rule with the wood. There was underwood cut every year on the farm where wood-land abounded, and Stephen always said, "Now, don't do the wrong thing, and break in to take what is not your own. I can promise

you it shall be offered first at a low price to you, and all
you wish for brought home to your doors; be satisfied
that the first choice shall be yours." Nor was he less
liberal in other ways: he would say, "I do maintain 'tis
a hard thing if a man who has worked for you for years
cannot come, when he sees a fair chance of helping himself in some little thing, and borrow a few pounds of his
master. 'Tis not likely but what he will repay it; and
even suppose that he should not, perhaps the loss of those
few pounds may not be that hurt to you through life,
that it might be to his spirit to think that he could not
make trial of what he thought would advantage him!"
Stephen acted on this feeling through life, and he said in
later years, "I have scarce ever known the borrowed
money that was not honestly paid back again; but then, I
suppose, there was a need in that, as in most other things,
to pray for that right judgment which does not come from
our wisdom!"

It was in such ways as these that, amidst the anxiety
of his responsible position, he proved that the poor, whom
his great-grandmother so tenderly cared for, had a home
in the compassions of his heart. But with all this considerate kindness, reaching beyond that which many a
better instructed Christian attains to, Stephen had an unyielding decision of character, which gave at times a
sternness to his aspect and tone, and which made those
who did not know him well, at times think him harsh. He
was like his mother in this; her aspect and words were

so decided and firm that it gave to a careless observer the outward appearance of sternness; but those who lived with Stephen, and all who knew him well, could at any moment turn him to a tone of softened feeling, by meeting the strong truth on which he might be speaking, with the same truth in its aspect of tenderness or compassion.

It is a remarkable fact, how often the circumstances of life are such as tend most to strengthen the strong points of character, which our wisdom would have thought could be better softened by being met in a different way. Stephen had a natural decision of character, that seemed to want the outward softening of some shield between him and the world, until his power was ripened by advancing years for the conflict; instead of which, he was called to enter upon that conflict while still in his youth, with a weight of care and responsibility upon him that, but for his trust in God, would have been overwhelming. He was younger than any one who dealt with him, younger than the buyer or the seller; and all who know what the merchandize of the world is, know that few who trade in it look out for any interest save their own; the young dealer may be obliged to enter on the market with but little experience, yet but few will have the generosity not to take advantage of his unreadiness; he may be fatherless and the son of a widow, but the world will beat him down if it can. This Stephen quickly found, and as he touchingly said, "It was not for myself that I had to make a firm stand, but for my mother, and a great family left dependent on me!" Finding how keen the world was to overreach if it could, he set himself with strictest care to put a true value on all he offered for sale, and having made his own estimate he never changed it. "That is my price—I take no less, I ask no more; you must do as you like about agreeing to it." "I was very young," he said, "and if they could once have turned me from my word, they would have tried me all ways." It was natural that this habit, once formed from necessity, lasted on when that necessity had passed away with his youth. But the high credit that he kept and left behind him was a testimony that no real hardness marked his dealings. It was the boast of his head horseman, who had worked all his life on the farm, that the corn his master sold from sample always proved "the right thing" when they carried it home.

Stephen's early friendship with Benedict, the blacksmith, told well on the farm, for his inventive mind had pondered long on an improvement in the share of the plough; he imparted his suggestion to Benedict, who said if Stephen would stand by he thought it was likely the thing might be turned out pretty right. Benedict did turn it right, and it turned such a furrow that Stephen saw complete success for the plough in the heavy land that they farmed; and so from that day each plough had the wrought-iron share, fashioned on Stephen's idea by Benedict, who never made a new one but he said master

Stephen must stand by or there could be no telling which way it would go. There **was** little question that the sturdy backsmith liked well to see the manly form by his forge, that in its boyhood had watched his bright sparks, and thought highly of Benedict's skill; and Stephen always yielded to the condition with a smile. And **though** Stephen and Benedict both rest now from their labors, yet the wrought-iron share they contrived with such care, **cuts its** deep straight furrow on the farm to this day.

But while active life, diligence, **and** family love blessed the farm, the angel of death again came to call one of its children away. It was Charlotte, tall and strong for her years, cheerful as the morning, **and** busy as the day; the cough that tells of consumption began, her strength failed her, and the doctor said she must die. That "must die" has a strange heavy **sound to** our ears; we might **well** think it should not be a "must" that tells us of the call to leave this world, when our Saviour has overcome the sharpness of death, and opened the kingdom of heaven to **all** believers; it may well be thought to sound strange to the holy angels, who know more than we do of the difference between this evil world and heaven, when they hear from our lips that sorrowful "must die," spoken of those who have only to pass through the valley of death's "*shadow*," to the open gate of the kingdom of heaven! When the doctor said that poor Charlotte must die, it fell on her ear with a solemn surprise. She had been always strong, active, and happy, and had not a thought about death. Their venerable minister departed when she was a little child, and since then there had been no one to tell her of heaven, nor to show her the way by which she might enter therein. She said it was God's will, and it must be as He pleased, and she hoped she should be forgiven before she was taken away!

Little fair-headed Matthew used to bring his father's old pony every morning to the garden-gate, with the saddle of white cloth that Margery had never used since the day she was a widow; and poor Charlotte was seated on it, and her little brother led it, that the rein might not tire her weak hand; he led her over the pastures, and through the home lanes, under the shadow of the trees that arched overhead, and climbed up into the bank to gather her the wild-flowers of the season; and so they went silently on until she was tired, and then he led her home, and she was laid down in the bed her mother had made for her in the farm-kitchen behind the door, where she could see all she loved around her, and never be left alone. And yet death is a lonely thing if heaven opens not to the dying eyes; the home may be around, but the link that binds the dying to it is melting fast away; the tenderest watchers may be near, but they are not treading the same path with the dying, and a step is drawing near which must lead beyond their sight for ever on earth. The only companionship must be immortal then. If the dying eyes behold one drawing near and saying, "Fear not, for I am with thee, I have blotted out as a cloud thy sins, and as a thick cloud thy transgressions; return unto Me, I have redeemed thee!" then the dying can rejoice and say, "O death, where is thy sting? O grave, where is thy victory?" "But how shall they hear without a preacher?" asks St. Paul. No living voice drew near to tell the dying girl of the "balm of Gilead, the Physician there." Stephen looked in grief on his sister; he knew what to do in the practical business of life, but he did not know what to do in the passive act of death. As he sat beside her he could only say, "It is the will of the Almighty, and we must submit;" and this was what the dying girl was doing, she was submitting: but there is a touching sadness in that which is only submission.

Then Margery said to Stephen, "You must go and ask our minister to come; 'tis not for the man that I send," she said bitterly, "but for the sake of the place that he stands in; since there's no hope of a better, 'tis all we can do!" Stephen asked, and the minister came, and read the beautiful service of the Visitation for the Sick; but the shadow of his presence darkened the chamber, and he came not again. The robins used to fly in and perch on the open door above poor Charlotte's little bed, and sing to her; and when she was dying, they kept watch by her pillow, and would not be driven away. The love between the farm children and God's creation was great, but all wondered to see the wild birds among the watchers by Charlotte's dying-pillow. And we may hope that He who said not even the sparrow falleth to the ground without His Heavenly Father, was near, though unseen; for He hath said, "It shall be required according to that a man hath, not according to that he hath not." But who will not consider how many, like this daughter of the farm, die in sadness for want of some one to guide them! Let us hasten to teach them the knowledge and love of their Saviour in life, and then it will be theirs to be happy in death. So another child of Margery's slept in the churchyard, and Mary and Elsie were the only daughters left in the home of their mother.

Then Nathaniel came back from his miller's apprenticeship, and built a mill in the parish, and a house as near as could be to his own mother's farm, and begged for his bright sister Mary to live with him and keep his little home. So his mother consented; and then she said in her wise heart, "I cannot keep all my five other sons to bring them up on this farm, for when they be grown I cannot hope to settle them in other farms of their own, and this could not support them all then." So she said that Daniel must go and live with Nathaniel and Mary, and learn of his brother the trade of the miller. Now Daniel was the life and the loved of the home; not a heart there but clung to him; the poor old people of the parish said, "You might always know when Master Daniel was coming, for his footfall was music, if such things could be!" it had a spring in it so joyous that before you saw whom it bore there came a feeling of cheer; his voice was blithe as a bird, and his smile made the home sunshine; no care rested on him like that which so early drew the furrows over Stephen's firm brow; work to Daniel was play, for his skill made him master of the best way of doing it, and his life seemed all energy, diligence, and love. All said that Daniel was never tired, never dull, never slow. When he crossed the home threshold from labor, it was always with some cheery word on his tongue; the home never seemed the same place if he did but chance to be out for the day. And when Margery said he must go, all wept as if their young hearts would break, and told their mother in their sorrow that if Daniel went away they could not be happy again! Daniel said not a word, except that if it was the wish of his mother he was ready to go. Margery was troubled, but she answered, "My poor children, ye fret for to-day, but I must act for to-morrow. I can promise ye will all see it right in the end, for I trust there's a higher wisdom than your mother's that orders for you." So Daniel went and lived with Nathaniel and Mary; and there were diligence and love in the little home of the miller as in that of the farm; but it was long before the farm children grew reconciled, though only a few fields lay between, and Daniel's step was often seen fast bounding over them home.

But while they grieved for the absent, Margery's children did not cling less to their home. Elsie was the only daughter left, and she never quitted her mother's side, except for a very rare visit to the near market-towns. Stephen had two market-days in each week, attending both the nearest towns on their chief business day; but nothing ever delayed him when his business was done. The home tea was made half-past five instead of five on that day, and Stephen was never absent. He often told with a smile how the market friends would vainly persuade him to stay; but he would take one glass of wine, which he always said, "was only for the good of the inn, for I never felt the better for drinking it, and I had a biscuit with it, and then off for my home. I knew they could give me nothing like a cup of my mother's tea; that was the best fare to me!" The market-day never brought to that widowed mother one anxious thought for her home-returning son.

On one of these afternoons, as Stephen was riding home from market on Starlight—the good horse was still in his vigor—he overtook a farm-bailiff, who had lately come to a neighboring parish; the bailiff was driving his wife home from market in his light cart, and Stephen overtook them ascending the same long hill that he had hastened up on foot when returning successful from the dishonest tradesman. He drew in his horse on the hill, and the farm-bailiff said, "You are early to-day, sir."

"I fear not," replied Stephen, "I reckoned I was late."

"Late!" said the bailiff, "why there's many of your standing would count it good time if they kept this side ten o'clock."

"Ah," answered Stephen, "there's one little word they never learned how to spell."

"What may that be?" asked the bailiff.

"H O M E," answered Stephen; "put those letters together and you get the best place upon earth! At least I know that for my part I am never away from it but I wish myself there. There's many a one can say he was never the worse for being there, who can't say so much for being away from it."

Now Stephen little knew at the time that he was talking to one whose wife had seldom the happiness of seeing him home on the evening of any market-day. The young farmer was soon off again on his horse beyond sight of the bailiff in his cart; but those few words he had spoken, gushing fresh as they did from the heart of the speaker, laid such hold on the bailiff, that he broke through, from that day, the habit of years, and returned an early and sober man from the market to his home; and the blessing of the bailiff's wife was one that added its tribute to many that were granted to Stephen. It is in this way we must all one day find that our influence on others has told for good or for evil, in instances without number, of which we were unconscious: the influence of what we ourselves really are is radiating all around us, while we think not of it.

CHAPTER XIII.

MARGERY had a high standing as a mistress, no less than as a mother. Her orders were short and decided, and obedience to them expected so promptly, that no neglectful habit had any time to gain strength. She had the advantage of being always engaged in the midst of her household, with her eye on their ways. Her own diligence, together with her high tone of authority and expectation, kept a bright polish on all the service around her; while the justice that marked her character, and the absence of suspicion—that darkest shadow we can cast on the light of another—made her to be served with an open-hearted courage and cheerful diligence that gave an added charm to the home. She had chosen as her own serving lad a boy of the village, named John Wilton; it was John's first place of service, and never boy had better training in all the moral duties that farm service requires. The lower work of the dairy, all the poultry, the young pigs, and the wood-house, were John's care. One hour the little active fellow came in with his faggot of batlings for the farm fires on his shoulder, another hour his open basket of eggs of that most attractive look which the farm eggs, fresh gathered from the nests, always have, a purity and transparency very unlike their deadness and dulness when the farm has made them over to the traffic of the market.

The farm was the whole world to John Wilton, and as he here found all his employment and interests, so his thoughts never went beyond it. When older, he changed his place of work from that of house-boy to day-laborer, then married and made a home of his own, but never changed in the faithful allegiance to his mistress who had first trained him up into service. John had rejoiced at the birth of each child on the farm, followed with tears each lost blessing to the grave, and risen higher and higher in his trust, until Margery was heard uttering her rare praise, and saying, "You might look far enough before you would find a better servant in his place than John Wilton." John made his own home the very pattern of industry; each child had to get through a certain amount of spinning in the week, or to go supperless to bed on Saturday evening. Rosy, well-fed, and warmly clothed, his children were the pride of his heart, and his home was all that honesty, industry, and cheerful service could make it. John resolved that, if possible, he would be an independent man, and provide against an evil day, so as never to have to ask parish pay. Wages then were not what wages are now; one shilling a day was the money earned by John in his place on the farm, but with this and home spinning he made enough and to spare. His place was that of head-woodman; but one day he had gone in as second horseman with the wagon to the nearest market-town, and as he was watering and rubbing down the fine horses of the team, that they might be more admired when he led them back through the town, a man standing near said, "We had such a tale told here last night as few ever heard before, as well-spoken a gentleman as could want to be; they say he's a Methodist, but I believe he's in the right for all that, and able to put the right way afore them that never knew it before."

"That's easy!" said a respectable man who stood by. "I could tell them that never knew it, the right way to walk in; but show me a man who can tell them that have known and left it, the way to get back to it again! I can tell you the main trouble lies there."

"Well, then, you go up and hear for yourself," said the first man, "for that's the very thing he framed all his discourse on. He showed up the poor prodigal, till I am sure I thought I was he; and he is going to lay out how he came back to his father on next Sunday night."

"No; is he?" said the respectable man; and John stopped rubbing his horses and looked up on the first speaker, for he also wished to make sure on the subject.

"He said so," replied the man, "and for my part I believe him."

Nothing more was said, except that John asked the man before leaving where the meeting was to be held, for he had secretly determined to go.

On Sunday evening he set out for the market-town,

without disclosing his purpose. Mile after mile, until from the heights on which he stood he looked down on the town, nestled warm in the valley below. It had once been a valley of light; lips had preached there the everlasting Gospel, which for so doing were burned to ashes at the stake on the very hill where John Wilton stood. The spire of its beautiful church still pointed like a finger to heaven, but the living voice was not there which once rang like a trumpet through its aisles, showing God's people their sin, and His Israel their transgression. The people stumbled on the dark mountains of ignorance; and of all the sons whom England's Church has brought forth, they had not one able to guide them aright. He whom John Wilton was hastening to hear was one whose object was to gather where the Church's hands were slack; to supply her lack of service. The room was full, and John saw both the men there who had talked together in his presence at the inn. The place of the Scripture that was read was the Prodigal Son, and the words were, his return to his Father. The stranger told how hard had been the heart of the prodigal, and cold as a stone, until that thought of his FATHER rose up within it, softening and warming it; then he began to look after his home, and to set out in the way that led back to it, and when any tempted him to turn aside out of the way he thought of his FATHER, and could not be persuaded. Then he told how some would have him wait a little, and not press on so fast, because there would be time enough yet; but he could not be hindered, for he thought of his FATHER. Then he told how he reached home at last, and how his FATHER embraced him, and forgave all his evil wanderings away, and clothed him in beautiful garments, and gave him glory and honor, and he went out no more, but dwelt happy for ever in the love and the house of his FATHER. And the stranger said, "I have shown you the love of the poor prodigal's FATHER, and if you could but get back to the heart of that Heavenly Father, you would find the same love in it waiting for you. If you come again on next Sunday evening I will show you the way by which you, like the poor prodigal, may get back to His arms and His everlasting home. John said it was heavenly, but he would hear a little more before he told his mistress and young masters where he had been.

The next Sunday evening John went as before, and the stranger read from the same place in the Bible, of the prodigal son. Then he said he had told them before of the LOVE of the Heavenly Father, how He hastened to welcome the poor prodigal to His arms when He saw him coming back in the distance; but, he said, I must tell you of something beside His LOVE, I must tell you also of His JUSTICE, and how it was the poor prodigal was able to stand before that. So he told them of God the Father's holiness—how He was of purer eyes than to look upon sin; told them of His holy law, which had only one punishment for every offence, and that punishment eternal death: "The soul that sinneth, it shall die." How was it then, he asked, that the poor prodigal ever got back to the arms of his Father? How is it that any poor sinner can ever get back to the arms of the Heavenly Father? Then he showed them One, the beloved Son of the Father, pure and spotless, and doing always such things as pleased Him; he showed them this beloved Son led as a lamb to the slaughter, dying on the cross for the poor prodigal; he showed them this Holy One bearing the poor sinner's punishment, dying that the sinner might live; he told them of the poor sinner washing away all his sin in the blood of that beloved Son, and so being made clean for the arms and the home of the FATHER. He told them that the beautiful robe in which the prodigal was dressed, was the robe of this beloved Son of the FATHER, that the poor prodigal was made comely through his comeliness which He had put upon him; and he told them His name was called Jesus, because He could save from sin, and that He was able to save unto the uttermost all who came unto God by Him; that the Heavenly Father would heed the poor sinner's faintest prayer, if it were asked for the sake of His Son, Jesus Christ. But the stranger said that though he had now shown them the heart of the Heavenly Father, and the way for them each one to get back to the arms of His love, through His beloved Son, Jesus Christ, yet they had not heard all that must be known about the poor prodigal,—they must come again on the next Sunday evening, and he would tell them then. So John thought he would not say where he had been, until he had heard this one discourse more.

When the next Sunday came he went again, and took his place in the room, which was always quite full. The stranger read again of the prodigal son, and then he said, "How came that thought about his FATHER, in the heart of the poor prodigal? it was not there before: he had lived a long time in that far country, and not longed once before to see the face of his FATHER. How came the thought to spring up in his heart, 'I will arise and go to my Father'? I will tell you how it came there; the Heavenly Father sent forth the Spirit of His beloved Son into the heart of the poor prodigal, and that Holy Spirit breathed in his heart those blessed words, 'MY FATHER!' and then the poor prodigal thought on the love of his Father, and said, 'I will arise and go to Him!' You are sinners, like the prodigal; have you got that thought in your heart? are you saying, 'I will arise and go to my Father'? If you are, then there is hope for you that God has sent forth the Spirit of His beloved Son into your hearts, crying, 'MY FATHER!' Do not delay; make haste, as the prodigal did; kneel down at the feet of the Father's beloved Son, Jesus Christ; beg of Him to wash you clean from all your sins, that you may be made fit for the arms of your Father; thank Him that He has sent His Holy Spirit to put that thought in your heart, 'I will arise and go to my Father,' and beg of Him to lead you in the way that you should go, and to strengthen you to walk therein, until you come to His Father and your Father, to His God and your God. But then," he asked, "is there any one here in whose heart there is no such cry as 'My Father!' no thought, 'I will arise and go to Him'? If such a one be here he must beg of God to send down the Spirit of His beloved Son into his heart, and then he will soon find the thought 'MY FATHER!' will wake up within him. 'Ask, and it shall be given you; seek, and ye shall find: for if ye, being evil, know how to give good gifts unto your children, how much more shall your Heavenly Father give the Holy Spirit to them that ask Him?'"

"Now," said John, "if I never hear any more, that's enough to save me, if God helps me to remember and obey it. I can see now what to pray for, and, what's more, I will never rest until I get it." John prayed—he prayed in his cottage, in the fields; he was always afraid of losing the hold of what he had gained, and this made him pray the more earnestly.

JOHN WILTON'S PRAYER.

"God be merciful to me a sinner! and send down the Spirit of His beloved Son into my heart, to bring me to my Father! for Jesus Christ's sake. Amen."

John Wilton prayed so earnestly and so often, that God answered him abundantly, and sent down the Spirit of Christ into his heart, and his whole life from that time was illumined by this divine light.

When Margery first heard that her favorite, John Wilton, had been off to the Methodists, she shook her head, and said, "'Tis not the first step, but all that follow after, ye must take into reckoning." She kept a strict look out in all that concerned John Wilton for a time, but when she saw that God's favor and the light of the divine countenance clothed John as with a sunbeam, and that all he did stood the test of that light, then Margery said, "It was a pity that such men as taught him did not stand up for the Church of their country, and teach some who would be better on the low stool for awhile."

Yet Margery was not altogether wrong in her caution, when she said it was not the first step, but all that followed after must be taken in reckoning.

The people of the town built a meeting for the good man who had taught them so well of an evening, and this made John wish to be in the town the whole day on Sunday. So he left all his children to his poor wife, who had no knowledge to guide them. His boys grew wild on Sundays, and broke away with evil companions, while John was keeping his Sabbath, with his crust of bread in his pocket, far off in the town. Had John only had the self-denial and the right judgment to spend the day with his family, taking them to church as before, and teaching them all he now knew at home, he might then have walked with his boys to the evening service in the town, and so have commanded his household after him in the fear of his God. But in this one thing he failed, and while his own path, in the eyes of all men, shone brighter and brighter to the perfect day, his poor sons became a curse to the place where they dwelt; for broken Sabbaths are stepping-stones to destruction: so it was that John Wilton had to see his children examples of evil, while Margery's became a blessing to the village of their birth.

It greatly pleased Stephen that his favorite laborer had become so thoughtful a man; he felt thankful to have a man of prayer on the farm, and he did not see any difference between his laborer's supplications and his own. It did not strike him that there was this difference between them—that his own supplications had reference to the life that now is, John Wilton's chiefly to the life that is to come. Stephen prayed, that he might order his affairs with discretion; John Wilton, that he might at last be received by God the Father, washed in the precious blood of the Son, and led by the Spirit of God. But though Stephen at that time saw not this difference, yet he walked by the light unto which he had attained, and to such the divine promise is sure, "He that is faithful over a few things shall be made ruler over many; for to him that hath shall be given, and he shall have more abundantly."

And so the fountain had been opened in the valley; and now the river began to flow on the high places. The valley to which John Wilton turned his steps lay far away to the west of the forest farm; to the east there rose a hill, on which stood a church, with farms and whitewashed cottages clustering around it. It had a happy look from the distance, when the sun gleamed on the high ground, and the white hamlet lay like a gathered family around the old church. It was but a little place and very poor, though in the days of Charles the First it provided and maintained a mounted horseman for the strife that then troubled England. It lay far from any high-road, and lawless men had made their haunt there, and it was left neglected and destitute. Once every Sunday, about noonday, the heavy door of the old church was thrown back upon its hinges, and a man booted and spurred entered in and performed the service, as it was called; it lasted as short a time as possible, and then he hastened on over hedge and ditch to serve another church in the same way. No eye of higher life looked down upon the lonely village, save when the neighboring gentry chanced to hunt across its fields; and what the state of the village might be seemed no concern to them—"Am I my brother's keeper?" Death at length summoned this hireling Rector from his charge; with all his broken vows upon his soul, he went to stand before Him whose dread tribunal can look more terrible to none than to the false shepherd of that flock for which the Judge upon the Throne gave up his life. "The Lord hath prepared of His goodness for the poor."

The new Rector could not enter at once upon its duties; so a friend, dear to him as a brother, undertook the little village for a time. There was no place in the parish in which the clergyman could live, so the new minister took a house as near to it as one could be found, and with his wife, whose youthful beauty had graced one of England's ancestral homes, he came to tend these lost sheep in the wilderness.

It was soon told on Margery's farm that things were now ordered quite differently at the church on the hill; and as there was only one service in their own parish each Sunday, Margery said to her children, "The best thing you can do is to go one part of the day to the little hill church now." So they went, and Margery kept house at home. Amongst Stephen's laborers there was a poor man who said to himself, "If my young masters take that trouble, why should not I?" Ben Hoffman by name, tall in figure, a silent man, industrious and steady. When he reached the old church porch he stood there amongst the men, who waited outside until the minister came. When Ben saw the new minister and his lady at his side, he took his hat from his head and bowed reverently to them; for he said, only to look on them paid him for his trouble in walking so far to church. The minister and his lady passed in through the old porch, he with his kindly smile upon all, and she in her beauty and tenderness. The men followed, and Ben went in with them. The second lesson was John xix.; and as the minister read of the cruel mockings and scourging, the crown of thorns that encircled the Redeemer's sacred head, the cry of "Crucify Him," and then the death of the Lord, the tears stole down his cheeks, and his voice trembled with emotion. The pastor's tears have oftentimes softened hearts, that but a little before seemed unready to receive the seed of the Word. Whether openly or in secret, they fall not in vain. The sermon turned to the same affecting subject, and Ben's sympathy was awakened. "How bad his words made me feel," said Ben, "and yet some way not bad altogether!" Ben went again and again, and the light of life dawned on his soul. He was a man of quiet temperament, by reason of which it might be that the new life he now lived was not so vivid and expressive in him as in his fellow-laborer John. But in a few years he became blind, and then the heaven to which his spirit was always looking up reflected itself in his countenance; such a calm radiance beamed there that you felt the spirit within dwelt in a region of sunshine and songs, beyond the earthly house of its pilgrimage; in looking on his face you thought of light, not of darkness, and the smile of that blind man was one that told its light was celestial.

The pastor who had led Ben to his Saviour was far away when blindness fell on the villager, having only taken charge of the parish until its new Rector could come; but year after year he sent help through Stephen to the blind peasant. Ben shared that pastor's children's bread, until, a few months distant from each other, both entered paradise.

CHAPTER XIV.

THE farm life flowed on with that calm current of change which brings its interest and anxiety to agricultural employment; the early and latter seed-time, the hay-time and harvest, the fields but just cleared when the plough again renews the soil, the felling and barking of timber, the sheep-shearing, the careful tending and rearing of all the young life of the farm for the different time at which each reaches its perfection, the constant work of the dairy; and on Margery's farm all this busy employment, this skill and anxiety, was cheered and strengthened by filial and fraternal affection. But while the whole course of nature follows on year after year in its season, "Man only knoweth not his time, it falleth suddenly on them." Death, to man, came not by God's order, but by man's disorder; therefore it has no certain season, but often calls us when least expected, and stands close beside us when we thought it far away. And now every heart in the farm circle ached, when the bright crimson on young Edward's cheek deepened and settled to a hectic flush, and consumption's cough told that his days upon earth would be few. Stephen had set his deep affections on the lad, he loved him as Joseph loved his Benjamin, and no wonder, for the boy had none of earth's strong passions, but the meekness and gentleness of a child in all he did and said; silent, yet so skilful in his work, mindful of orders, and full of quiet observation, no wonder all tenderly loved him, and could not think that seventeen summers was to be the term of so sweet a life on earth. Stephen looked upon him day by day with that questioning solicitude, which seemed silently to say, "Who can tell whether God may be gracious unto me, that the child may live!"

One thing in Edward told of more than earthly feeling, his Bible was the object that he seemed to care for more than anything beside. When he could not work in the fields, it was sure to be beside him; he would open and read, then sit thoughtfully until he read again. Yet he spake not of what he read, nor of what he hoped or feared; the silence of the mother's lips seemed to seal her children's also. Edward had not known the venerable clergyman whom his elder brothers and sisters had loved and learned from; a very different man had received him at the font, and baptized him into the name of the Father, the Son, and the Holy Ghost. But though man changeth, God doth not change; and the good-will of our Heavenly Father, declared by His Son Jesus Christ, and sealed by the Holy Spirit of promise, comes not by man, but by the eternal purpose and grace of God. Edward had grown up in a home where the Bible was honored, the Sabbath kept holy, and prayer continually offered; and before his young life faded or his strength was weakened by disease, one able to show him greater things than those that had yet been taught him, came to the eastern hill, and every Sunday saw Edward, with Elsie and his brothers, worshipping there. The new Rector had now come, and taken his duties upon himself, and his observation often fell on the lad's expressive face, the first traces of consumption as yet only heightening its beauty, and giving lustre to eyes full of attention and quiet thought; but he was one amongst many strangers who now came to the church, and the Rector lived at a distance of seven miles from the parish and nine from the farm, so that intercourse did not seem a probable thing.

When Edward grew too weak to walk to church, he never complained of the loss, never expressed a wish about anything, only had his Bible always close beside him, read in it, and sat silent and thoughtful. Stephen had known from a child that the Bible told the way to reach the kingdom of heaven. He could well remember how his great-grandmother found all in the Bible. And now he saw young Edward caring for nothing but that Holy Book. Yet he did not feel happy about him; he watched the boy, and there was no brightening in his patient face; it did not seem to him as if he had found what he wanted. Stephen would have given all he had to have comforted the lad, but he did not know how; he had not thought about meeting death himself, and he did not know how to help another to meet it: he still supposed the only thing to be done, was to submit to the will of the Almighty; but that young patient face, with the look of sadness upon it, was almost more than he knew how to bear, and he could only lift up his prayer in the words he had learned from the collect, "O God! we beseech Thee leave us not comfortless."

When Edward grew weaker, he was laid in the large crimson bed in the favorite guest-chamber, and some one of the home always sat there beside him. Margery would certainly have sent, as before, for their minister, but it had greatly displeased him that she should send her family to another church, though all worshipped in their own whenever it was opened for service. In his hasty displeasure he had said that he would never enter Margery's dwelling again, and it was always a principle with Margery never to make any one go from their word. "If it be a good word," she would say, "you are bound to help them to maintain it; and if it be a bad one, you are not to interfere between the word and Him before whom it was uttered; it is for the Almighty to turn it back; it must wait for His time." Therefore Margery sent no request that the minister would come; but still in her heart the thought that troubled her most was that her child would die, not like a lamb of the fold, but a lost nurseling in the wilderness. Never absent from the church of his fathers, she felt it strangely hard that he should die so neglected. She had yet to see how in this "the ways" and "the thoughts" of the Most High were not hers, because they were "HIGHER!"

It was the second watch of the night, the watch towards morning, and it was Stephen's turn to take it. Elsie had kept the first watch, and she now left the room softly, for Edward was sleeping. She went to lie down for an hour or two, before rising again to the dairy churning at four o'clock; Stephen stepped in as softly, and took the arm-chair by the bed. When he had taken the watch before, it had generally been the night watch, as they called it, from nine o'clock until one o'clock, and then Edward had always been wakeful, and had liked Stephen to read to him, for he seldom slept much before midnight. He liked Stephen to keep the first watch, because he always knew the chapters and psalms he most wanted to hear, and could pray many of the Church prayers beside him, which the others did not seem to know so well how to do; but this night it happened otherwise, and when Stephen went in, the dying lad had fallen into his long morning slumber. A midnight hour without sleep once saved a nation. (Esther vi. 1.) So now, on the contrary, the sleep God giveth his beloved (Psalm cxxvii. 2) proved the occasion of enduring blessing. Stephen sat down by the bed, the Bible lay on the little round table by his chair, and the one dim night-candle was burning. He sat listening to the breathing of the boy, so different from the gentle slumber of health; he felt how vain it was to think to save from death, and in his heart he said, "O merciful God, must the child die alone? No minister come to offer up a prayer for him to Thee?" While he was sitting in this mournful thought, young Edward woke, and, looking up and seeing that it was Stephen who sat beside him, he said, as he was wont, "Read, brother." Stephen turned to the lad's favorite psalm, the twenty-fifth; it was the psalm that he chose to have read to him every day, always saying that Stephen must not go out in the morning until he had read him that psalm. Stephen turned to it now; but before many words had been read, Edward was again sleeping. Stephen read on to himself, "Show me Thy ways, O Lord, teach me Thy paths." When he reached the verse, "Consider mine enemies, for they are many, and they hate me with cruel hatred," his thoughts turned, as it was natural they should, to the only enemy they had in the world; one who might have been expected, from the place he had filled, to be their best friend. While he thought on these things, he turned to the fiftieth chapter of Jeremiah; it was a chapter he had often read and thought upon as descriptive of the sad condition of his parish, and now he turned to it again to find sympathy in the knowledge of the Most High. "My people have been lost sheep, their shepherds have caused them to go astray, they have turned them away on the mountains." As Stephen read he wept, and then he prayed, and still his tears were many. He who had subdued oppression with the sword of the Spirit, he who had pleaded his own cause fearlessly and alone against the false witness of man, now "wept and made supplication like Jacob, and, like him, he had power with God and prevailed." Few moments in any life could present a more touching aspect than this; the young man, in his strength and activity, keeping watch by night in that dimly-lighted chamber, beside the death-bed of the younger brother of his home, turning to the Word of God for the sympathy earth could not give, and, with supplications and tears, beseeching God in behalf of the lad.

Then, in that long watch, while Edward still slept, he looked again on the chapter open before him, and read the words, "In those days, and in that time, saith the Lord, the children of Israel shall come, they and the children of Judah together, going and weeping, they shall go and seek the Lord their God, they shall ask the way to Zion, with their faces thitherward." It seemed, truly, a description of his own state at that moment, and the thought rose within him, "'In those days they shall ask the way!' then if we be like them, surely we may ask it also! if our minister won't come near to show us, we must ask of one that will. There can be no manner of doubt that we may, for does it not say, 'They shall ask the way'? There is but one that I know of who can show us, and I believe that he will; but, let that be as God pleases, I'll not be behind His Word in asking!" It was the first time that the thought had occurred to Stephen of requesting a visit from any other minister than their own, but in the sorrowful extremity of that night it came to his soul in connexion with the words that he read, and at once he resolved to follow it out in the faith of the Word of his God. He had heard the voice behind him saying, "This is the way, walk ye in it." He longed for the day to dawn. He could not watch the sunrise, for the eastern window that once let in the early radiance had been darkened, but he saw the slanting sunbeams fall on the southern window's white blind, and could hear the cheerful sounds that told of morning's advance—the head horseman at the farm by four o'clock, then the call of the cows, and Elsie's voice below. As soon as he could, he gave up his watch to Philip, and hastened to settle his business for the day, that he might not be hindered in starting for his drive of nine miles to the house of the new Rector of the neighboring church, who had now taken into his own charge the parish that lay on the high ground to the east.

There was then in each social tie more of a patriarchal character than can often be found now; and in all the rural districts there was a comparative sitting still and at rest, each taking what was found around him, without going far to seek a supply. But it surely is not an English feeling that ever questions the lawfulness of freely entering any house where want, sickness, or death looks vainly for counsel and comfort in the hour of need. If the Englishman's cottage be his castle, and he may shut its door against whom he pleases, so may he also open it to whomsoever he will, or the principle fails of all force; and while the administration of the sacraments must be local and individual to each parish and its minister, the comfort wherewith any are themselves comforted of God must be open from one heart to another, free as the tender mercies of the Most High, which are over all his works, and unlimited as the universal brotherhood of man.

Stephen was always prompt to execute his purpose; he would say, "I once set that word before me, 'Whatsoever thy hand findeth to do, do it with thy might,' and as sure as ever I failed to follow that word up closely, I gave time for a hindrance to drop in." Therefore the newly risen sun saw Stephen on his way. Then he said to himself, "This is surely a great favor I am going to ask. This new clergyman might well say to me that 'tis not for him to look after other men's lost sheep. I am sure I couldn't blame him if he did, for he must have enough to do to look after his own. "Yet," again he thought, "to see how the Saviour travelled the country if so much as a poor sick child sent to ask Him! and by what I can see and hear, this new clergyman follows very close upon Him." So discoursing with himself, he reached the house of the minister, was shown at once to the study, and the hand of welcome extended to greet him.

"I am come after troubling you, sir; but I have a young brother who now lies dying, and we have no one to speak a word to him for his good. We are poorly off in our parish, and our minister has offended himself with us, and says he will not enter our house. If it would not be too much trouble to you to come over before my poor brother be gone, we should all esteem it the greatest favor in the world."

Happily that minister was fully persuaded that **he lost not his right as an Englishman because he was a** Churchman: **nor** did he think that the Word made any exception when it said, "Pure religion and undefiled before God and the Father is this, **to visit** the fatherless and widows **in their** affliction;" therefore he unhesitatingly promised **to go,** and Stephen hastened back with lightened heart to the farm.

When Margery heard that the clergyman would come, and certainly arrive before long, she **sent and** called all her children each one from his employment to the chamber where their young brother lay. At length, on the opposite hill, above the green valley, they saw **the** hired gig which brought the clergyman and his **wife,** for when **a** visit involved effort like the present he could seldom venture without her. The hired horse knew his driver, and the ascent to the farm being steep he made a halt, at which silent hint the clergyman alighted and walked. The fair-headed Matthew was keeping watch at the window, and when he saw the mutual understanding between the clergyman and the horse, he turned away in entire satisfaction, and rubbing his hands together said, "That's the man to come here, I can see at this distance!" and the dying boy looked up in expectation from his pillow. Margery went down with Stephen to receive the clergyman and his lady, and conducted them up to the chamber. Then entered those footsteps of blessing, never familiar but loved, and most loved where most familiar! It was the clergyman's habit to see the sick apart from their families, that they might speak more freely, but it was not possible to think of dismissing all those statue-like figures that had taken their places round the walls of the room on the large oaken chairs, with seats of crimson, that stood round this the favorite guest-chamber, each with a face full of reverence, yet sad as if every thought and every feeling were concentrated on the interest before them. There was everything to win and assure the dying lad in the aspect and tone of him who now sat beside him; and the tender, beautiful smile of her he brought with him was a softened sunbeam, that did not flit across the surface of suffering and sorrow, but penetrated and lightened its gloom. That minister's teaching was simple as his high commission, "Go ye into all the world and preach the gospel to every creature;" simple as the divine declaration, "Look unto Me and be ye saved," "The blood of Jesus Christ cleanseth from all sin." Young Edward had heard the same voice declaring the same precious truth before, but now it was addressed personally to him; it was the dying boy's want to be encouraged to cling to his Saviour, to look to nothing but Christ. The words of truth and love breathed for him, fell like the summer evening dew upon the thirsty drooping flower · in the balm of that dew the fair blossom of his young life closed up to sleep, and reopen at the resurrection of the just in perfected beauty and fragrance. The clergyman came again and again, and a heavenly gleam lightened those last days in which the living watch by the dying. The boy never yielded his love for the twenty-fifth Psalm, he still would give his charge that Stephen should not go out without reading it to him; but he now added the same love for the fourth chapter of the first of Thessalonians, and that also **must be** read to him daily. But the tide of his young life ebbed fast.

One day he said to Stephen, "Read, brother."

"What shall I read?" Stephen asked.

"Read, Them that sleep in Jesus will God bring with Him."

Stephen read, but earth was fading into heaven; the boy raised his arms, could not speak, they fell back, and his meek spirit was gone, gone to Him, the meek and lowly in heart, who had taught him his ways upon earth, **and** whose presence he now beholdeth in heaven.

No time could efface from Stephen's remembrance the tenderness and the anxiety of his love for that brother. He had trained him to the skilful exercise of all his home work, and he had wrestled with heaven for the brighter light that so tenderly shone on the last days of his earthly life. Stephen would speak of him as years passed away, **of** the prayers and the tears that young death had cost him, and would say, "He was surely the meekest spirit upon earth; if ever one had the spirit of a little child it was he; and our Saviour says it is them that shall enter the kingdom, so I think we may say HE IS THERE!"

CHAPTER XV.

STEPHEN stood as it were side by side with the Roman centurion, Cornelius, "a devout man, and one that feared God with all his house, which gave much alms to the people, and prayed to God alway"—to whom the angel said, "Thy prayers and thine alms are come up for a memorial before God; now send men to Joppa, and call for one Simon." Cornelius sent for his own instruction, Stephen for the sake of another, who received the blessing, but Stephen found it not then.

Margery now went with her sons to the church on the distant hill; Matthew drove her there; and she heard the words of truth from that voice which had spoken heavenly peace in the ear of her dying child. She sat with her family in the Rector's pew in the chancel; Stephen always occupied a corner where few liked to sit, so he made it his own. The church was well filled, and Margery's sons made a great addition to the melody there; the clerk led the singing from the far end of the church with a solemn and musical voice, the village people joining as they best could read or remember the hymns; the children of the Sunday-school raised their clear joyous voices, and Margery's sons, with practised ear and steady tunefulness, blending with the Rector's family, balanced the young treble from the chancel and the broader tones beyond, filling the old church, so long silent and desolate, with "that holy, heavenly melody, the music of a thankful heart." Oh! blessed Sabbath-days, how many now made perfect give thanks for having seen ye! It was no little charm to Margery's children that the voice they now listened to had music in its tones. Stephen would say, "No instrument can match that voice!" Philip would say, "it seemed to him nothing could be very far wrong where that voice could be heard!" Nathaniel, that "it was the voice of a good man, and what music could be equal to that?" and Elsie, that "to her thinking, there could be no voice like to that upon earth!" And so its tones became dear, while as yet the highest truths that it taught were but seen from afar.

Nathaniel was the only one of Margery's seven sons who had been trained to his employment away from his home. The reverence for the Sabbath, and the church of his country, in which he had been brought up, went with him when he went; and the town where he served his apprenticeship was blessed with teaching in its church which shed a clearer light on Nathaniel's soul than as yet had shone upon Stephen's. He came back to his native parish the same in outward aspect, and most ready in address of all Margery's sons, humble and guileless in spirit, to worship again in his parish church with his mother, and again to join his powerful bass voice to the choir, still formed by the brothers of his home; but with a far clearer knowledge and deeper feeling of the one only way of escape from sin and its condemnation. The growing ignorance and evil in the parish deeply grieved his always compassionate heart, and it became his constant prayer that God would enable him to accomplish some means of instruction, for the poor ungodly children around. There was a laborer on the farm, an old man, who could not only read well, a rare attainment in those days, but he had also an intelligent mind, and a heart enlightened and warmed by divine truth. So Nathaniel consulted with Stephen whether the old man's farm labor should be lessened to three days in the week, and the other three be given by him to school-keeping, for the sake of the poor ignorant children; who might also be assembled by him every Sunday to attend the service at church, and on the other part of the day, when the church was not opened, be further instructed by old Linstead in the school. Shephen's warm response at once encouraged Nathaniel; the two brothers took the care and expense of the school upon themselves, and children of all ages, except the very young, were soon gathered around Linstead, learning the heavenly truth he knew well how to teach. The children made a great addition to the few who now entered the parish church. Nathaniel instructed them in singing, they soon caught the sweet psalm tunes, while old Linstead in the week-day taught them many a hymn, which he thought matched the tunes full as well as the psalms arranged by Tate and Brady, and might, he said, come nigher to the understandings of the young. So Nathaniel thanked God, and Stephen greatly rejoiced in the good work of his brother. "My brother's school," he always called it, because the thought had been Nathaniel's. And the tear rose to Margery's eye when she saw her sons, pressed round as they were with the world's care, opposed where they had most right to look for help, and yet spending their thoughts and hard-won earnings on the blessing of the poor and ignorant around them. And now, as you passed the village-street or near by cottage door or window, you were not unlikely to hear young voices singing at home the hymns of praise learned at school, instead of the evil sounds that before broke on the ear.

The Rector of the parish on the eastern hill was at this time obliged to live seven miles from his church, and there came a Sunday on which he was unexpectedly too ill to go over as usual in the morning, and unable to obtain other help; so he said to his wife, "I wish you would drive there in the pony-chaise, and call on the people; and then, if possible, I will come over in the afternoon in a post-chaise for one service." Little Spedly, the tailor, was growing an old man at this time, but having heard that this parish church was "a heavenly place" now, he thought on that morning that he would ride over on his donkey, and judge for himself. When he reached the church he heard that the Rector was ill, and would not come until the afternoon service; so, not wishing to return disappointed, Peter Spedly thought where he could bestow himself for the time. The village had long been a haunt of wild, ungodly men, who as yet refused to hear the voice of the charmer, though he charmed never so wisely. One of these men was a gipsy, of great stature and strength, and terribly noted for crime; he had settled himself in the parish as convenient for his manner of life; the cottage he occupied stood close to the church, the door of which he never entered. He was of the true gipsy race, and his children beautiful specimens of their tribe, with bronzed complexion, eyes of darkest brilliancy, and blackest hair that clustered in thick curls about their heads. They soon found their way to the Sunday-school, unhindered by their parents; but nothing could win the gipsy within the walls of the church. It was into this wild home that Peter Spedly, the farm tailor, limped on his crutch, to ask rest, it being near to the church. The gipsy was hospitable, and Spedly was welcome. While he was seated there resting his lame leg, the wife preparing the dinner, and the gipsy, unwashed, unshaven, and in terrible week-day undress, sitting smoking by the fire, there came a gentle knock at the door. "Come in," said the gruff voice of the gipsy, and a lady entered, "dressed so fair," in a white muslin pelisse, and with a face of such sweetness and blessing, that Peter Spedly, who had never travelled far, and had always thought his mistress, Margery, the picture of all womanly perfection, had a secret rising belief that he now saw an angel. He looked round at the gipsy, who did not even take the pipe from his mouth, then at the gipsy's wife, who went on cooking the dinner, and amazed at seeing no notice taken, he himself bowed as low as he could. When he lifted up his head the beautiful being was not gone, but seated in a chair very near the fierce gipsy. Spedly fixed his eye upon her, and wondered what would happen next. Then she began to speak; she never said a word, to Peter Spedly's surprise, of the rude unready way in which they had received her, "but she told of heaven, just as if she had but then left it," and told of Him who was the Lord of it, and of what He had done for sinners, and begged so earnestly of the gipsy to turn from his Sabbath-breaking and sin, and to make his prayer to Him who died on the cross, saying He would certainly receive him, that Peter Spedly, who had never heard such words before, was quite overcome by them; his eager attention caught them all as they fell; and his neighbors bore witness that he was another man from that hour, living ever after by the light that fell on him from the words he then heard. But the gipsy still paid no attention, and his wife went on cooking the dinner. Then she who sat beside him, and must truly have looked a being of light and love, by that fierce squalid man, tried hard to persuade him to come on that Sunday to church, that he might hear what had been done and suffered by Jesus Christ, for all who come unto God by Him. The gipsy said, he did not want preaching, and was not coming there; but Peter Spedly felt glad that he had travelled himself so far, on purpose to attend the service at which the gipsy refused to be present. When the gipsy refused, she who still pleaded with him said earnestly: "I will tell you how your minister cares for your souls; he is ill to-day, and could not come over early, so he sent me. You know he is not a rich man, and he has a family of children to provide for, and yet he thinks so much of your souls that sooner than leave you one Sunday without a service, he will hire a post-chaise, which you know costs much money, and come over because of his anxiety for you!" This was a plain fact to the gipsy; he threw down his pipe, said at once, "I will go!" and then stretching out his arm, called in a firm voice of command, "Wife, bring me my shirt!" and Peter Spedly moved from his chair in surprise, and when he looked round she who sat by the gipsy was gone. So that afternoon the tall fierce-looking gipsy came into the church by the side of the little lame tailor, and listened to all that passed there. A few days more, and the officers of justice arrested him, and his sentence was transportation for life. Oh! who can tell, when beneath the captive's chain, so galling to the wild, athletic gipsy, what echoes from the words of peace heard on that Sabbath might awake a new and better life within his soul!—The words of tender truth and persuasion from her who sat beside him that day in his cottage, the service that followed in the thronged village church, the

8*

prayers, the hymns of praise, and the gospel of glad tidings that told of heavenly liberty to the captive, and the opening of sin's prison to them whom its chains had else bound eternally. Often when the hallowed thoughts of her who that day pleaded and prevailed, followed the poor outcast gipsy, she trusted that she had been sent, as little Spedly first imagined, a messenger to him from his God. It was blessed to think that such words of grace had been poured on his soul; it might be that the hand of justice was sent then with a final arrest, lest temptation and successful sin at liberty at home should blot from his soul the remembrance of what he had heard. And perhaps when death closed the eye of the gipsy, as it must now have done in the land of his banishment, his spirit saw again the calm vision of that sweet village church, and the love he there heard preached in its freeness might in adversity's discipline have been sought and found; and though possibly another invitation never fell on his ear, that one may have proved his eternal salvation. Well had that injunction been obeyed, "While we have time and opportunity let us do good unto all men."

But while on the east and west of the farm, light was kindling; while on the long dark night of ignorance and sin, stars were brightening, which when they set on earth would rise eternally in heaven; one who had long been shining on in the gloom, was darkened by an unexpected cloud. Old "Faithful," the village harness-maker, the chief favorite of all Margery's children, was in trouble and could not be comforted. He had grown old in his honest dealing, and though not rich, had enough in old age to support him; he still made and mended harness, for his trade to the old man is often like a friend who has helped him through life, and whose quiet company would be much missed by him, and therefore tradesman and trade still live on together. So it was with old Faithful; and the respect that all felt for him was pleasant to the old man. But an acquaintance, it might be a relation, asked him to sign a bond of security to the Government, to enable him who asked this great favor to take a situation, which could not be entered on without a surety. It would have been happy for the harness-maker if he had then consulted his young friends at the farm; Stephen, who so diligently read the law of his God, would have soon settled the question, but he did not do this; in an unguarded moment he signed, and he who had nothing in the world except his small honest earnings, became surety to a bond of one thousand pounds. The man for whom he had signed soon proved unsound in principle, and the Government demanded their bond. A thousand pounds from the old harness-maker, a thousand pounds or a prison! What a harvest of grief and desperate sorrow must sometimes be gathered from a single word, a single act, that would never have been uttered or committed if Stephen's prayer for a right judgment in all things, had been the prayer of daily life! The poor harness-maker was overwhelmed with distress; and for a time he sank under it, like Peter on the rough waves of Galilee, when he saw the wind boisterous and forgot Who stood by him in the storm. A prison, and arrested by Government; disgrace! loss of liberty! misery!

And this to be the close of a life so industrious and respectable. Dark rolled the waves and the billows over the heart of the old man. In his temporal despair he found that to trust in the Lord, and stay his troubled soul upon his God, was beyond the faith he had yet attained; like Job, his feeling was that he chose death rather than life. But though for a little moment he lost his own conscious hold of his Saviour, that Saviour unloosed not the Almighty Hand that held him; underneath him even then were "the everlasting arms," and the tempter could not pluck him from their eternal embrace. The Holy Spirit, the Comforter, for whose divine presence he had often prayed in better days, forgot not his supplications, but calmed his soul in this extremity of trouble, and by His unseen influence sustained his failing heart. The poor old man sat within his home, silent in misery. He had none to whom he could look for counsel or comfort; many were distressed for the old man, but no one could say to him, "Weep not;" his burden, brought on him by his own error in pledging wealth he did not possess, seemed heavier than he could bear. There were many to censure others; those who were bound to see that no one signed a bond beyond their possessions had not done their duty;

the old man blamed himself; but it was plain to all that the open door of the prison stood before him. Then a gentleman passed the window, and stood at the door of the harness-shop, lifted the latch and came in.

"Well, how are you? I am come because I heard of your trouble." It was the Rector of the church on the eastern hill; it could not be guessed how he heard of this distant grief, but sorrow often borrowed wings in its haste to reach his listening ear. The iron bands of that heavy woe loosened their grasp round the soul of the old man at such tones of sympathy; he poured out his complaint, and the clergyman sat by him listening. Then, when all had been heard, he said tenderly, "Have faith in God; you have fallen by an error, but God is still able to make a way of escape for you; put your trust in His mercy. I will do all I can."

The clergyman returned home and wrote to the Government. Day after day he watched for a reply; a week passed, but no answer came. Then, fearing for that trembling old man in this terrible suspense, he took the same coach that had carried Stephen to London, and went up himself to plead for the poor man. He went to an eminent clergyman, whom he knew to be acquainted with the First Lord of the Treasury, obtained a letter of introduction from him, and waited on Mr. Vansittart the next morning early. The Lord of the Treasury was at breakfast, but he admitted the village Rector to an audience, and rising as he entered, asked with the courtesy of the great man, "What is it that has brought me the honor of a letter from Dr. Dealtry?" Then briefly but eloquently the cause of the old harness-maker was pleaded before him.

But the countenance of the Treasury Lord was decided as he replied, "It is no mercy to reprieve in these cases; they so frequently occur, that the true mercy is to enforce the penalty as a warning to others."

One strong word in answer; it must be the last that the intercessor for the poor harness-maker may venture. "If the penalty be enforced, it will kill the old man, and I am sure you would not wish that!"

There was no doubting the truth of the declaration, made by a voice that well knew how to stamp reality on the facts that it uttered. The Lord of the Treasury rang for his secretary, sent him with the poor man's intercessor, and desired full particulars to be entered in the Treasury against the harness-maker's name, that full consideration might be given to the case by those who had power to remit the penalty. The secretary's heart was touched with compassion; he took the greatest interest and care in the entry, expressed more freely than his master could his hope for the result, though none could question Lord Bexley's pity for the poor. So by the next coach the village Rector returned, and hastened to the old man as the bearer of Hope. What is Hope to the spirit almost sinking in despair? they know who have seen such gloom lightened by its beams; and they who have not cannot be told by words what it is. So the old man bore on in hope. And soon the Government mandate came down; the thousand pounds was exchanged for twenty, and by that **payment as** much safety to be secured as if he had never signed the bond. The twenty pounds was the seal of his freedom, made him realize the fact, and swept away all misgiving, leaving the old man unshadowed by a fear; while his deeply disciplined spirit rose brighter from the furnace of trial, like gold purified seven times in the fire.

CHAPTER XVI.

THERE was great joy over the old harness-maker's escape from a prison; the sympathy felt for him had been great, but no one had known how to help him, until the God whom he served sent His servant, and delivered him from the fate to which his own unwary deed had so nearly consigned him. The old man had been the light of his darkened parish, and during his long consistent life had taught the holy religion he professed, no less by example than by precept. He had been betrayed into an error, but all could see how surely God had delivered His servant's soul from death, his eyes from tears, and his feet from falling, still to walk before Him in the land of the living. The welcome tidings reached the farm, and every face there brightened in thankfulness and joy.

But tribulation is God's servant, sent by Him to dwell upon the earth while sin abides here. And, therefore, when its work is done in one home, it turns to another, and often goes where those who see it enter think it least needed, and often when least expected by those to whom it comes; they are happiest who bid it welcome for its Master's sake. Tribulation, having worked patience, experience, and hope, in the heart of the old harness-maker, now turned again to the widowed Margery's home. A year had not passed since young Edward's death; and all well remembered that, on the day when they gathered round to take their last fond look of his sweet face as it slept the sleep of death, Daniel alone shed no tear, but stood with folded arms, looking down long and earnestly upon that young silent face, as if he could not cease to gaze upon it. Margery was seated near, calm in her sorrow; she had mourned a husband, and all other grief passed over her only as the returning shadow of that woe. The brothers and sisters stood around the sleeping form, weeping their farewell, only Daniel wept not; and at length, looking up, he calmly said, "In a year I shall be where Edward is!" It was a sudden shock that stayed the tears of all, and sent a chill to Margery's heart, but no one spoke; and he who had uttered the words turned calmly away. The months passed on, no one forgot, no one spoke of it, all thought it could not be; but when nine months were gone it was said that Daniel had taken cold, it did not leave him, and he was not well; he soon returned to the farm, not with his buoyant step and mirthful tone, but calm and grave, and when he entered, he looked at Margery and said, "Mother, I am come home to die!" And so he came again back to the love that had never ceased to feel his absent presence; the eyes that, as Margery said, had lost too many looks each day, to see if business or opportunity might drop a chance for him to make for home; he came, whose step, as Elsie said, had always turned work to play, and made him in his busiest ways seem keeping holiday; he came back, with the cold of only a few weeks upon him, but how changed—gravely calm, as one who knew that for him the end of all things earthly was at hand, and wished that all who loved him should know it too; yet not as one alarmed at the sudden call to die, but warned himself, and able to warn others of death's near approach. There was grief in the home, on the farm, at the mill, in the village; the driest eye could drop a tear for him, for all around him, perhaps, there could be hardly found the living thing he had not smiled upon. He only did not seem to know how all were mourning at fear of losing him; he looked as one who had other thoughts to think, and work to do. Truly God had been good to him, in sending him to dwell with Nathaniel. Elsie, and Philip, and Matthew, who had said they could never be happy again if Daniel were sent from the home, could see it now, for Nathaniel best understood and could best speak of the things that make peace between the soul and its God. And more than this, God had given that warning to Daniel, while he was yet strong and full of activity, impressing on his mind the fact that his death was near; as if taking tender notice of his joyous guileless spirits, and the charm that earthly life had for him, God had, by a voice within, warned him, as few are warned, to prepare to meet his God.

He soon felt too weak for an arm-chair in the farm-kitchen, and they laid him in the large crimson bed in the favorite guest-chamber, to die. "I should like to see him, brother, if he would take the trouble to come once before I die!"

All knew who alone that "him" could be; and Stephen hastened on Starlight to the distant home of the clergyman. He came, the messenger of peace and assurance. "If with the heart thou believest unto righteousness, and with the mouth makest confession unto salvation, thou shalt be saved."

It was not many days before the clergyman came again, for never were the dying forgotten by him. "I was sick and ye visited Me," will be echoed at the last great day by numbers, who, left as sheep without a shepherd, would but for him have had no earthly comforter! When he came again, he brought one of his youngest children with him, a child of four years old, little Mabel, and Elsie stayed down in the farm-kitchen with her, and gave her gingerbreads out of the deep closet by the great open chimney; and she heard her father's voice praying in the chamber above. When prayer had been offered, he sent for little Mabel; Elsie took her up stairs, and she saw the dying man, and her father sitting beside him; her father called her and put her hand in Daniel's, and she asked, "Are you better to-day?" and Daniel smiled, pleased to see the child of the friend he most loved. The dying youth soon departed from earth, to go, as he said he should, where young Edward was; where "they who have waited on the Lord shall renew their strength, and mount up with wings as eagles, and walk and not faint, and run and not be weary."

The little home at the mill sadly missed the lost brother. But another home, not far distant, was waiting for Mary; she was affianced to one whose industry, and integrity, and kindness of heart, won for him the respect of all who knew him; so Mary was married, and her bright face made sunshine in the house of her husband. Then Nathaniel chose a wife from a farm not far distant, one who had a heart to pity the poor, and brought her home to the mill. The eldest of Margery's seven sons had married some time before, and made his home on a larger farm at a distance from his native village. He was the only one of all Margery's children who ever settled beyond reach of their mother; and he in old age, as a widower, returned to be nourished from the home of his birth.

Time had brought changes at both Benjamin's and Margery's paternal homes. Margery's parents died in old age, and their farm was occupied by a stranger. Old Benezer too was gone from the wolds, his venerable head laid at rest in its quiet grave; for the record of earthly life must still be the record of death; though could we see the other side of death's shadow we should read the reverse, and see how, in heaven, the record of earthly death becomes there the bright register of immortal life. Benjamin Northwood, Margery's father-in-law, also was dead, and his sons could not long carry on the farm by themselves. A short time brought farming with them to an end, and now a sale was to be held at the paternal home. The great-grandmother's blessing had passed on to another generation; it was an ornament of grace to Stephen's head, as he stood the stay and the staff of the widowhood of his mother. Stephen had no thought of attending the sale; it would have cost him much feeling to see the farm that had been his great-grandmother's home, yield up all that it had to the highest bidder of money. But he said to his mother, "Though we don't go to the sale, there's one treasure left there that we ought to speak for and buy in!"

"What is that?" asked his mother.

"Poor old Sam Grist," replied Stephen; "he has spent all his strength on that farm, trusted his masters with his earnings—of which now, I suppose, he will never see a penny—and I would not for the world have him left to strangers."

"What would you do for him?" asked Margery.

"Bring him home," answered Stephen, "and feed him on clover!"

"That's a wish to which I shall never put No," answered Margery.

So the question was settled, and Stephen drove Starlight—the good horse being now in his old age—to bring back poor Sam Grist. He reached the desolate farm; no sound of busy husbandry was there, no stirring life around it or within. But he drove to the house, expecting to find some one left there in charge. As he drew up, he saw poor old Sam Grist seated on the stable-step, with his head bowed down low. He looked up at the sound of Stephen's voice, rose, and came slowly to meet him. It was the day after the sale, and not a creature was left on the farm for the kind heart of the old man to cling to. The pens were empty, the stables deserted, the poultry all gone, even the dog-kennel forsaken, the faithful watcher of years led away by another, and his chain lay forsaken on the ground. The last "lot" had been sent for, and Sam Grist—who had never worked on other land than that farm, and who had tended by turns every creature reared on it—had sat down, alone and desolate, amidst the wreck of all his interests, his honest earnings, and the only home of a lifetime. He thought on his first mistress, Esther Northwood, and the blessing that sprang where she trod, and grew up under her hand. He thought on his second mistress—her daughter-in-law, and how her quiet spirit had been troubled, until at last it found comfort that was not of this world, and then was taken from the evil to come. He thought of Christiana in her pleasant little farm, and the kind message she had sent to have him come and bide a time with her and her husband, until he could look round and see what might still offer for him. But he shook his head at that thought, and said, "I cannot make a being there; old and poor, all my wages spent by them that helped break their poor mother's heart, none paid me for long, and scarce decent clothes to my back; no, I cannot turn in there!" Then Sam Grist thought of the churchyard where those he most honored lay sleeping, untroubled by all the desolation around him; and that seemed to him then the only rest for his old head, he wished it were laid sleeping there. Who could wonder that the faithful old man, himself the victim of wrong, felt like Solomon when he said, "I considered the oppressions that are done under the sun, and beheld the tears of such as were oppressed, and they had no comforter; wherefore I praised the dead which are already dead, more than the living which are yet alive." But it was a greater than Solomon who could say to the desolate, "Weep not," and He was waiting now to speak peace to the troubled spirit of the old man.

Starlight's step on the road in better days would have wakened attention, but what the good horse could not do, its master's voice did. Stephen's call aroused the faithful Sam Grist from the cold stupor of desolation, and he came to meet him and Starlight. Sam Grist took hold of the reins, but he did not pat and welcome the good horse as usual, and it was touching to see the poor animal rub his lips on Sam's arm, and take his coat-sleeve between them, as if to say, "What, have you no welcome for me?'

Stephen was affected at the sight of the place and the old man left there alone; the memories of the past, in contrast to the facts of the present, overcame him unawares.

"What, all gone but you, Sam? not a feed for old Starlight?"

"Ah, master, the cheer is clean dead; there's nought left to be had."

"Step up then with me, Sam; we'll drive to the inn and stable him there, and you shall dine there with me, for I've business with you."

It was cheering to see the old man's lightened aspect, at this something to do for and with one of the family he had served from his birth; he stepped in beside Stephen, saying he was little fit for it, the three days' sale had done badly for the best clothes that he had; and then he added, "I can rub down the old horse while he's taking his feed, he won't fancy another now his eye has once turned upon me!" Stephen left Starlight with Sam in the inn-yard, ordered dinner for two, and then walked off to the churchyard to look again on his great-grandmother's grave; its grassy knoll lay verdant, beside it the peaceful grandmother slept, and not far off lay the faithful Benezer. He dropped a tear on the grassy sod that covered the saintly relative who had taught him in childhood to love the law of the Lord, and to pity the poor; and returned to the inn by way of Christiana's little farm.

"Now, Master Stephen, how glad I be to see you in here! If you could but have done us the favor to stable your horse in our yard, and take up with the plain fare at our table, I'm sure 'twould have given us the greatest pleasure."

"Thank you all the same; but I had business to-day: but if you can step up to the inn an hour from this time, I shall be happy to see you there before starting, which I must do pretty near by that time."

On Stephen's return, he sat down with Sam Grist to dinner. Sam thought that an inn dinner must be a festival he could not look fit for, and begged to "take a bait to the stable with Starlight," but Stephen said, "I am master to-day, and I'll have you sit down with me." He had been unable to tell the old man on first arriving the object of his coming; he felt unnerved himself, and could not venture on more; he knew that Sam Grist had yet made no lodging elsewhere, his worldly goods were all wasted by others, and the farm being empty his farewells could not be many. But now, after their short dinner, he told him his errand. "Well, Sam, what should you think brought me here to-day? I am come from my mother to take you back to her!"

"Ah, Master Stephen, I would go with greatest of pleasure, and let myself to serve you in the least place on your farm, but there's no work now left in me. I'm strengthless and penniless, and scarce clothes fit to wear."

"I don't want workmen," replied Stephen; "I have plenty of them, and too many sometimes of such as some are! You may walk about all day and see what each one is after, and if any be not the better for your eye upon them, why that's no fault of yours, so you come home with me."

"Ah, Master Stephen, such goodness can't be; 'tis too much for me!"

"You look, now," replied Stephen, and he untied an old shawl, out of which he lifted a great coat. "This was my poor father's own coat; it has lain by ever since he was taken from us, and my mother sends it for you; she says, had my poor father been living he would have cared well for you, and she will see the thing done all the same by you herself; so come, put on the coat, and then we can be starting."

When Sam Grist saw the coat, it was like Joseph's wagons to old Jacob, his spirit revived, and with the tears and sobs of a child he let Stephen put it on; in those warm tears he wept out the cold world from his heart; and so, warm within and without, could now think of nothing but the starting with Stephen and Starlight. Christiana came up, and her kind heart rejoiced in strong congratulations on Sam Grist's happy fortune. The old man sent a few kindly messages to one and another, helped to harness Starlight himself, stepped into the high gig after Stephen, who, making him comfortable beside him, drove the old man away from the scenes of a lifetime, now embittered and desolate, to a home where care and kindness awaited him.

"He treads so nimble," said Sam Grist, ' as if he'd

make me believe I had rubbed his old limbs young again! and how handsome he looks when he's groomed as he should be!"

It was plain, by degrees, that a sense of some energy and power was stealing over the warmed heart of the faithful old man. None knew better than Margery how to make a faithful servant welcome—without saying too much or too little; she made her high estimate felt, and Sam Grist found his place in her household as naturally as if he had always had a home there. He thought the farm all perfection, said that wherever he trod it seemed to him the footprints of his dear old mistress had been;— the true dealings of the farm, its evening prayers, and the poor who came to it, as they did to his old mistress in days that were gone. And when the evening music was sounding, he sat in the back kitchen with eyes shut and hands resting on his staff, for then he said it seemed to him as if he were come pretty near upon heaven, and heard the sounds of them praises that his old mistress did go to join in up above. He was willing to live now, he said, as long as it pleased God that he should, for, as his old mistress often said, "My cup runneth over." And when the call came, he should like to go up on them praises to heaven! And when at last his strength failed him, he said that "to see such a heap of kind creatures come waiting upon him made sickness wholly a pastime!" And so at length, full of days and of thankfulness to God and to man, the faithful old servant, who had been long taught by the same venerable woman who blessed the childhood of Stephen, departed in peace, and was laid in the village churchyard amidst the graves of the household.

CHAPTER XVII.

ON a morning when the farm was rejoicing in the sunshine, and the promise of the fields that the sunshine was ripening, a stranger was seen entering the gate that opened upon its farm and the valley. He was a man of fine height, as Elsie said, and could be seen from that distance to be all over a gentleman. The farm lay so apart from all casual guests, that any arrival was always watched with curiosity and interest. The visitor was on foot, which also excited surprise; but one of the laborers, coming in by the field, explained that fact by saying that he had been seen to arrive in a post-chaise that morning at the Rectory, and it was supposed he had been breakfasting there. This information was no happy herald of his errand. Stephen received him at the garden-gate, Elsie at the door, Margery in her farm-kitchen. He bowed slightly in return to the widow's curtsey, but his manners were cold and severe. He declined the seat offered him by Elsie, and turning to Stephen inquired, "Are you the manager of this farm for your mother?"

"Yes, sir."

"Then I must request you to conduct me entirely over it.

My authority for desiring this is an order from the managers of the estate, the Commissioners of Woods and Forests."

Margery saw that the austere stranger was come with no good-will to her and her home. He left the house with Stephen, and Margery sat anxious within.

Oh! widowed mother, whose trust is in God, He shall deliver thee in six troubles, yea, in seven there shall no evil touch thee; thou shalt be hid from the scourge of the tongue, neither shalt thou be afraid of destruction when it cometh. Are not thy children in league with the stones of the field, and the cattle of the field at peace with them? Surely then thou shalt know that thy tabernacle shalt be in peace! Yet it was a long painful morning to Margery; no dinner-table was set as usual at half-past twelve on that day, for all waited in anxiety and suspense. At last, Elsie saw the stranger and Stephen coming home by the pasture called Flowering. He stood a moment and looked on the house, and as he entered all were struck by the paleness of his countenance. It might be the heat of the sun on the fields he had crossed. "Would you please to take anything, sir?" asked Margery, in a tone expressive only of solicitude for the stranger. He made no answer, but seated himself on the table in the southern window, struggled a moment with emotion that would not be restrained, then burst into tears. All stood around in sympathizing surprise at the grief they understood not. Margery never wept without knowing why, but the eyes of her children filled to overflowing at the sight of the tears of a man and a gentleman. In a few moments he recovered composure, and turning to Margery he said, "You have a bitter enemy indeed!" Then drawing a paper from his pocket, he added, "His statements as fellow of his college had weight, and I came down here to-day to serve a notice upon you to quit, and only went round the farms first as a matter of justice. But, indeed, all is far from what I expected to find it. Be assured now that my coming can only prove for good; I shall take back such a statement as can only establish you here. But the thought of what I had come to do, as I returned to the house and saw you again, for the moment overcame me." Margery could give no answer but tears; and her children wept with her. The stranger waited a little, and then said, "Let me cheer you; the threatened evil had passed before you knew it was come! I will sit down to table with you if you have a meal ready." The stern reserve, in which he had armed himself for his expected painful task, was gone, and he was, as Elsie said, "one of the pleasantest of men." He was himself a landed proprietor, and had been requested to visit the farm, from his accurate knowledge of the cultivation of land. On returning to the trustees, and being asked what he had done, he replied, "Assured the widow that nothing is less likely than that she should ever be turned out of the estate, or her children after her!" The trustees were not a little surprised. But he gave in full particulars, and undertook to visit the farm yearly. So no weapon formed against the trusting hearts of the widow and her children could prosper, but every tongue that rose against them was condemned. From that day neither Margery nor her sons had a moment's anxiety as to their standing on the estate. The God whom Stephen had believed and honored when the danger was seen, spread His shield over the home when no effort of his own could avail. And he who wept for the widow, from that hour became a friend, and had reason in long after years to bless God for such friendship as he found at the farm.

> "Alms all around, and hymns within,
> What evil eye can entrance win,
> Where guards like these abound?
> The prayers of hungry souls and poor,
> Like armèd angels at the door,
> Our unseen foes confound."

"Happy are the people that are in such a case; yea, blessed are the people whose God is the Lord."

The children of the Rector on the eastern hill, all held their own place in the warm regard of Margery and her family, and little Mabel was allowed the joy of many a visit at the farm. To her it seemed a paradise, each wood a garden, each bank a planted border, each streamlet her young delight; and the creatures looked as numerous as in her picture-book had come to Adam to be named in Eden. One great charm of the farm to little Mabel was, that the dulness of night was not there. Elsie often set the first breakfast the last thing in the evening, telling Mabel not to wonder if she heard noises below, because the horsemen would be up by twelve o'clock in the night, preparing their horses to carry out the corn, and in at breakfast by two o'clock in the morning. Then the first cock crowed at one, and crowed twice at two o'clock—on through the dawn keeping the hours. Elsie rose at five o'clock, and then came the farm boy with the cows, shouting his call as he brought them all in, amidst all the voices of waking creatures—geese, ducks, and hens, stepping out in the morning air; even the satisfied grunt of the farm pigs was not discordant there, heard with the bleat of the lambs turned out on their fresh dewy pasture, and the song of the birds from the orchard and garden below. All this Mabel knew was going on, however unbroken her slumbers might be, and to her it seemed a most pleasant way of lengthening the enjoyment of that happy thing called LIFE. The favorite guest-chamber was made little Mabel's own room. The large bed with crimson hangings had been moved to another chamber, and a new tent bed was there, with unlined chintz of a white ground, strewn with green leaves. Bed was piled upon bed, all made of softest down feathers from the fowls of the farm, and when Elsie laid Mabel to sleep in the centre of this circumference of down, and drew the green leaves all around her, Mabel thought nothing could be more like a bird's nest in the wood. The crystal waters of the farm, than which none could be clearer and colder, were poured out by Elsie, when she called Mabel in her little milking-bonnet at five o'clock in the morning, and Mabel's small wardrobe laid ready, up to her white frock and blue sash, which could be tied in front and then slipped round behind, as Mabel at the farm did all things for herself. Her white tippet and hat had their place in the parlor, and her little pattens just inside the door. On the lowest shelf of the parlor cupboard stood the little antique tumbler, that Mabel had her new milk in each morning in the cowhouse. The cupboard was full of glass and china; many a curious goblet was there, and tumblers of old quaint devices, some long and small that baffled the thirsty, others twisted and spiral, and others adorned with ground figures. In their father's time, when the harvest-home was kept by the family, as well as by the laborers, he had the strong old ale of the farm drunk from these quaint spiral glasses—quite excluding the possibility of excess. But Mabel's was simple and pretty, a little glass goblet for Blossom's new milk. Reaching it down, she went next to the back kitchen, where Margery was always busy in her large-ringed pattens, scalding milk-pans in readiness for the new milk coming in. Margery always stooped to kiss Mabel and bless her, and Mabel put her arm around Margery's neck to return the morning kiss that she gave her, and thought Margery beautiful with her firm and grave face, and tall figure—her neckerchief of whitest muslin, and a red handkerchief pinned over the shoulders of her always black gown.

Then Mabel stepped out from the back-kitchen door into the sweet breathing air of the morning, all fragrant with the breath of the cows waiting about on the straw of the farmyard, and the scent of clover, or hay, or whatever pleasant fodder might be filling the mangers and cribs, for the cattle. The cow-house would not hold all the cows at one time, half waited outside for their turn, but Mabel was glad if Silvertongue, Thistledown, and Skippet were within, because they were apt to crowd round the door, too intent on their favorite Elsie, to attend to civility and move out of the way, especially Skippet, who had a very earnest stare that Mabel never quite understood, but Elsie always heard the click of her little sharp pattens on the stones of the near stable-door, and looked out, and told Skippet to mind what she was after and stand out of the way, at which Mabel walked manfully in. Each cow had a history and disposition of its own, and Cloe, the farm-maid, and Peggy Berry the farm-helper, had many a tale to tell Mabel, as she sat on the clean straw on her little three-legged stool, behind the animal she thought it safest to trust, though no cow showed ill-humor when Elsie was near. Mabel listened to the tales that chronicled the love of the creatures for Elsie—who smiled and said nothing, but leaned her forehead against the animal's soft side, and milked her brimming pailfuls. Mabel drank the warm frothing beverage, and in spring watched the calves at their play, in the pen that opened into the cowhouse; and then went in at six o'clock, with Elsie to breakfast. Breakfast at the farm was a substantial repast—it was the principal meal of the day, and proportionably plentiful. The clear home-brewed ale filled the tumblers more than once before Elsie poured out her fragrant tea; meat and cheese were succeeded by the pile of hot buttered toast, and the slices of bread-and-butter, with all the accompaniments of an hospitable table. But Mabel had her own little glass jug of Blossom's new milk, her thin slice of ham, or a new-laid egg—which Matthew boiled for her while breakfast went on, and her chair was set between Margery and Stephen.

All the winter long it was still a six o'clock breakfast, and then, of course, it was breakfast by candle-light; but this was delightful, for no one at the farm was afraid of the cold. Margery said, "It was one of the good gifts of God to a healthy body and soul;" and the great logs of wood crackled and blazed, and glowed up the huge chimney; and the house dogs lay in front of the fire, just lifting up an eye to catch the first notion of any one moving out; the shutters still shut, and the white-fringed window-blinds down. But Margery said, she "thought it no merit ever wholly to block out the heaven," so no shutter went higher than the third window-pane, and the first rays of sunrise laid their soft light on the window-blind, and little Mabel at her own discretion blew out the candles, and the daylight came in.

Breakfast for the farm fowls came next, and Mabel

took them under her care. She ran down the stone steps to where the heap of refuse barley lay safe hid in the nearest cellar below, and filled her can, with a wish that each fowl should be satisfied. It was a pleasant sight to her to see them running and flying from every side at the sound of her call, especially in spring-time, when all the young broods were there; the golden goslings, soft waddling ducks, and prettiest of chickens, all following her as their best friend. But one unfortunate morning she did not latch the little wicket-gate, and a mother duck pushed it open to follow her, and one duckling, making haste after its mother, was caught in the gate as it closed again, and lay writhing with a broken head on the ground. Mabel lifted it up, and hastened in with the little duck in her bosom, to tell Elsie it must die: but Elsie said, "No, there's no occasion for that, ducks live through stranger misfortunes than a crack through the head, it only wants nursing, and will thrive well enough yet." Elsie made it a flannel bed in a round basket by the fire, for she said "warmth was healing," and she fed the duck with such food as would best help recovery. "Do you really think it will live?" Mabel asked, as she watched by the duck. "Yes; live, and very likely to be the best duck in the brood! it will lose its right eye, and be sidus-headed, but that will not trouble it when it once gets about!" The duck lived, as Elsie said, and was a very handsome duck, but it lost its right eye, and held its head awry; it retained a great attachment to Mabel, always turning its one black eye to look after her, and waddling to her whenever she appeared in sight. And as Mabel had lately learned, with much trouble, the names of the constellations, she called the little duck "Georgium Sidus," because Elsie had said that to be "sidus-headed" must be always its fate. And one of England's pastoral poets, being a kind friend of Mabel's, and listening to her tales of the farm, introduced the sidus-headed duck into one of his lays, and so memorialized it above all its fellows.

When the farm-fowls were satisfied, little Mabel came to the dairy, where Elsie was sure to be busy with either butter or cheese. Elsie's cold rosy hand made butter in perfection, and Mabel always found her part to do also; with Elsie's help she fashioned the fresh butter into swans, with a double-sided mould, swans with long arching necks, and great wings to float in the crystal waters, with a sprig of parsley here and there on the surface, in a large circular glass on the table at tea, on every festal occasion. To break up with her fingers all the soft curd for the cheese, was not less pleasant to Mabel; and Philip cut large initials of her name, to be laid on the soft curd of every cheese that she made, before the heavy press was lowered upon it, that the expected excellence of her cheeses might not pass unnoticed, when sold or cut for home use.

On three days in the week the work of the dairy was followed by the occupation of baking. The household was large, and sometimes the different people who came in the course of the day would be from twelve to twenty, and not one be sent empty away. Stephen would look at Elsie's hands laden with food, and say, "I never can think wherever it all comes from!" and Elsie would answer, "Well, but it DO come!" and Stephen's satisfied smile proclaimed Elsie's logic unanswerable. So baking was a busy, cheerful business at the hospitable farm; there were Margery, and Elsie, and Cloe, and Peggy Berry, and Mabel with her part to perform, in making loaves of all sizes, cakes of various description, tarts, and tartlets, of orchard fruits and home-made preserves. The huge brick oven arched the flames back again, until heated above and below. Peggy Berry and Cloe fed the oven, and Mabel stood between Margery and Elsie, on a stool to reach the broad sideboard of whitest deal, where the hospitable baking went on. Mabel's choice was, in summer, to make the harvest cakes; these were little loaves of bread filled with plums, made in harvest as an added meal for a man in the fields; and Matthew always said he knew when Mabel had made them, because no pony was wanted to ride from one plum to another; for Margery let Mabel take her handfuls without count and at will, therefore there were no such harvest-cakes at the farm as those made by Mabel. In winter Mabel exercised her skill in apple turnovers, a large species of apple puffs. As all waited on themselves at the farm, Mabel carried her own productions to the mouth of the oven, for Peggy Berry to put within; and on one occasion, holding her dish tightly with both hands, as not being aware that a dish required no tighter hold than a book, an unknown crack yielded to pressure, and leaving half the dish in each hand, the turnovers fell on the sanded stone floor. The little baker looked round in dismay, but Elsie answered to her look, "Why, you have only made wholly a *turnover!*" and gathered up the contents of Mabel's dish, saying, "What was the harm of a little clean sand!" and turnovers and sand went into the oven together. Every one wished for turnovers when they appeared at table, and on Mabel saying it was a good thing they could be eaten after such a misfortune, Philip answered with a merry smile, that "He did not see how it was possible for a TURNOVER to have been managed better!" So work went smoothly on in a home where each one knew how to turn into play any household misfortune.

When this cheerful business was concluded, the day was still early for those who had six o'clock for their breakfast hour. Philip and Matthew were generally back by ten o'clock from their first rounds on the farm, for now that they only were left with Stephen they assisted him in the oversight of all, only turning to the plough when occasional necessity required. Philip and Matthew had grown up side by side in their home, and their love for each other was like David and Jonathan's. Matthew had Stephen's quickness and naturally hasty spirit, but always followed by a gush of forgiveness that never bore an ill-will. Philip was full of humor and thoughtful observation, and the very soul of gentleness and good-will to all. The Rector of the eastern hill called them "the Gemini," so rarely were they to be seen apart, and seeming to have but one will to guide them in every thing. While Elsie's heart leaned on Stephen, who turned to her also in all things; and so, while household love reigned over all, each heart had its stay, and that fellowship with another that every human spirit needs for its full exercise here.

As the early farm morning wore on, Philip would take Mabel for a walk, or Matthew arrange for a ride: either walk or ride had its charms delightful to the child. In the walk, Philip guided through the wild paths of the woods where the sweetest flowers grew, and the bird's nests might be seen above them, and each little songster be recognized by its note. Or the hazel-nuts hung in rosy clusters, and the hare was discovered peering above the brown furrow. Nor was the winter walk less delightful, along the field paths above the ditches, where the crimson fungi grew, that Mabel, in botanical ignorance, called cup moss, on the dead and damp twigs; or, when the old year was gone, and the cheerful new year in, the eager search in the wood banks for the first primrose —sweet herald of the spring. One day in the wood Philip found a young ringdove, which had strayed from its nest. He brought it home to Mabel, and the bird took kindly to its young mistress; it sat on the back of her chair in the day, and when she walked out it went contentedly on her finger; it seemed to find life as pleasant as did Mabel at the farm, and showed no disposition to forsake its new home. Another thing that made the walk with Philip most pleasant, was the friendship of the village children with him; many a kind look and word was given or asked as they passed, nor could any wonder that he gathered around him the love of the village.

One spring morning Philip said at the breakfast table, that a forest tree would be felled before eight o'clock, and asked if Mabel would like to be there. It was a woodland sight she had never seen, and she was delighted to go with her yeoman protectors to the wood. It was an exquisite morning in May; the flowers were all drooping with dew, to the spangles of which the early sun gave the splendor of gems. As they went on in the wood the chorus of song gew more thrilling; that joyous song of the morning, which, perhaps, no one can imagine who has not stood early in the depth of wild wood in spring. Philip and Matthew trod down a pathway for Mabel, and held back the hazel and eglantine; and so all made their way, until they reached an open spot where moss and flowers alone formed a carpet. The forest tree stood there in its grandeur, the woodmen had already laid the axe to its root, but they were not near then, and the noble tree looked unconscious of the fate proclaimed by the gashes already cut at its root. Not a single leaf had yet unfolded upon it, but its countless buds were rich in promise of foliage, and gleamed bright against the blue sky above them. Mabel had a seat on the stem of a tree already cut down and barked; and from the copsewood one nightingale answered another, until Matthew's quick ear could reckon five around them concealed in the green mist of young leaves. But now the woodmen came, crushing down with heavy tread the light anemones that clustered above the mossy ground; they looked up at the tree, then stooped to unfasten and prepare the long coil of rope that was to guide it in its fall. The sight of the woodmen brought suddenly to Mabel a feeling for the fate of the noble tenant of the wood, and in these last few moments a bullfinch perched on one of its branches, and poured forth his plaintive song. Mabel saw his crimson breast glowing in the sunbeam, and listened to him singing there alone, and a sadness came over her, for she thought, "It is the last little bird that will ever sing from the tree!" It seemed a touching farewell to the noble forest tree, which for so many years had been a shelter and home for the birds of the wood; perhaps this little bullfinch remembered its last year's nest in its foliage. But the men threw the rope, and the bird flew away; the men plied their sharp hatchets, and the nearer birds in the copsewood ceased their song in surprise. At last the tree swayed, a few more strokes and it fell; its huge stem came down with a crash that was terrible, crushing its own branches, and breaking the young trees down beneath it, then lay stretched on the ground, the prostrate giant of the wood. It was too much for Mabel.

She knew not before that there was sorrow to be felt in the fall of a tree; and never more from that day would Mabel look on the felling of timber.

CHAPTER XVIII.

THE management of horses on the farm seldom took the form of conquest and subjection, it had the character rather of personal friendship, which was but rarely broken by an opposition of will. The horses were most of them born, and at that time all broken in and trained, on the farm. Matthew maintaining that if you had the horse from a foal there was but little necessary in the breaking him in, except the giving up your rest by night, (horses being more easily managed in the dark,) and not losing either watchfulness, or command of your temper; these three requisites, with a knowledge of horses from childhood, he said, was pretty much all that he had found wanted to bring them to the perfection of training that could be shown on the farm. The eighteen fine carthorses were worthy of admiration, both in appearance and conduct, but the favorites were the beautiful hunters, reared for sale. A race of them flourished, all bearing the same name of Wrangler, and in disposition and faithful attachment they could hardly be excelled. Mabel's visits gave a good opportunity for showing the readiness of the horses to include in their allegiance and attachment one who, apart from their own good-will, could have held no authority over them. But the farm gave beautiful glimpses of the promise, as yet unfulfilled, when of the brute creation it is said, "And a little child shall lead them." And the farm gave constant evidence how faithfully the brute creation, even now, will return the justice and the kindness of man.

Margery's white embroidered saddle had long hung unused on its peg; it was now lifted down, and she gave it to Mabel. Matthew saddled the Wrangler, dressed himself in Stephen's red martial cloak as a habit, hung loose chains on the saddle, and with whatever else might be thought most unaccountably strange, rode the hunter, to try if his spirit were proof against fancies. Returning home with a good report, all was ready for Mabel. Mabel and the Wrangler were friends already. Elsie took her every morning to the great chest of oats, at which she filled both her hands, and then called to the Wrangler, who, stooping down his high neck, put his small nose into them, eating up all his oats almost without spilling one, then waited for her to caress him; he considered himself her especial friend, and if she bestowed notice on any other horse he showed every sign of impatience until she turned to him again. Such a friendship existing, every considerate attention was to be expected from an animal so intelligent, and these expectations were never disappointed. All the wayside incidents that were wont most to discompose the young horse, would be almost unnoticed if he had Mabel in charge—a cart rattling behind, another horse passing by, or even a red cloak, which from the excitement it usually produced was supposed to remind Wrangler of the hunt; proof against all discomposures, he cantered quietly on, never changing his pace except at the request of his young rider.

One of the race called Black Wrangler was a horse of great size and strength; his neck clothed with thunder and his eye bright with the quickness of lightning. All would sometimes step out from the farm to see him loosed from his stall; he would rush round the farmyard, his nostrils dilated and his eyes fierce and terrible, but at the least signal from Matthew he would turn instantly in his maddest careering, rush up to his master, and rearing over him drop his paws above his shoulder, and stoop his head to caress him. Black Wrangler trotted a mile in three minutes, and notwithstanding his formidable appearance, Matthew said he was ready any day to drive him without reins to the distant town, quite certain of guiding him only by the whip and controlling him entirely by his voice, so complete was the understanding between them. He looked almost too formidable to ride, but his small feet stepped lightly as if treading on down; little Mabel shared his friendship, and he would canter for her mile after mile without changing his pace, as if his only care were the perfect contentment of the young rider he bore.

But the chief favorite of the farm was a horse of remarkable color, one of the same race of Wranglers. Before he was broken in for the saddle, and while as yet only led out to accustom him to the road and the rein, the servant who led him proved unworthy of his charge, a rare occurrence on the farm; he did not return at the right hour; in the evening, as all were watching at the door, the horse and the man were seen on the opposite hill. The man had evidently been stopping at some wayside inn, and disabled himself for his duty; he descended the hill with a tottering step, the beautiful creature behind putting his head now on one side of the man and then on the other, to keep him from falling. All determined to see what the intelligent animal would do to the end. In the valley the stream turned off through deep banks below the hill, on which stood the farm-house and stable; the unconscious man took the bed of the brook instead of ascending the road, and the faithful horse followed him; at this all hastened down the hill, and looked over the steep bank into the brook; the man had caught his foot against one of the great stones in its bed and had fallen, the horse stood stooping over him, striking his fore foot on a stone by the man's prostrate head, as if to awake him. There were many witnesses to this act of fidelity, and Margery, who had watched from the door, after that day manifested more interest in this horse than she had ever given expression to for any animal before. The beautiful creature seemed to know his mistress in a way scarcely to be accounted for, as she rarely saw him except in harness, or when saddled for Mabel to ride. He had on most occasions an exuberance of spirit, that had made it no easy task to break him in, and now, having but little work and much play, he had nothing but his sense of allegiance to keep it in subjection. When waiting harnessed it was almost impossible to hold him, and few but those well acquainted with horses would have wished a seat by his driver; but when his mistress wanted his services, he appeared quite another animal. Margery had grown heavy in figure, and to get into the gig became a difficulty to her; a chair and footstool must be brought, and even then it was managed slowly. When the Wrangler was led up full of spirit and play, if Margery were going she went up to his head, and laid her hand on his neck—in a moment he steadied into a statue; all the deliberate process of the chair and footstool went on without haste or fear; Matthew had time, not only to get fairly into the gig, but to button up the apron; the Wrangler did not start until the order was given; he would then trot quietly on, neither too fast nor too slow, but as equal as time in the measured pace that he went; and when with help of chair and stool his mistress alighted again, the only reward that he looked for was the commendation of her hand. It seemed as if he silently said to Margery, "We all know on the farm that it is you who have trained us up masters so just and so kind; and you shall see that we understand well the difference between good usage and bad, by our making most obedient acknowledgments to you." It was glory to Matthew to see his fiery young hunter subdue itself in that way to the service of his mother, for more than silver and gold to her children was the sense of that mother's approval. The one thing that all dreaded was the day when some one would offer a high price for the hunter, for then he must go. It is often the trial of the farm that it rears its favorites for the hand of another. The purchaser pays his good price, and little thinks, it may be, how the heart of the seller is not with the money that he holds in his hand, but with the favorite of the farm now sold from it for ever.

Mabel had gone on a visit near London, and one day when walking out she saw a horse in the distance, like none but the farm's favorite Wrangler; his peculiar color made her think so at first. An officer was riding the horse quickly down a slope, but the moment he reached Mabel the creature stopped and turned to her; poor Mabel also stood still, but the officer, little thinking that the child was a friend recognized by his horse, put spurs to his side, and the Wrangler took wings and was out of sight in a moment. Then Mabel wrote to the farm to ask if indeed the Wrangler was gone; and Stephen wrote back that, "it was true they had sold him; he had been reared for the gentry, and it was but right they should have him. An officer had bought him, and they had been told he was gone up to those parts. But no horse ever cost more at the parting; their mother shed tears for him, not one of the family could see him go, and no one on the farm would consent to lead him away; so it was to be hoped they that had him would know how to use him, for never could there be a horse to deserve better of any hands he might fall in."

It was no wonder that it seemed to some as if the God of creation owned the filial obedience of Margery's children to their mother, by honoring them with a power, which all who saw felt peculiar, over the animal creation around them.

Dinner was a simple repast at the farm, hospitable and cheerful, but of no very distinctive character. When Mabel was there the farm dessert followed, of home-made wines and fruit from the garden or orchard; but the tables were removed before the dessert was brought in, the centre of the pleasant room left free as usual, and all again occupied chairs round the wall. Stephen sat within for awhile after dinner, and took pleasure in teaching Mabel many practical facts of agricultural life. Margery and Elsie worked at this time, and Mabel worked also. Elsie bleached and made all the home linen; its stockings also were knitted, and many pleasant household things contrived and done. At three o'clock all the horses came home, their day's work was done at that hour; two and two the nine pair of fine horses drank water at the brook, bathed their limbs in the pond, and ascended the hill. At this hour, when Mabel grew older, she went off to the cottages, leaving the farm busy refreshing its tired horses. If it were the poor of the village Mabel wanted to see, she went alone; but if they lived at a distance Matthew drove her; or if it were winter, and the fields heavy with mud, he saddled the farm pony, which she only rode on these cottage errands; and then Matthew walked by its side, and held it for her while she made her long visits by the sick, or the aged, or the ignorant. Old age, and childhood, and youth might be dying, and no one but Mabel to visit them. Margery loved her with a tenderness that yielded up many a strong feeling to her; for she unconsciously violated many a surface feeling of Margery's when she broke through the strict household order, or decked the walls with her fancies; but Margery always said, "'Twas the child's hand that did it, let it be as she left it." And so that strong heart enshrined her in tenderness, and always called her "the child;" but it pleased Margery well that she should visit the poor. Stephen was glad, and always thought that a way could be made out for Matthew to give time to attend upon Mabel; and Matthew thought that nothing could be of so much importance as to visit the poor ignorant people, where there was any one who could speak a word for their comfort. So the love of the farm strewed Mabel's pathway with roses.

Going out or returning from her afternoon's excursions, she called at the church farm upon Margaret, and would often persuade her to come down to tea. The five o'clock tea was the rallying point of all interest and cheerfulness. The day's work was then done, except in haytime and harvest, and social converse brightened all. The tables from under each window were lifted for the third time in the day to the centre of the room, covered with crimson cloths in winter, and in summer with blue, and laden with home-made provisions. Brimming tumblers of ale, a large section of cheese, ham of Elsie's own curing, bread, butter, a variety of cake, the pile of farm toast, beaten down and dried, making a dish only farms can prepare, intermingled with the home-made preserves and the flowers of the season. Elsie did not pour out her fragrant tea until the conclusion of the repast, when the more substantial fare had taken the first course; but Mabel had her little glass pitcher of Blossom's rich milk, and her seat by Margery's side as at breakfast. All conversed on the interests of the day, and seldom could any home table be more enlivened than was Margery's, where native refinement shed a charm beyond all that mere education can supply, strong common sense, and most gentle wit enriched the social converse around it. The throne of her country stood close beside its church in the royal heart of Margery, and not less firmly associated and established in the hearts of her children. The farm was all over Conservative. Every wainscot panel in those days gleamed in blue,—the Conservative color of the county. Stephen thought nothing but blue worthy to be looked at in dress; his coat was blue, of a darker shade than the wainscot panels, but still truly blue; his neck-tie was blue; his best waistcoat of pale blue, half concealed by the breadth of the frills that fell over it; his very handkerchief of blue. He never considered Elsie dressed unless her gown was of blue; and he sometimes smiling said, that when he chose a dress for Mabel it should be the richest blue that the country could produce. And when a politician argued with Stephen, on the ground that the whig candidate then canvassing was a better man than the Conservative, Stephen listened, as he always did, in attention that never lost the speaker's meaning, and then answered, "Sir, the family has always voted Blue, and the family always will vote Blue; and if the man be not what he ought to be, they that are about us must look into that." The walls of the farm parlor were hung with framed representatives of the royal family; only one or two amongst them laid claim to the title of *portraits*, but they were reverently hung up as high as was possible, and gleamed amidst antique embroidery of Jacob first looking at Rachel, and all the patriarchs in various occasions of their pastoral life. And at tea, it was very affecting to Mabel, to see every best cup and saucer and every best plate still mourning the Princess Charlotte, with a likeness of her upon each: every cup, saucer, and plate inscribed "Princess Charlotte, died on the 6th of November, 1817." But after England's crown descended on the royal brows it now encircles, the china that mourned the Princess Charlotte was never used again.

Nathaniel would often step across from the mill to join the evening anthem and hymns, and his good and bright discourse gave a hallowed turn to the topics of home.

Then in summer there was evening work in the garden, the training and tending of flowers; and in winter Margery always said, "Now, child, come and read." And all at that maternal call took their chairs into an exact semicircle around the glowing hearth, while Margery and Elsie's knitting-pins rang music in the firelight, and Mabel sat on a stool just within the great open chimney, whose inner walls, where not black with the wood smoke, were also painted bright blue, and hung with spurs, bits, and all the steel harness of the horses glittering in the wood flames. There Mabel sat close to Margery's armchair, and read aloud, to the interest and satisfaction of all. It was always some holy book, for Margery cared for no other, and Stephen, and Elsie, and Philip, and Matthew, and Mabel, and Margaret when she came down, were all of the same mind, and so the later hour of the evening passed away until the great clock in the corner struck nine. Stephen and Margaret crossed the valley for evening prayers at the church farm, and the servants came in at the home, where Philip reverently conducted the service.

The servants remained after prayers to take their supper in patriarchal style in the same room, at a separate table spread for them. Then Cloe, the maid, set seven basins in a row on the white tablecloth, and Elsie stood before the row, crumbling in a large farm loaf, with her quick hands despatching all business while most would still have been considering what next must be done; the great saucepan, full of boiling milk, was lifted by her, and a broad stream descended into each basin of the row; but Mabel's was a little basin of china, red and white, and the crumbs in her basin were small, and the stream was poured gently,—then Elsie put in the spoons and handed them round. The man-servant, Jonathan, had one for his supper, and Shurtel the boy—Shurtel's name was Shealtiel, so entered in the church register, but the name being long he was called Shurtel on the farm. His brother's name was Maher-shalah: but Shurtel only lived in the house, and though not equal to what John Wilton had been, he earned some praise for his care of the creatures in his place as yard-boy.

After this infantine repast the day was done, and the household retired to rest. Elsie never laid down to sleep until she saw each head reposing on its pillow; then she retired to hers, and slumber and silence settled down upon the active cheerful day at the farm.

CHAPTER XIX.

ON a summer day in June, a carriage drew slowly up the steep hill to the farm. All knew whom it bore, and came out to the garden gate to meet its arrival there, each with that aspect of deep feeling which repeated bereavement had made natural to them—in sympathy with grief. The old coachman opened the carriage door, and the minister's lady first alighted. She who had come to the farm in the hour of its sorrow, now came in her own deep anxiety, to be welcomed and cheered by its sympathy and love. She met Margery and her children with the same sweet smile—no personal anxiety ever banished that, when others could be cheered by its light. Then Elsie gave her hand, and the old coachman held his arm to a young and lovely form, whose wont it had not been to lean upon others, but with a springing step of tender joyousness to tread the earth, which was to her young heart a garden of delight. But now as she left the carriage, she gave her hand to Elsie, and leaned on the old coachman's arm, then stood erect and looked around on the fair scene of hill and valley, grassy turf, and waving grain, like a freed bird who yet feels its wing is broken and its flight cut short. Beautiful she looked, and unlike earth, as those around her thought, and the radiance of her smile brought tears to their kind eyes. She stooped to caress the farm dogs who fawned at her feet, and then was soon seated in Margery's arm-chair by the open parlor window, the southern breeze blowing back her sunny curls and fanning the hectic of her cheek. Mabel stood beside her; it was her elder sister, the brightest sunshine of life to the child, the object of her deepest affection. Her mother had brought her to the farm to see what such change might do. Margery and her children welcomed them with their true but silent hospitality, glad to give the best their home could offer to those who had brought to them a heavenly benediction. The farm was worthy to receive her, rich as she was in natural gifts, in loveliness of person, heart, and mind; a child of song, free and sportive, yet clinging in deep tenderness to all the objects of her affection. She, like Margery's children, possessed that peculiar gift of subduing animal life to gentlest control; creatures that others feared to approach were playful and safe with her. And she had yet a higher grace, and could soften into gentleness fierce, rugged human natures, winning them to kind response. It was no wonder that her sixteen years of life had been full to her of love and blessing, of gladness and of joy, so that when she found her call had come she said, "I have always been so happy, or I might wish to die!"

But she who had learned to live, could not find it hard to learn to die. She who had feared no danger to bring others to the Saviour's feet, who had ventured in the strength of love, the might of gentleness, where men might have drawn back, she could find no terrors between her young spirit and its home in its Redeemer's bosom; though the sudden call to part with all most loved on earth, at first looked sad to her in all the joyousness of youth; and her deep affection for her mother made her say, "If I could but take you with me!" But as heaven drew nearer, she saw it was not death, but life and love made perfect, to enter there; and her spirit turned to meet the unveiled glory of the Lord.

On her first coming to the farm she could walk out amongst its creatures, and make them all her friends. The summer air blowing softly on the hill's southern side was life to her, and though her thrilling voice of song was hushed on earth forever, she loved the farm evening's hour of sacred melody, chose the hymns, and listened from the open parlor with delight.

Margery did not give the favorite guest-chamber to her; death had been often there; it was in that room the mother of the dying girl had seen the youth and beauty of the farm laid on the bed of death; association would be sad there. So they prepared for her the pleasant south-western room. When a few weeks had passed, her drooping strength failed suddenly; Philip, used to tenderest nursing, carried her to her chamber, and she rose not from her bed again until angels bore her spirit to the skies. All through the weeks of suffering, in which mortality still bound the immortal spirit, Elsie was ready day or night with her gentlest nursing; and every evening the farm brothers, with their instruments, stepped softly up the stairs, and sang one evening hymn outside the chamber door.

"I am at the gate!" she said, and her freed spirit entered in to be forever with the Lord. She had been born in glowing August, when the corn was ripe in all the country round the wild home of her birth, and she passed away in the same month, when all the golden sheaves as yet were standing on the farm, herself first gathered to the garner of her God. Two days before her seventeenth birthday they laid her in the tomb, and many mourned on earth, but there was joy in heaven.

The snows of advancing age had fallen white on Margery's head, and strewn their silver hue above Stephen's early furrowed brow. Philip's manhood was advancing, and Matthew was no longer young, though his mother called him still "the Boy." Mabel often wondered that Stephen, who was so true and kind, and freely talked to her of every earthly thing, yet never spoke of heaven, nor of Him who gave His life to open Paradise for all who come to God by Him. And when she spoke of that better life to come, and the grace that alone can make us ready, it always left him silent—silent as one whose heart had no response. It was a mystery to Mabel, at which she often wondered. But God had taught Stephen from his youth, and as yet he could not learn of man.

Now a sudden illness came upon him, and brought him quickly face to face with death. He had often seen death drawing near for others, but now it came for him; he felt himself approaching the immediate presence of the Almighty, and he trembled as the light of the divine Holiness fell on him. He looked into his past life with the deepest anxiety, to see if it could stand in the judgment before a holy, heart-searching God; he had never silenced the voice of conscience within him, and now it spoke louder than ever; it pointed solemnly back;—his eye seemed constrained to follow it; it showed him sin; it showed him that he had lived for earth, not for the eternity that he knew laid before him; it showed him thoughts and affections taken up with the business of this world, not with preparation for the next; it showed Self in his heart more than God; he felt, "I am not ready to die, not prepared to meet my Judge; He is holy, I am sinful; I have read before that God is of purer eyes than to behold iniquity, and cannot look upon sin; I little thought that word pointed at me! I see it now; oh! I cannot stand in my sinfulness before him; I dare not think of appearing before God." Stephen poured forth his prayer for life, and he determined if God in mercy raised him up he would never sin again! He could see now what sin was; he saw that it had its root in the heart, and he determined he would keep his heart with all diligence; he would live for eternity, live to God; he tried to fulfil his duty to man, and now he would fulfil his duty to God; he saw that was what death demanded, and he would have it ready against death came again. And there was more truth in his feeling, than in the feelings of those who blindly lean on a hope they have not made their own, who never cleanse their way as Stephen had tried to do by the law of God, and yet trust to an indefinite pardon at the end. So far as Stephen's light went it was true light; he saw the requirements of the divine holiness and the divine justice; though he knew not yet the fallen heart's inability to meet them, nor the way divine love had provided, "that His banished might not be expelled from Him forever."

Mabel looked up to the white curtained window of Stephen's room at the church farm; watched Margery's silent anxiety; stood by her as she gave charge to Shealtiel on the pony, with the basket on his arm, to follow the doctor home quickly, and lose no time in returning with the change of medicines, that perhaps might give relief. Relief was given, the sickness abated, and Stephen recovered.

Many in sickness have felt as Stephen felt, and resolved as he resolved; but returning life has dimmed their quickened sight; they have sinned again, and not felt the sin; forgotten God, and conscience not reproved them; transgressed his holy law, and justified the transgression. But it was not so with Stephen; the light that had shown him his own sinfulness, and the requirements of God's holiness, was no momentary flash of conscience;

but "the light of the morning spread upon the mountain;" nor yet "a morning without clouds," but still the dawn of that true light which never sets again in darkness, but "shines brighter and brighter to the perfect day."

One fact is strikingly illustrated by the resolution Stephen had made, a fact that observation constantly discovers—how difficult it is to act in heavenly things by the rules that govern us in earthly! Our principle of action may be a true principle—such as diligence, watchfulness, trust, love, effort, supplication, but we do not apply it in heavenly things; in the attainment of them we are slothful, negligent, unbelieving, cold, spiritless, silent, and yet we expect success to attend us. Oh, strange delusion, that the eternal is to be won with more ease than the temporal; the heavenly treasure with less effort than the earthly! Stephen did not fail in diligence, or watchfulness, or effort—all these he had always applied to his spiritual as well as his temporal life; but he forgot his childhood's precept,—"It is better to trust in the Lord than to put confidence in man." He rose from his sickness trusting in his own power to attain the holiness of heart and life which he saw to be necessary. He trusted in himself, and came back to the world resolved to work out a righteousness of his own in which he might venture to die. So true it is that we can trust God with anything sooner than ourselves; we may be willing to trust Him with everything earthly, but the soul he died to win we keep in our own hand, thinking to save it in our own way; therefore we never know the love of God to us, never know the love that flows from the sense of the "much forgiven;" and therefore, alas! we may have one day to say, "The summer is past, the harvest is ended, and I am not saved!"

It was now that Stephen's spiritual conflict began. It was no longer for earthly success that he wrestled, but for spiritual victory—for a conquest over his own sinful nature, for a righteousness in which to stand before God, for a heavenly Inheritance. He roused his whole resolution to the effort; he became a jailor to his own spirit, repressed all its mirth, and curbed his quick temper with a double bridle. His step lost its energy, his eye was fixed and thoughtful, he grew silent and self-absorbed. Many a friend questioned with him, and tried to wake up his lost cheerfulness, but he answered to all, "Let me alone, I am not the same man I was; I shall have no more, I can tell you, of what once pleased me well." Yet victory drew not near, it gleamed not even in the distance, nor ever cheered the heavy strife with one bright earnest of success. Sin was with Stephen still. Conscience could show it when he lay down to sleep; and when he rose conscience could only warn him still that he must conquer in the strife, or meet the terrors of the Almighty when again he was called to die. He saw too clearly to think for a moment that He could reach the Mercy of God, by turning away from His Holiness, therefore he would not yield up the effort; yet the day came not in which he could say, "I have made my heart clean, I am pure from my sin;" vainly trying to "bring a clean thing out of an unclean," he saw not yet "that more excellent way."

The winter months passed heavily; duty had a stern look, and life seemed a weary load. But all outward circumstances remained unchanged, and Stephen still filled his constant place in the parish church, and his corner in the chancel on the eastern hill.

One Sunday, as he walked to the distant church, he said to himself, "What will the end be of all my endeavors? This strife with myself is the hardest thing I ever tried at in life; the whole world would seem an easy thing to match against the struggle I have held with my own heart, and I don't see but what it gets worse rather than better; but yet give it up I cannot, for if I do it must be certain that death will find me unready." Weary and heavy laden, he knelt down in his corner in the chancel, and prayed, "God be merciful to me a sinner." The words of the text were that afternoon, "Will He plead against me with His great power? No; but he will put strength in me." Stephen heard; and it seemed to him as if his own troubled heart poured itself out in that absorbing inquiry, "Will He plead against me with His great power?"—it uttered all his dread; he had seen how great that Power was, "glorious in Holiness," and the one apprehension of his soul was of the hour when it would meet and plead against him as a sinner. When therefore he heard the question answered, and that "no," in all its truth and simplicity fell on his awakened conscience, it seemed to him like the final answer from the judgment seat of the Eternal, confirmed as it was by the justifying reason—"He will put strength in me!" He listened to the unfolding of the Word of Life; the awakened conscience described, the sinner whose eyes are opened to see the requirements of God's holiness, discovering that if that power pleads against his sin he must be condemned and crushed by it eternally. The anxiety with which the question is asked, "Will he plead against me with His great power?" the answer to the inquiring conscience, "No." What then will He do? "He will put strength in me"—salvation can be only His work! "When we were without strength, Christ died for the ungodly." "The life I now live in the flesh I live by the faith of the Son of God, who loved me, and gave Himself for me." "Thanks be unto God, which giveth us the victory through our Lord Jesus Christ." "We are more than conquerors, through Him that loved us." The preacher's style was full of Holy Scripture; each sacred verse as it fell shed another ray on the soul of Stephen, which the text of the sermon had kindled with the light of divine love.

When the service was over he rose and left the church, changed as one who, struggling with innumerable foes and despairing of victory, beholds them suddenly swept away from before him by an invisible power; so did that wave of Divine love which now overflowed the soul of Stephen, bear back on its bosom every foe and every fear, leaving him alone with the sense of "the height and depth, the length and breadth of the love of God, which passeth knowledge." Humbled yet happy, repentant yet assured of forgiveness, he realized the truth of the declaration, "We that have believed do enter into rest;" the rest of faith before the rest of fruition. To use his own expressive language, "I watered the road with my tears; that "NO" had turned my darkness to light, and shown me where my hope lay. From that day I walked to and from that church alone; I would have no company; it was enough for me to consider what I was going to hear as I went, and what I had heard as I came back again. My 'Zoar! I called it; and often as I look upon it, when walking to it it first came in sight, I said, 'Is it not a little one? O let my soul escape thither and it shall live!'"

In the June of this same summer Mabel was again at the farm; she was still a child in years, but sorrow deepens life far more than joy, when sorrow's discipline is blessed by Him who bore its heaviest grief for us; and so it had been with Mabel, who to the joy of life, had added now the grief of separating death.

> "And side by side they flow,
> Two fountains flowing from one smitten heart,
> And ofttimes scarcely to be known apart,
> That gladness and that woe."

She had reached the farm on a Saturday, and it was

now the Sabbath evening, not yet the hour for the farm hymns of praise, so she went alone, as she was used to do, to the Seringa Arbor, to read her Bible there. Nature in its loveliness—its songs and fragrance—was around her; of its past perfection and its future sinless glory she read in the Bible's open page. Then she thought of the farm, where she had come again to stay, and was ever welcomed as the child of its affections. "Why was it that where human kindness reigned, none ever spoke of heavenly love, nor brightened at allusion to it?" While thoughts like these were asking unanswered questions in her heart, she heard a step near the trellis-work, and Stephen stood beside the arbor. He had never come before to her retreat, and she was glad to see him now; he stood beside the honeysuckle in thoughtful silence. Mabel observed the softened smile that lighted up his face; she had yet hardly seen him except at church, as he spent the Sunday with his sister, until the evening, when they both came down to tea, and now she thought he wore another aspect than she had seen before; he was silent a little while, then turned as if to speak; she saw that something touched him deeply, and put her hand in his. Then he said, "There is a text in Ruth, and I say it to you, 'Whither thou goest I will go; thy people shall be my people, and thy God my God!'" He said no more than that one text, but in that touching utterance to the child before him, he broke through the reserve and silence that had held expression so strongly back. The sense of Divine love had made him ready to confess his Saviour before men; and with the child of the farm, from that Sabbath evening hour, he held through life unbroken intercourse of hallowed thought and feeling. Eternity may lie open within the heart, a change greater than that which brought the world out of chaos take place in the nature and the destinies of the spirit of a man, and yet all be hidden at the time from the nearest observer, open only to the eye of Him who made man for Himself.

CHAPTER XX.

THE miller's school was like a little guarded fold in the midst of the wilderness. Old Linstead, with his mild venerable aspect, and gentle persuasive authority, gathered the young of all ages around him, and taught them the knowledge which, truly to know, is Life eternal. And often in the summer time he took his eldest scholars with him, and crossed the fields to the Rector's Wednesday evening service in the village church on the Eastern hill. It was a beautiful sight to see the fine old man, of aspect so intelligent and benignant, coming in to worship, accompanied by his elder scholars. On Sunday they never left their parish, attending its church, and spending the rest of the day under instruction at school. One extract from the old man's diary will show the intelligence and grace of his mind. He kept a record of his work, and of one of his pupils, who for a time disappointed his hopes, he writes, "She appeared a tender plant, that could not bear the sun. In the time that green leaves shaded it, the plant grew; but the sun rose above the trees, and the plant faded in the heat of the day. But evening returned and the plant revived, because the root was not dead."

At length the ceaseless opposition manifested towards the school, the master, and its patrons prevailed. Nathaniel and Stephen had established and carried it on for years as Christians, as Churchmen, as Englishmen; therefore to find a handle against it was not easy, but a false accusation did what truth could not do; the meek spirit of the miller, broken down by the ceaseless contention, yielded up his school, and the children were gathered and instructed no longer. "What it cost my poor brother to keep it on as long as he did no one can tell!" said Stephen; "but, verily, his work was with the Lord, and his reward with his God!"

Mabel, when fourteen years old, had a serious illness; as strength slowly returned she was sitting in her armchair by the large open window of her chamber, up to which the roses climbed, breathing their fragrance for the young prisoner within, when she heard the sound of wheels, and saw the Wrangler in the winding lane that led to her home. Matthew was driving Elsie, who came up to the chamber. Elsie said that her mother's health had been failing for weeks, which prevented her coming before; but that morning she had called Elsie to her, saying, "It does not signify about leaving me, I will have you go and see how the child is, and bring me back word again." She then ordered fruit to be gathered from the garden, and taking one of her own red silk handkerchiefs that she wore over her shoulders, she pinned up in it the polished hoofs of some of the young cattle that had been reared on the farm, and with her love and her blessing to the child, sent Elsie with her gifts and inquiries.

Mabel longed to see the friend of her childhood, once more to embrace her and receive her strong, tender blessing; but weakness banished this hope to a distance. The accounts from the farm continued the same, until one day Elsie suddenly saw the shadow of death fall on the face of her mother. Elsie well knew that shadow, she had often seen it before, and she knew that when it fell death could not be distant. She was alone with her mother, but, though her heart sank within her, it did not alarm her, for Elsie never trembled at death. Stephen soon came in from the hay-fields, and when he also saw that shadow on the face of his mother he trembled exceedingly. Men can look upon death in heroic daring, but when the king of terrors suddenly crosses the quiet threshold of home, they are often unnerved by the face of the foe. Elsie bade Stephen not tremble but come and take her place; then he wound his arms around his mother, upholding her, while Elsie made ready her most hopeful remedies. In Stephen's arms rested the mother to whose face he had looked up with such reverence and love for more than half a century, whose every word had been to him as a law, whose authority he had revered as much in manhood as in youth, in whose honored name and for whom he had done all things; the head, the stay, the shelter of all! But blessed for him was the certainty, that not one drop of bitterness had he ever poured in the cup of her widowhood. He had stood alone and fearless beside her, and fought a safe pathway for her through all that troubled or opposed. If those who can still look upon the face of a mother, could anticipate the moment when that look must be their last, when no atonement can any longer be made for rebellion, unkindness, neglect; when the wounds—of all wounds the deepest that the child has made in the heart of a parent—can never by after tenderness be healed, would not such reflection save a remorse that earth has no joy to obliterate?

Elsie's remedies restored animation, and life gleamed again in the face of their mother. All her children were sent for, and the in-gathering of the fields left alone to the laborers.

Mabel had a secret misgiving that Margery was worse; for there is an instinct in nature that none can define, whose spiritual mysteries none can explain, but which often awakens the sympathetic cord that vibrates unseen between man and man. Mabel's mother, to relieve her anxiety, drove over to the farm. No one appeared at the gate, or the door, to welcome her approach. As she entered, Cloe, the maid, came forward, and said her mistress was dying. She went up to the chamber. Two of Margery's sons—themselves grey-headed—were supporting her; her other children knelt around the bed, their tears falling like rain. It was a scene never to be forgotten—the death of the patriarchal mother! A smile gleamed from the dying eyes as that best of friends entered, and the departing spirit was satisfied with the heavenly truth she uttered beside it. But in the morning the dying mother said to Elsie, "I hear the child's voice below; I knew I should see her again!"

"No, mother, I doubt that she cannot be come!"

"But I know it is her tongue! go down stairs and see."

It was death disencumbering the sense, for no other ear could catch the least sound like the voice of the child whom Margery's strong heart had enshrined in its tenderness, and who was lying it might be then in prayer for her dying friend, on her little white couch far away. Margery then spent some time in silence, a sacred silence which no one disturbed; then raising her eyes she looked round on her children, said tenderly, "I have done what I could for you all, now I leave you to God; may His blessing rest on you!" and her spirit slowly struggled from the fetters of mortality.

Weeks passed before Mabel reached the farm. There was a deeper tone in the welcome all gave her, yet solemn and sad; and her childhood's friend lay sleeping in the churchyard, encircled by the fields and above the green valley of the Home. Elsie told of her calm illness; Stephen, how no worldly thoughts ever troubled her; that since her strength first failed, long before, they never had one ten minutes' talk upon business. She had kept her house in order, long expecting the summons. The bees had given warning of the loss, alighting in a swarm on the ground at Margery's feet, the last time she walked out with Elsie. But Elsie had not told them of the sorrow that had come, and all the bees forsook the hive or died in it. Margaret, at the church farm, told hers, and they stayed as before.

When Mabel went again some months afterwards to stay at the farm, she felt how beautiful was the only change that had come: a hush about the place, the current of active life flowing calmer, and each face reflecting a heart of deepened thought within.

Sunday had always there, been "the holy of the Lord, honorable;" the farm had not done its own ways, nor found its own pleasure on that holy day. There was no mother now, by her firm authority, to keep the sacred hours; but the only difference seemed that her children, bereft of their earthly stay, drew closer beneath the overshadowing wings of the Eternal. All customs were the same. The family breakfast hour had always been at seven instead of six o'clock on that morning, in order that all the farm work might be finished beforehand. By seven o'clock the twelve cows were milked, the milk poured out in the dairy in the pans prepared the day before, and Elsie, in her Sunday dress, ready for breakfast. By seven o'clock Philip and Matthew had seen to whatever might be necessary amongst the cattle; and had put on their Sabbath garments. All now was early as before, all wore the same aspect of Sabbath rest, yet were all less silent deeper yet brighter in their tone—as of those who walk not by the rule of an absent Lord, but dwell beneath the presence of a near though unseen Friend. Stephen's spirit had long before broken its chain and walked at liberty; or rather the hand of divine love had opened its prison doors, and shown him the pathway of Life. Elsie, bereft on earth, looked more entirely to heaven, and a peace, the world could neither give nor take away, deepened all the cheerful energy of her life.

It was beautiful, as the Saturday advanced, to see how the farm business settled down into the calm eve of the Sabbath. Stephen would not allow any business transactions on Saturday afternoon; his laborers were all paid at five o'clock on the Friday afternoon, not only for the Saturday's repose at the farm, but that each cottage might have a day before Sunday on which to expend its little weekly income. By noon on Saturday, Stephen had laid aside, as much as possible, all worldly occupations and cares; the stir of life quieted down, and a feeling of repose stole over the farm. Stephen looked as if the world's six days' chain were already broken, and his spirit calmly rejoicing in the rest of his God. He sometimes said, "If I did not begin my Sabbath on the Saturday, there would be but a poor chance for me: I have too great, and too changing a concern on my mind to roll it all off in a minute. Why, if worldly thoughts will press hard on Sunday sometimes, as it is, how would it be if I had not shut them outside before that day came in!"

In summer, Stephen would sometimes go aside on Saturday afternoon to lonely places, unseen; but this was not necessary to his spirit's repose; he would often sit in the farm kitchen for an hour at a time, lost in thought and in prayer; if suddenly spoken to, he returned to the world around him with a start, as if from sleep. To Mabel he said, "What could I do, with something always going on before my eyes, if I had not trained myself to be alone even when others are near?" He always brightened as Saturday rolled the world from his brow, his playful humor still enlivened his words, while the calm aspect of thoughtful rest marked his sense of the sacred hours that were near. This truly was "calling the Sabbath a delight!"

Elsie hasted on Saturday, and dressed the food of two days in one. On Sunday, the servants, no less than their masters and mistress, kept holiday.

To give Stephen's Sabbath morning, we must return to old Linstead's family. He had not long survived the breaking-up of his school, and the grief felt by his masters and himself on that occasion. Stephen watched over the old man, and cheered his last days by the earthly kindness most valued by him. Linstead had a home with his son, who was a laborer on the farm, and a great favorite there; his master's interest was his own; and the fine English peasant was respected by all, because his hands were never slack in their labor, and his heart never unfaithful to the trust that reposed, without questioning, in his honest dealing. But it was not diligence and honesty alone that endeared him to the farm, it was his filial respect for his parents. He rented a beautiful cottage, of Stephen's own building, on the edge of a wood, and one of its pleasant chambers, overlooking the glades of the oak wood, was given by him to his parents; their bed was warm and soft by the labor of his hands; their clothing excelled by none in the parish for comfort; and their food all that old age most required. He would never receive any parish allowance for them, saying, that while he had a penny his parents should share it! his spade was often heard at work by moonlight, and again by three o'clock of the morning, in busy seasons of the year—yet he stood the broadest shouldered, and strongest man on the farm; all could see that "the commandment with promise" shed its blessing on him. His children were trained to wait on their aged relatives; and the step and smile of their master oftened brightened their home.

The death of old Linstead broke down the feeble strength of his wife. Unable to read, and her son unable also, Stephen took the aged widow especially under his care. On Sunday, Margaret at the church farm never failed in having breakfast ready by seven o'clock; at both farms all sat down at the same hour to the early Sunday repast. And at half-past seven every Sabbath morning, Stephen started for the woodland cottage. All the cottage was ready for the master's early visit, and in the chamber the bed-ridden widow expecting the step she had loved from its childhood. It brightened her eyes to see the master enter, in his Sabbath dress, all of blue; "already wearing the crown of glory,"—that the silver head is declared to be when found in the way of righteousness, with the smile of the Sabbath beaming bright on his face. Kneeling at her bed he read the prayers of the Church, the litany, and collects, and all such petitions as he thought most suitable for the occasion. He once smiling, said, "Yes, I *open* the book, not but what I have said all those prayers often enough to remember them, I hope, without the help of a book; but still I do open and read, and surely we may say that no other prayers of sinful man can ever reach up to them!" Then he read the lessons and the Psalms for the day, refilling the lamp of the widow with the light of the living Word. It was a remarkable fact, that for eight years he never missed this Sabbath morning visit. No sickness, no accident ever disabled him; he himself allowed no hinderance that man could prevent, and his God kept back every other. He who, fifteen years before, poured forth supplications and tears in doubt and distress by his young dying brother, now kneeled at the bed of the peasant's widow in the calm light of "the assurance of hope unto the end."

In those days it was a beautiful pathway that led to the cottage, descending from the village churchyard abruptly to the valley, over a narrow bridge, where the stream, with its everlasting voice, broke over the stones and bent down the long blades of grass beneath its crystal current; ascending again by a road that curved round the hill, under the fine trees that there sheltered it, until reaching the solitude of the beautiful wood, by which stood the cottage—its casements open to the carol of the birds, the play of the squirrel on the oak boughs, and the coo of the wood-pigeon who often built near. Through all seasons, for eight years, Stephen trod that lonely pathway. Once, in after years, as Mabel walked there beside him, he said, "I never tread this roadside without a Sabbath feeling! It has been, I may say, a high-place for prayer! So many years I trod it, never meeting a creature, blessing God that the Sabbath was come!"

Mabel had forgotten how many the years were, and asked Stephen to tell her. He answered with a smile, "A whole year of Sabbaths I and that old lady kept sacred together! Never for eight years, did eight o'clock on Sunday morning see me anywhere else; and so we may hope all those supplications were not offered in vain."

When Stephen returned, Margaret had the farm kitchen ready. The little round table that held his large Bible was set by his arm-chair, and he had an hour of peaceful retirement alone. He had already chosen one portion of Scripture for his Sunday morning reading and meditation, and he never changed it through life.—The forty-second and forty-third Psalms. Once when speaking to Mabel, he said, "Take those two Psalms in one, and where can you find any portion more fitting the hour? Is not the soul then set free from the world, and does it not pant for its God, as the poor hart for the streams? Are we not then going up to appear before God? and if we can remind Him of the tears that no eye has seen but His, sure He won't forget, if we can put it to Him from His own Word!" So continuing the Psalm from memory, he in this way went through the whole with his own touching commentary.

Soon after the death of their mother, the Rector of their parish, whose every effort against them had only been turned into good, gave a terrible expression to his feeling of aversion at seeing them in the church. This was final; no choice now remained for them; in sorrow, not in anger, they turned from the sanctuary, where they had worshipped God from their childhood, their seats were left empty, the melody silent, and now twice every Sunday they walked to the church that Stephen called his "Zoar." They always came on foot: Elsie said that to be driving to her made it seem not like Sunday! Through mud or through snow they walked the long distance, while in summer the pathway was firm and pleasant through fields. But though none came so far, they were always the first; some time before the service they were seated in the church; and Stephen came long before to listen and learn with the children. He said that, "For his part, the lessons taught to the children in the chancel pleased him well, and he always should say, that if you could not sit down and learn with the children, how were you going to order the entering as a little child into heaven? and yet our Saviour had said, that except we did become as little children, we should in no case enter therein!" So Stephen came long before the service, and sat in his corner in the chancel, his silver head stooping, and his listening spirit gathering up the crumbs that fell from the children's table. He never forgot Mabel's love for the spring-time, and before she could find the first primrose, violet, or cowslip in the hedgerows, she was surd to see a tiny nosegay in her seat in the chancel, gathered and placed there by Stephen—Sabbath blossoms in his pathway. It might have seemed as if each flower in its season first bloomed on a Sunday; Mabel could so seldom find them before she had first had them gathered for her by Stephen.

There was no lack of cheerfulness in the Sabbath mid-day repast; it was the most picturesque dinner of the week, though the only Sunday labor it gave was to set it on table. Another table was spread in the same room for the servants, with the snow-white cloth and Sunday viands of the farm; the servants in their Sunday garments taking their repast at the same time, that all might again be ready for church. And then the family assembly at the cheerful evening tea, followed by the anthems and hymns of the home. Notwithstanding Stephen's love for the metrical version of the Psalms he had sung from his childhood, he delighted in the hymns of the church on the Eastern hill; and always hearing them there to his favorite old tunes, and in congregational harmony, they became to him as the songs of the house of his pilgrimage. And so closed the Sabbath evening, with its hallelujahs of praise; to these they would welcome any who had instruments or voice and a good will to join them: glimpses of a hallowed Sunday evening for some who might never have known it elsewhere.

One of Stephen's favorite verses was the first verse of the fifteenth Psalm—

> "Lord, who's the happy man that may
> To thy blessed courts repair?
> Not stranger like, to visit them,
> But to inhabit there!"

With a face beaming with feeling, he would repeat

> "Not stranger like, to visit them,
> But to inhabit there!"

Well he knew the stranger's feeling, compelled as he now was to pass by the church of his parish and wander on to another. There were but few who knew the conflict of feeling that often weighed him down as he thought on these things. Yet God had given him his "Zoar," and Sabbath after Sabbath he returned to it again, as the dove to the ark of its refuge; and so truly was his feeling one with the breathings of the Royal Psalmist as to the House of the Lord, that he once said, "O, it is seldom that I do not let fall a tear, when Monday morning calls me back again to the world!"

CHAPTER XXI.

NO gloom of bereavement hung over the farm. The life that is made gloomy by sorrow, is seldom if ever, deepened by its discipline. A tone of quietness and tenderness pervaded the home; a calm that often stilled all into thoughtfulness, told more than words could express. But the seasons came and went, and labor has its blessing, because unto man the true Noah—Child of rest and comfort, has been born, to comfort us concerning our work and the toil of our hands, because of the ground which the Lord had cursed.

Harvest at the farm had all the spirit and charm that could be yielded by agricultural life. Stephen stood like Boaz amongst his men in the fields; or like Joseph amongst the patriarchs, with Philip and Matthew for the Benjamin of his heart. The men, who so many years had reaped the same fields, and started on the first harvest morning to put in the sickle—with green boughs and songs, the reaper king at their head. And as each sunset closed in, the peasants, losing their weariness in the joy of the harvest, gathered to some field near the home, or the brow of the hill above the green valley, there forming a circle with the reaper-king holding his sickle in the centre, and singing together the old songs of the harvest; in the chorus that divided each line, all bowing low to the ground, as they lengthened out the deep bass "HILL-LAHT" that rung through the welkin, and proclaimed far and near the harvest-men's joy. And when the last wheat-field was cleared, the wheat harvest done, all were called from within to see the reaper-king stand aloft on the stack, with the last sheaf in his arms, and the harvest song was sung, and a cheer echoed over valley and hill, as, stooping on the pinnacle of the round stack, he laid the last sheaf in its place. Then refreshment was brought for the men, and Mabel filled the cup for the reaper-king, and all left them then to their cheer. The largess money (money given by way of congratulation by strangers or friends to the harvest-men in the fields) was all saved by Stephen's advice, and a supper provided at the village inn—the landlord of which was a tenant of the farm: and the men, with their wives and children, met there to celebrate the occasion in English fashion, with beef and plum-pudding; all returning together to their homes before ten o'clock in the evening.

At the farm, when the harvest was over, a supper was given to the men. Mabel was there at the first after Margery's death, and when supper was over Stephen asked her to open the Bible and read. She read the Parable of the Marriage Feast,—the man who had not on a wedding garment; Stephen stood beside her chair while she read, and while she tried in few words to explain it to the men. Then Stephen said that he liked the old English songs well enough in their way, but to his mind it was a hymn that was wanted for harvest; as he could not find such an one amongst those that were sung on the Eastern hill, he should wish that Mabel would sit down and write one, to the particular tune of Bethlehem Judah, for them all to sing every year as the harvest came round. Mabel excused herself, but Stephen would admit no excuse. It was plain, he said, that it was a good thing much wanted, and therefore there could be no reason why it should not be taken in hand directly and done. So Mabel went to the pastures, where the little river flowed peaceful beside her, and wrote the harvest hymn for the farm.

HYMN WRITTEN FOR THE HARVEST HOME AT THE FOREST FARM.

To the Tune of Bethlehem Judah.

Let us now praises raise
For the joyous harvest days;
Unto Earth's Eternal King
Let the full thanksgiving ring.

He who blessed the springing ear,
Now with plenty crowns the year;
Food and Gladness cheer our Board,
Let our Harvest praise the Lord!

And, my soul, thyself prepare,
For thy harvest draweth near;
Angel reapers ready stand
With the sickle in their hand.

Does thy life bear heavenly grain,
Such as angel hands will claim
For the garner of their God,
For the Holy One's abode?

Faith, and Love, and Hope, **and Prayer,**
Are the fruits thy life must bear;
Watered by the Word of God,
Washed in Calvary's cleansing **blood.**

Oh! my soul, thyself prepare,
For thy harvest-time is near;
Then the reaper's work shall thee '
Bear to immortality!

Praise the Lord, His praises sing,
Loud the Hallelujahs ring!
For with food and gladsome cheer,
He hath crowned our Harvest year!

It was not alone in its hospitality, that the farm showed its liberality; it wore in all things the aspect of "the cheerful giver," whom it is said, "the Lord loveth." Stephen had been heard by the poor, saying, as he turned from the cottage door of the sick, "I don't ask you what you want, but I tell you whatever you feel that you want send up for it, and it shall be given you!" Whatever cause of charity was pleaded, publicly or privately, was sure of the support of each one at the farm. They never made their subscriptions large, because Stephen said that might be apt to discourage some who could not come up to it, but secretly the sum was much increased.

When all England competed in one great show for prizes on the cattle of its farms, the Forest Farm sent up a horse. Philip, Matthew, and the farm man went up with it. The day of examination passed, and the next morning, when all the horses were led to their separate booths, the first prize flag waved over the Forest Farm stall. The farm brothers came home with the honor and the prize, and the horse that had won it worked as one of their wagon team for years. But a portion of the gold of that prize was sent, without name, to the work of Foreign Missions, as a thank-offering to the God of the whole earth—whose are the cattle upon a thousand hills.

When Stephen first visited the poor, he found the sick and the dying almost without covering on their beds; not because wages were low for the time, but because, whenever a people are left uninstructed in true religion, the comforts and blessings of social life will be found to waste away from amongst them. Stephen had no rich friends to appeal to, none but his God and his own family to lean on; but strong in faith of the increase on diligent labor, and the blessing of God that alone maketh rich, he rested not until every cottage in the parish had two warm blankets as its store.

Yet no one would have been more distressed than Stephen, had rent, tithe, and taxes, not been ready to the hour; he felt his position required that they should be, and they were. Each hand in the home was the the hand of the diligent, each heart the heart of the liberal, and of such it is divinely declared the hand of the diligent maketh rich, and by liberal things shall the liberal stand.

One day, as Stephen showed Mabel some beautiful vegetable produce of the garden, she exclaimed, "Oh, I wish I had a cartload to give to my poor people!" She was only at the farm for that day, and great was her surprise by eight o'clock the next morning to see a laden cart at the gate of her home, filled with the produce she had longed for, and strewn over with bunches of cowslips, which Stephen had called the village children to gather. When Mabel spent her birthday at the farm, Elsie gave a feast to the old people of the parish. Those who could not walk were brought up in carts; the blind came, and the lame; and the long tables were spread for them. Mabel read to them from the Bible, and a daughter of one of the fathers of the Church Missionary Society being there, interested the aged people with Missionary histories; then they were feasted on Elsie's best ham, and bread and butter, and drank many cups of tea, and Philip and Matthew waited on them. One of the number was an ungodly old man, who had shown a bitter enmity to Matthew; but all at the farm said, "Make no difference, let him come with the others: if we want to do good we must not stand upon enmities!" So the old man came amongst them, and Stephen's face beamed with a joy that might have kindled the dullest beholder. The farm brothers brought their instruments and played and sang to the old people, who at last departed by daylight, pouring out their assurances that they had never known such entertainment before. Then Stephen presented Mabel with the costliest Bible the country town could produce, saying, as he gave it, "We beg you to accept this Bible, which we wish to give you, because you have helped us better to understand the precious truth that lies in it!" And not long after, on his return from the market, he brought back an illuminated Prayer-book, thinking, as he said, that where the Bible was given the Church Prayers ought to follow not long after; and he had brought the best he could find, because he considered those prayers could never be written on paper too good! So Mabel had Bible and Prayer-book, the gift of the farm. At her next birthday, the last spent by her within reach of the farm, when she came down in her home to the eight o'clock breakfast, she found two pheasants, both of brilliant plumage on the table for her, and a little note tied to their feet, which she opened and read. It was the speech of the birds: "Dear Miss, we were flying in the forest woods early this morning, and now we are come to welcome your birthday!" It must indeed have been an early flight, for it was the first of October. Philip, who was the sportsman, had been up before dawn, attended by Matthew, shot the birds, and sent them off by express, to greet Mabel at breakfast. Such was the cheerful liberality of the farm.

The old harness maker had long departed to rest, safe for ever in the paradise of God; but Peter Spedly, the little tailor, was still living at upwards of ninety years of age; and Benedict, the blacksmith. Two greater contrasts in figure could hardly be seen. Spedly extremely small, with the limbs of a child, a little withered bent figure, lame and bald-headed; Benedict, broad-chested, tall, and large in stature, with a noble-looking head, down which hung locks of white hair. Both had their welcome for Mabel; Spedly loved to talk to her of what a heavenly place his young master's farm had always been, as none could fully make known! And on market days, Mabel was sure to find him seated on the foot of his very small bed, to see his "master" drive by; but this dear earthly subject never hindered the heart of the old man from its welcome for the Word of his God. While Benedict loved to tell of the heavenly blessing Master Stephen had brought him, instructing him in the way to the Kingdom; and the tears of the fine old man fell fast above the open Bible as he spoke of these things. And many there were, beside Benedict and Spedly, only waiting for the living voice to bring them the glad tidings. The little child of eleven, dying on her tiny bed in the old cottage loft, unable to read, for she was too young for the school of the miller when it was open, and it had now been given up for years; with no one able to read to her in her home, a timid child with silent lips, looking up with her dark expressive eyes, never asking a question, only listening to all that was said. Until, as death drew nearer, Mabel asked, "Tell me, Mary, can you believe that Jesus Christ died for *you?*" The tears gathered in her large eyes and overflowed as she answered, "You tell me He died for sinners; I know I am a sinner, so I hope He died for me!" A little further on lay another **dying girl**; her open heart welcomed all that told of a Saviour, believed in His love, and entered into rest. "For of such is the kingdom of heaven!" But between the cottages of the children a farmer lay dying; one who had lived for this world alone, and was suddenly startled by finding the next opening upon him. In his anguish of soul at discovering his danger; **earth, which he had** labored for, melting fast from his grasp; **and Eternity, which** he had never prepared for, **waiting now** to receive him; he could not control his expressions of despair. Stephen went to him, and now begged **Mabel** to go. The contrast to the gentle aspect of the dying children was a terrible one. At sight of Mabel he clasped his hands in agony, and said, "Oh, I have sinned beyond forgiveness or hope!"

"Say not so," replied Mabel, "there is forgiveness with God. And the blood of Jesus Christ, His Son, cleanseth from all sin!"

"Are you an angel sent to tell me that?" asked the poor dim-sighted sinner.

"I am a forgiven sinner," answered Mabel; "cleansed from all my sin in the precious blood of the Saviour; and you may be what I am, if you will only look unto Jesus, and pray to Him to take your sins away."

"Pray! yes, pray; that is it! O pray!" exclaimed

the dying man in unutterable agony. Mabel knelt; and with a desperate effort he raised himself on his knees in the bed, with clenched hands and upraised face; the very sight was appalling; and used as Mabel then was to the aspect of death, it cost her best efforts to command herself.

"You are too ill to kneel," she said; "I am kneeling for you, lie down again, and try to pray with me."

"Not kneel, when it may be my last prayer!—I who have lived without prayer! If 'tis fit for me to pray, 'tis fit I pray kneeling! Oh, pray! pray!"

Mabel prayed—"Enter not into judgment with thy servant, O Lord, for who shall stand in Thy sight when once Thou art angry?"—"*Enter not into judgment!*" groaned the dying man. Mabel prayed again, "We have sinned, and done wickedly, and our misdeeds prevail against us; our sins are more in number than the hairs of our heads, therefore our heart faileth us; but Thou art a merciful God, and full of compassion; Thou sparest when we deserve destruction, and in Thy wrath Thou thinkest upon mercy. We have destroyed ourselves, in Thee only can our help be found. We are not worthy so much as to lift up our eyes unto heaven, but we come unto Thee in the Name of Thy well-beloved Son, Jesus Christ—in whom Thou art well pleased. Oh, hear us, for His Name's sake, we beseech Thee! Wash us in His most precious blood, and we shall be clean; purge us with his Spirit, and we shall be whiter than snow. Blot out as a cloud our sins, and as a thick cloud our transgressions; enable us to return unto Thee, for Thou hast redeemed us, O Lord, Thou God of Truth. Oh, merciful Saviour, who can pluck the brand from the burning!" *"The brand from the burning!"* echoed the man. "Stretch forth Thy pierced hand, lay hold of this poor sinking sinner, and deliver him from going down to the pit, for Thou hast found a ransom! The Lord hear us for the sake of Jesus Christ, who died, the just for the unjust, to bring us to God. Amen."

The dying man sank back exhausted, and after reading a few verses from the Bible, Mabel left him. On her next visit, the same eager despair rose before her; vainly she tried to calm his sin-awakened soul, that he might be able to understand the things belonging to his peace; his agony of feeling appeared too convulsive for him to be able to look steadily at any object before him. It seemed a fulfilment of that awful verse, "Fear, and the pit, and the snare are upon thee, O inhabitants of the earth." As he grew weaker he grew quieter, but whether the light of life ever dawned on his soul, the last day alone can make known. Well might the Apostle ask, "How shall we escape if we neglect so great salvation?"

A little further on lay a very different scene. Mabel went to visit a dying woman, the grandmother at a farm. More than ninety years of age, most of her faculties were gone, sight entirely lost, and she lay helpless in her bed. At the top of the stairs Mabel heard her low sweet voice saying, "Saviour! Bless Him! died for me! glory be to

God most High, and on earth peace, good will to men!" Night and day, shut in from almost all contact with the outer world, the dying saint cheered her spirit with whatever she could remember of holy words—her songs in the house of her pilgrimage. She never asked day or night for any earthly thing, only held converse with the heaven to which she was so near. No one could tell the comfort, her married daughter said, when they woke in the night, to hear such heavenly sounds in the darkness beside them! Mabel sat down by her bed, and repeated slowly and distinctly, "The Lord is my Shepherd, I shall not want."

"He be! He be my Shepherd! Oh, how true! I don't know a want!" And turned her sightless face, expecting to hear again.

"He maketh me to lie down in green pastures."

"Heavenly places! oh, my Saviour! blessed be God!"

"He leadeth me beside the still waters."

"He gives me water, living water! I shall thirst no more!"

"Yea, though I walk through the valley of the shadow of death, I will fear no evil, for Thou art with me."

"Night and day! He never leaves me nor will forsake me! Oh, how He comforts me!"

So, as Mabel uttered the holy words, the saint, almost in heaven, broke forth in her glad paraphrase. Mabel stooped and kissed her brow, so furrowed and so white! She felt the kiss, and said, "Bless you, my angel, though

I don't know, for I can't see who you be! I only can see Him whom the darkness hideth not, and who turneth the shadow of death into the morning."

This APPROPRIATION is the secret of dying!

CHAPTER XXII.

EVERY feeling of their patriarchal mother's had now become as a sacred legacy to her children. Her sayings were chronicled in memory, and quoted with, "Our mother used to say;" and every household contrivance of hers had more charm for them than any novelty art could produce. People looked for changes; expected that, now the elder generation had passed away, the family would take an onward step with the advance of the age, adopting a more modern style; but no such changes came. Margery had taught her children to labor, working with their own hands, that they might have to give to him that needeth. To Elsie the household broom and brush, the washing-tub and ironing-board were all familiar as the needle. "The open door stood free to all, for it recked not of a foe;" bell or knocker there was none, and freely entering, you as freely saw all that was going on within. Yet when Elsie was dressed in her afternoon gown of pale pink or blue print, and her cap— it might be of bright yellow flowers, notwithstanding Stephen's objection to yellow—perhaps it happened to be the only one the travelling merchant brought to the door

—when she sat down beside you, with needle or knitting-pin, or without either, for she was not wedded to manual employment, you found that you had beside you a heart so comprehensive, that you could confide to it the anxieties of a lifetime; a judgment so mature, that having asked Elsie's opinion you hardly wanted another; and a sympathy so responsive that, let your difficulty or trouble be what it might, you were sure of solace from the brief-pointed words of Elsie's lips. The friend of a lifetime, never failing in affection, judgment, or sympathy—such was Elsie; and the same might be said of the brothers of her home. Rich—because they had to give to them that needed; for he who can freely give is rich, whatever be his worldly store; and he who cannot freely give is poor, whatever be the aspect of his outward life. Margery's children earned by a diligent hand every gift they bestowed; their substance was increased by the blessing of God, and never wasted by the fashion of this world. Elsie would say, "Where fashion reigns, woe to work!" They thought the worn and soiled garments of labor no dishonor. Philip would say in his mirth, "It always seems to me, it must be a deal harder to speak up to the mark out of fine clothes than out of common ones!!" If they could clothe the naked, it was because they could wear the plainest working raiment themselves, and wait for a new suit for years. If they could feed the hungry, and give to him that asked of them, it was because they thought it sufficient to follow the simplest habits of life; proving the Truth—that "before Honor is Humility." They stretched not themselves beyond the rule of their station; more or less wealth made no personal change in them; therefore they were able to stand as the children of the Highest—good and kind to the just and the unjust.

"I should think you will soon venture on a new fender?" said an acquaintance, seated by the farm-kitchen fire. "If I gave a guess, I should say that this was half the steel rim of a waggon-wheel!"

Stephen smiled as he answered, "Well, certainly, you could not guess nearer the truth! It was so long ago, as when I was a boy, that our mother wanted a fender, and saw that half rim of the waggon-wheel lying in the farmyard. She could see in a moment the use of anything, let it be what it would. So she said, 'Bring that half steel rim in, it will make a fender quite good enough for me!' and so it has been there ever since, kept bright as you see, and there it is likely to be, for I think we may well put up with what did for our mother!"

"Yes," added Matthew, displeased with the visitor's interference, "you may change, and likely enough for the worse! That half rim of steel from the waggon-wheel does all that is wanted and no more, which, I suppose, can't be said of all the fine things in use now. Here we come in with wet boots from the land, and they dry in no time, because there's nothing standing up between them and the fire!"

So the half steel rim of the waggon-wheel is the family fender to this day.

All kept its neat order within and around. On the farm no neglect met the eye to bear its sad witness of the hand that was gone; you only read the home's bereavement in the deeper feeling, that ever after shadowed each thoughtful brow. The one exception to the neatness still kept was in the waggons and carts of the farm; they in time looked neglected and shabby, with their paint worn away, not worthy of the beautiful horses that drew them. As Mabel one day stood watching the fine team, returning with the empty waggon from the town, she said, "Why do you leave every waggon and cart looking shabby, for want of fresh paint? it did not use to be so."

The tears started to Stephen's eyes as he answered, "That's a thing that ought to be attended to, it is true; but we have never known how to take it in hand, because we cannot paint on again the name of our MOTHER!"

But as the time wore on, Elsie sometimes found her single strength overdone, especially in the household work of the spring, when the dairy and poultry required more care; so her brothers said it was quite time to think of what could be done to lighten her labor, and Elsie said that one thing would tend greatly to that; if they would paper the parlor and both the guest-chambers, and so save the whitewashing of their walls every year. Stephen decided at once that it was the thing to be done, and chose the papers the next time that he went to the market-town. So the parlor was hung with birds of paradise perched upon trellis-work, and the ceiling papered with blue, for Stephen said, "he never thought a room papered unless the ceiling were done with imitation of the sky." Smaller birds of paradise, on lighter trellis-work, covered the white walls of each guest-chamber; and for Mabel's own little sitting-room, which lay between the guest-chambers, Stephen chose a satin paper of white ground, strewn with moss-rose buds, and its ceiling was also papered with watered sky-blue. The rooms looked exceedingly well; and Mabel persuaded Philip to hang all the representations of the royal young family, a little lower down on the walls; and Elsie carried off the portraits of the Jewish patriarchs to the chambers above.

This made a relief in household work for a time; but one spring the two farm laborers, who always white-washed the large kitchen, left streaks on the walls, and it must be whitewashed again. But Elsie said to her brothers, "You will be very much to blame if you do not paper the walls of this room right away." But what description of paper, they asked, could it be? Elsie answered, "I cannot have you bringing home any of those delicate colors. I can never bring my mind up to the care of them here, nor would they be suitable to an old Roman fireplace like this. You go and bring home a nice dim color, that will wear and look well!"

Stephen said, "His mind was that no paper could be suitable to a farm-kitchen, unless it were covered with represensations of the creatures that ran about the farm-yard." So Philip and Matthew went to fulfil their instructions. In vain the town upholsterer inquired of his brother upholsterers, no such paper could be found. But Matthew said, "It was his brothers mind to have it, therefore he supposed it was the upholsterer's business to try for it." The upholsterer acknowledged it was; he sent to London, London sent to Paris, and finally a splendid pattern came down, quite to Stephen's mind, but not to Elsie's, for the fine cock crowing on straw was drawn on a white satin ground. So the specimen was pasted over the back kitchen door, and a second attempt made for something less delicate. A paper was at length found covered with strips of land, and blue sky in between, the land covered with churches, houses, men, women, and cattle. It was also all of one sober shade, a quiet drab, except the blue sky. Elsie agreed that this would do, and the cheerful kitchen grew darker and rather quaint under the change; but streaks in the whitewash would be saved evermore.

One purchase more, Elsie said, and the house would again be set up to go on as before. A new tent bedstead was wanted for the south-western chamber.

"Had Elsie not better go herself," Stephen asked, "to choose such a critical thing?"

"No," Elsie replied, "no occasion for that. Any simple tent bedstead, one as good as another."

Stephen went to the upholsterer, a man whom he much

respected. All who worked for the farm seemed to meet its fair dealing with integrity on their part. Stephen asked for a tent bedstead. Then the poor tradesman told Stephen what a trouble had befallen him. Some one of the resident gentry had ordered a bedstead of best mahogany, and all things to match; the greatest care had been taken in meeting the order, but some fault was found, and it was returned on his hands. "I should like just to show it to you, sir!" Stephen went in his sympathy to look, thought the bedstead a good one to wear, greatly felt for the tradesman's disappointment, and said, "I suppose I had better stand your friend, and take this one." So the mahogany bedstead came home to the farm, Stephen saying, "The money was more to the poor man than just now to us, so I took it off his hands." Unlike all the other simple beds of the farm, its weight and heavy drapery darkened the chamber; but it left a neighbor's heart lighter, and that was the chief concern there.

Amongst the fields of the farm, and only hid from its windows by one of its beautiful woods, there stood a thatched cottage, in which lived a hard-natured man. He had toiled all his days to earn and save what he could · slow in movement, slow in speed, and without any expression on his uninviting face, he seemed little more than a moving form; yet he managed to gather together more money than his neighbors, he had bought cottages, and passed for a rich man amongst the poor Mabel sometimes attempted a discourse with him, but she could get little from him beyond "no," or "yes;" his wife was a pleasant woman, cheerful and active, and their cottage very pretty with its flowers without and its comfort within. Certain payments fell to the old man as holding property in the place, and Matthew being at the time road surveyor called on him with the rate. At a demand for money, the apathy of the old man kindled into anger. Matthew made call after call, getting only the language of ungoverned resentment. By patient perseverance the rate was at length obtained each time it became due, without a legal summons, the old man knowing the claim to be just; but Matthew felt hurt at the wrong, and Stephen indignant at the treatment received by his brother. In the next cottage to the old man's, a poor woman lay dying, and Mabel used sometimes to ride over from her home on her donkey, attended only by her dog, to the poor woman's cottage. They were sad visits to her, the bitter tears that fell, and the still more bitter lament made in anguish of heart, "No man has cared for my soul!"

On one of these visits she saw the old man next door, seated in his arm-chair supported by pillows, paralysed and helpless. A mournful object amidst all the verdure around him, as he sat just within the threshold of his cottage, the air blowing on him, and the bright flowers of his garden blooming before him. Mabel looped her donkey to the pales and went in, but the spark of mental intelligence seemed gone. After her visits she rode on to the early dinner at the farm. Seated with the family there, she said how shocked she had been to see the state of the old man. "Yes," Stephen answered, "and the treasure he had laid up here moth and rust have destroyed; he has not enough left to support him."

"What will he do then?" asked Mabel.

"Oh, he will not want," replied Stephen; "there are those that have enough and to spare."

"Are you then rendering good for evil?" asked Mabel.

"No, it's Matthew," Stephen said, "who has taken the care of the poor old man; it was Matthew he so reviled, and therefore Matthew said that care ought to be his!"

"That is fulfilling the law of Christ!" Mabel answered with a heart rejoicing in the beauty of such Christian love.

But Matthew, as he passed his hand across his eyes answered, "I thought that was no more than what ought to be."

From that day, through ten long helpless years, the old man was nourished from the farm, and Stephen would sit beside him, read to him, and kneeling pray for him, until slowly, after years of stupor, light dawned on his soul, his tears flowed in contrition, his blessings were poured on the grey-headed sons of the farm, and his spirit seemed feebly yet believingly to grasp the hope set before it in the gospel; in the calmness of repentance he continually poured forth his prayer; the apathy of his nature was gone; and few who knew him could doubt that the constant instructions and supplications of Stephen, won both the old man and his wife to their Saviour.

The business of this world Stephen thought no reason for neglecting the souls of his neighbors. He would say, with his countenance all beaming in heavenly expression, "When I open the Bible I find the best men there the busiest! What are we to say of Moses, who ordered all for a nation, and in such an unsettled condition as Israel was in the wilderness? Daniel too, only just look at him, and David; yet see how God was honored by them! so if I think at any time that I am hard pressed by the world, I have only to look there, and what then can I say?" That parish pastor's lost blessing, his lost crown of rejoicing—where must it eternally rest? surely on the head of Stephen, in starry brightness for ever! The words of the Judge are already uttered, "Take therefore the talent from him, and give it unto him that hath ten talents, for unto him that hath shall be given, and he shall have abundantly; but from him that hath not shall be taken away, even that that he seemeth to have."

Yet none more deeply felt than Stephen the sense of transgressions; notwithstanding his cheerful aspect in social life, he could often say in his brokenness of heart, "tears have been my meat day and night." One evening Elsie and the farm brothers were expected to spend the evening at the home of the Rector of the Eastern hill, and Mabel was happy looking out for her friends. They came, and surely the welcome had good reason to be warm that awaited them. Stephen looked unlike any one else in the world, his universal blue relieved by the broad snowy frills plaited by Elsie, that folded over his breast, and his long silver hair above a face on which the cares of this world, and the radiance of the next had both set their impress; it was earth that had furrowed it so deeply, it was heaven shed the light that illumined it. But this evening he looked grave and absent. It was not his wont to wear that aspect with friends, still less in the home then receiving him; but nothing that evening could rally his spirits, not even the old Psalm tunes that he loved, though he had often said he would walk miles any day to hear them on the piano, for he thought that one instrument far excelled all their melody, though of flutes, serpent, bassoon, French horns, violin, and flagelot. Spirits they had attuned to the melodies of their home—a pathos of deepest reverence in their piety, a purity of most harmonious cheerfulness in all their gentle mirth. This evening Stephen listened and praised, but it was as one who repeats words that he knows have been true in the past, and so may be safely used in the present; he did not seem really to enter into anything then before him.

After a few weeks Mabel was again at the farm; she no longer shared Elsie's care of the poultry and dairy, other and deeper interests awaited her now. Philip and Matthew went out as usual the first thing after breakfast, but Stephen spent the hour from seven until eight in converse or reading with Mabel, who sat in Margery's armchair, and made garments for the poor, as Stephen's great-grandmother had done in the days of his childhood. It was too early for any callers on business, and Stephen took the lead in the heavenly converse. Mabel, who once had wondered at his silence, was always herself the learner now. It was then that Stephen poured forth unfettered the spiritual riches of his soul. Sometimes melted to tears as he dwelt, with all his natural eloquence, on the love manifested in the life and the death of the Son of the Blessed; sometimes wrapt into sacred joy, which awed Mabel as she listened. His words, had they been written, might have kindled other hearts; but no record could have given the man—the eye, the tone, the bearing, that to simplest words gave a force inexpressible. Mabel, who once had wondered at his silence, now wondered still more how it was that he drew so abundantly of the river of God's pleasures. And she always observed that the morning hour stood alone; when he came in again the dust of earth had dimmed the reflector's vivid power; cheerful, responsive, and ready in all social and hallowed converse, yet not again, as in that early hour, lost in the glory of the Lord.

On this visit Mabel took her work as usual after breakfast. Stephen was silent for a while, then referred to the evening he had spent in her home, said "he could not enjoy it, he had done a wrong thing on that day, and there was that in the shadow of a sin which the light couldn't shine through; it did not signify what any might say, but until you could see the putting away of the sin by the blood of the cross, there could be no peace in the conscience that the Holy Spirit had quickened."

"The occasion had met him suddenly, as he supposed many could say. A most insulting message had been sent him, his hasty spirit had risen, and he had sent back a message of defiance; the message had been sent as an insult, and he had sent back anger. But, oh!" he said, "how soon he felt darkened, and how often it had weighed him down since! Well," he said, "might the blessed Saviour say, 'Ye know not what manner of spirit ye are of!' You might get clear of most things, but to draw the foot clean out of self was the hardest trial of all! and we might well often sit down and consider what it was that our Lord said to Peter, 'When thou art converted!' why Peter had long been a disciple, and had felt and said great things, yet there was a fall waiting for him. Perhaps we, like poor Peter, may have thought great things of ourselves, while yet our Saviour may be saying to us, 'When thou art converted!'" As Stephen talked, his face again lighted up, and the shadow of the sin of words hastily uttered, passed away from a heart always repentant and always forgiven.

And now the time had come for Nathaniel's guileless

spirit to return to its God. To him who had lived as a Christian, it was gain to die. His treasure and his heart had long been in heaven; and though he had not yet reached man's threescore years and ten, yet he was one for whom there seemed a peculiar truth in the beautiful lines,—

> "The less of this cold world, the more of heaven;
> The briefer life, the earlier immortality."

The sin and ignorance around him, and the yielding up his school, his life's chief effort for the good of others and the glory of his God, had clouded him with sadness. He spoke trustfully rather than brightly, and looked earnest and thoughtful. Like his mother, he entered on no wordly business, only once he said to Stephen, "Brother, you will see some day that I was not fit to live!" Stephen looked at him, and he replied, "You will know what I mean some day, and then you will find my words come true." Stephen remembered the words, but feared them not. It was remarkable that while Nathaniel's life had been so guileless, he had yet always distinguished, with an exactness but seldom expressed, between the natural benevolence of character and the graces of the divine Spirit. "But that is only nature!" was an observation so often on his lips, that it became a household saying. He met his death in humble thoughtful silence; but as all stood around him a beam of bright yet softest light fell on his brow, passed slowly across the dying face, lingered on the lips, and then was gone; and his ransomed spirit had departed with it. Stephen thought upon young Edward's favorite text, "Them that *sleep* in Jesus, shall God bring with him."

Stephen and Philip were left his executors, and when at length they opened the miller's books, they found that he, who from the extent of his business might have lived and died a rich man, had only left a quiet maintenance to his widow and child. Page after page registered the unpaid debts of the poor. Where ignorance of divine truth prevails, there it will be found that ungodliness, and want, and debt abound. Nathaniel often said, "Poor souls, they have none to teach them better!" and as one pound was added to another in his books against them, still he could not refuse them flour when they came for a sack. "Bread is the very staff of life," he would say, "and we cannot tell exactly how the case may be with them!" When Stephen saw this he said, "Now I know what my poor brother meant when he said, 'I am not fit to live!' and sure enough it is not the truest kindness to let the poor heap up debt; but his nature was such he could not deny any the thing that they wanted if he had it to give. And he 's gone where all will deal well with him now." Yet to his widow and child he left a maintenance, and the Blessing of the God of the Poor.

CHAPTER XXIII.

"WHERE is Master Philip? The pit has fallen in on poor Robin Rutt, and he does nothing but call for Master Philip to come! I am going for the doctor, but please to say if Master Philip will run across, they will almost be there by that time at the cottage."

"Could you go too, Elsie? I seem to dread it alone."

"Oh yes, I can go; but don't you wait for me, I'll be after with a few comforts as quick as I can."

Now Robin Rutt was a man of whom no one held a very high opinion. He had no love for work, and no skill when put to it, so that he seldom got beyond breaking stones on the road. Slothfulness was a crime in the statute-book of the farm; Margery would say, "Never was there a truer word written than 'He that is slothful in his work, is brother to him that is a great waster.' And to waste the least one of the good gifts of God, is nothing less than an insult to the merciful Giver. Don't suppose that because you shut your eyes, therefore the God above does not see! So sure as the least thing is wasted, there is some poor creature lifting up a cry, that your waste would have satisfied. And the God above hears it too!" Therefore, as Robin was reckoned slothful amongst men, he was no favorite at the farm; and the poor man knew it well. But he also knew that tender-hearted Charity dwelt there, and like many more he believed there was no hand like Master Philip's for gentleness and skill, so as they carried him home he still called for him. His quiet industrious wife had not heard the tidings, until she saw the men bearing him home on a shutter; but in the distance behind him, crossing the field as fast as the mud would allow, came Philip and Elsie, and it kept up the faint heart of the poor woman when she saw "such dear comfort was near!" Philip knew, as well as a carpenter, how to take down and put up a bedstead, so with the help of the men who had brought Robin home this was done in no time, that the poor man might not be laid in the cold chamber above. Elsie had brought a couple of her own whitest linen sheets; she made up the bed, and the doctor arrived, having been met on the road. He laid poor Robin Rutt on his bed, who looked up in such patience and paleness, thanking all around him, until Elsie wiped away her tears, to see him whom they had never thought highly of, suffer so meekly! When it came to the necessity of removing the hard leather boot from off the crushed limb, Robin said, "I beg pardon, but I couldn't stand any hand but Master Philip's for that! I know it must be a bad job any way, and I can best take it from him!"

"Well, Robin, I am sure I don't know," said Philip, as

he kneeled ready to assist by the bed, but skill and tenderness triumphed; he who had helped to tend every injury to the cattle on the farm, and handled each one so that the creature often turned a mild eye of thankfulness on him, was no stranger to wounds and bruises; and heard the blessing of the poor man, as the crushed limb was released. The kind-hearted doctor was affected at seeing the farmer's skill preferred to his own, and he made every attempt to secure his rightful preëminency—by tenderest handling, and dressing with that best healing ointment—of kind assuring words. Elsie had wrapped a bottle of her home-made wine in her white linen sheets, and from time to time she gave the poor man a spoonful. At last all was done, and the doctor ordered quiet. Robin Rutt looked his thankfulness, as his eyes followed Philip and Elsie to the door. Philip would step across on a morning, and Elsie at even-tide, to see how Robin might be. In a few days all danger was over, and the poor man lay on his bed full of thankfulness. Then Stephen said, "Now, if ever, is the time to do him good for the future; I don't see but what we might teach him to read!" So a thin book of light weight was bought at the market-town, with letters and short words in large print on its pages. Robin Rutt learned much quicker than any one could have expected. When he sat up again in his chair, Stephen gave him a large-print Bible, in which he soon made out a chapter, and each chapter he learned to read was read by him so often, that he knew it by heart; and his face lighted up with a brighter intelligence, and his words were so expressive of thankfulness, that Stephen said, as many have said before, and as many more would say, could they but show the same mercy as these English yeomen—"There is more in poor Robin than ever we thought to find there!"

Then Philip said, "Robin, I don't know, but I fancy if I made you crutches, you would soon step about on them."

"Well, sir, 'tis likely, I think, if you took it in hand!"

Now Philip had made a succession of wooden legs to suit the growth of a beautiful lamb that had only three; it was the finest lamb of the flock, and lived on the grass-plat, and drank milk from Elsie's hand, and was a favorite with all at the farm. So Philip was skilful in such work, and now he made a pair of good crutches for Robin, and he still cut and tried them, and then cut again, until, hopeful of success, he carried them over to Robin.

"Now, Robin, you must try, though I am but a clumsy tradesman, I fear!"

Robin leaned his weight on them, then exclaimed, "There now, 'tis a fit; just into my arm-pits! why, they don't feel like wood—'tis a sure thing they'll walk if I can hold to them!"

Robin crossed his cottage floor; and sat down again with a tear of gratitude brightening his eyes. In six weeks he reached the farm on his crutches, carrying his Bible tied up in a handkerchief, and said he should wish to read to all the masters together. And in six months poor Robin was well, and a far more active and better man than ever before. So happy is he who has a good Samaritan to pass by his way! So blessed are they who, in life's active charity, *consider* the poor!

"Would it be possible for you to make a visit some evening to the farm?" Mabel asked of a clergyman, who had lately come to a parish, distant ten or twelve miles from her friends.

"Yes, I will gladly pay it a visit, and let you know when I can fix a time."

This clergyman had a most clear and impressive way of explaining and applying Holy Scripture; and as Mabel saw in that parish what it was to have a famine of the Word of God, in the ministry that ought to provide it, she longed, whenever it was possible, to supply through others that great necessity. The clergyman wrote to fix the day; a little boy went from the farm to meet him on the way, and guide him through the many crossing lanes; and Mabel set out from her home, accompanied by a friend to whom the farm was greatly endeared. As she reached one cottage door after another, she stopped and said, "If you like, you can come up to the forest farm this evening at six o'clock, to hear the Word of God read and explained. You can tell one another, and let all come who wish." And so, inviting her friends by the way, she arrived at the farm. It was then but four o'clock, so she said, "I want you to put the horse into the gig, and drive me to fetch old neighbor Gay this evening to tea."

"Oh!" exclaimed Stephen, "you may well spare yourself that trouble, for you will never get the old lady to come."

"I don't know about 'never,'" replied Mabel, "for if I only get rid of that first letter 'n,' what good success may I not hope for then!"

A cheerful hope was always the best argument with Stephen if he doubted success. Matthew said, "As you please;" and so the horse was harnessed in; not one of the Wranglers, but a sober-minded old pony who had forgotten all frolics, and thought standing still the best play in the world. As all watched the departing gig from the windows, Stephen shook his head, and smiled and said, "She will not succeed there, I can venture to say!"

Neighbor Gay was a pleasant old woman, living on a comfortable little independence, quite alone in the world. Her small house was the most picturesque of old places, standing far back in as picturesque a garden. Neighbor Gay lived in her "keeping-room," and showed Mabel the inside of her pretty bow-windowed parlor sometimes, and the very pretty old prints that hung on its walls; always pleased at Mabel's pleasure, whose delight in pictures was great. All was old in the dwelling, all the flowers were old-fashioned, and the pathways were made of little round pebbles laid side by side in long rows. Neighbor Gay, bent down with old age and feebleness, never now left her home; she sat in her arm-chair, with a round basket of work, and three books, always carried in the same basket: the Bible, the Prayer-book, and Bunyan's Pilgrim; from all these she read at intervals, by the help of her very large spectacles, and said she wanted no better company; but Mabel was not quite happy about her. So this evening, when the distant clergyman was expected, she drove to the little gate, overhung with heavy drooping trellis of honeysuckle and hops; and walked along the garden pathway—where every round pebble was wedged in its place, to the door of the little house, which was open, and neighbor Gay seated near it, at work in her "keeping-room."

"Bless you, my dear! why, I didn't know you were over."

"I am only come for this one evening; a very good man, a clergyman from ten or twelve miles away, is coming over to tea at the farm, so I drove up here first to take you back with me, because, you see, it is a great occasion, and you must be there."

"My dear, I couldn't walk the worth of a tenth part of the way; I haven't been out I am sure I don't know when!"

"You are not to walk, no one ever thought of that; Mr. Matthew Northwood is now at the gate, and the steady old horse in the gig, waiting ready for me to drive you down."

"The gig, my dear! why folks would say I had lost all my senses, to see me go romancing like that."

"But, neighbor, this good clergyman will read the

Bible, and explain it; and you know you have no teaching like that to lighten you here."

"My dear, I wish well to the church, and only think it a pity that every one that stands up in it be not like to the good man you speak of; but I cannot go riding after him, let him be what he will."

"What, not this little way? with me to drive you so carefully, and Mr. Matthew Northwood to walk by the side?"

"But, my dear, I don't want the good man; here I sit with my books, and get light out of them."

"Yes, neighbor, but don't you know that sometimes the candle wants snuffing? and you have no one to do that for you here."

"Yes, I have you! and every time you step in you leave me more cheery than before you did come."

"Oh! but I am so afraid when you come to the valley of the shadow of death lest your light should not stand the darkness there, but go out, and you know not which way to turn! It may burn pretty well now, but if it be not the true light it will go out then! and this good man would show you what the true light really is!"

"Would he, dear?" said the old lady, moved at Mabel's earnestness; "well then 'twere a sin not to go, if I could any way; though how it will be ordered I am sure I can't tell. Liddy, girl I say, come and get my best gown; here's the chief folk of the parish all a-waiting for me!" So with steps up to the gig, and Mabel from above, and Matthew and Liddy from below, the old lady climbed in.

"Who ever would have thought it?" she said, when safely started with Mabel, and Matthew leading the old horse to make assurance doubly sure. "Dear me, how beautiful the land do look; and the air, how sweet and nice it is to be sure!" So, praising all things, and enjoying to the utmost this unexpected romancing, old neighbor Gay, driven by Mabel and led by Matthew, arrived at the farm. All the household came out to receive her, but Stephen smiled at Mabel, and said, "Now, I suppose it will always be EVER!" The kind and warm greetings kindled up the half-stagnant life of the old woman to the fullest sense of enjoyment, and the clergyman arriving they all sat down to tea—Mabel between neighbor Gay and Margaret—who had come down from the church farm to join the pleasant assembly.

While they were seated at Elsie's cheerful table, Stephen looked up, and as his eye fell on the green slope leading down the valley, he said, "Look! who are coming now!"

A company of people, all dressed in Sabbath garments, men and women, were descending the hill.

"What is this?" asked the clergyman.

"Well, sir," replied Stephen, "I suppose you must ask Miss Mabel that question; we know nothing about it!"

"I only told the poor people," Mabel said, "that they might come and listen, when you read and explained the Bible this evening."

But now another company appeared in the distance.

"Who are these?" asked the clergyman, "that flock as doves to their windows? I did not come with any expectation of this; and to read the Bible in your house to such a company of people would expose you to a penalty."

Poor Mabel knew nothing of penalties; and at that formidable word she looked up anxiously at Stephen. The tears were in his eyes as he watched the poor people flocking up the green slope, and more of them still appearing on the opposite hill, and he at once replied to the clergyman, "Well, sir, as to the law, I can truly say we knew nothing of their coming; but you see they be hungry and thirsty, and none to supply them; and seeing how it now stands, I can only say we shall not grudge the penalty, if you be willing to open the Bible before them."

And **now** the great back kitchen had filled, and the poor villagers were crowding outside, to be ready to listen to the message of God's mercy, from one whose name they had never before heard in their retired homes. All had hastened at Mabel's call, one had told another; the men had not stayed for their supper, nor the women to finish their day's work, but all had hasted and washed the day's toil from their hands, and put on their Sabbath garments and come. And now an arm-chair was placed for old neighbor Gay, and Mabel led her in; then the **poor** men climbed on the back-kitchen boilers, and **thronged** round the windows, and those crowding outside with village courtesy still let the women in, who filled the passage and sat two and two up the stairs to the chambers above, wherever they thought the voice of the good words could reach them. There was no space to give the clergyman chair or table, he stood pressed around by the throng. He read the thirty-second Psalm, dwelling chiefly on the verse, "Thou art my Hiding-place!" Breathless stillness hushed that village multitude, broken at last by low sobs; a niece of the farm, in the bloom and freshness of her youth, had come on a short visit before taking her first place of service, as lady's-maid in one of Scotland's ancestral families. She had never before heard such words; and overcome by feeling she pressed through the throng, to go out and weep alone. To her it was the call to her Saviour, and it came with a power more attractive than all the enticements of this world. With those words of love and mercy written on her heart she went to her distant place of service, won the love of her young mistress as a friend no less than a servant; then died in the illness of a few days, soothed to the last by the tender tones of the mistress she loved; laid in her coffin by the head of the baronial family she served, who in the absence of all her friends did this office of a kinsman for her; walked by her sleeping remains, borne by the household servants at their own desire, and made her grave among the tombs of his family. She the most deeply impressed, and the first called from earth of all on that evening assembled.

Neighbor Gay poured out a thanksgiving to think that the had been present on so blessed an evening! The poor stole in thoughtful silence away. In the cottages and in the fields you heard mention of the words spoken on that evening; and months after, as Philip passed under the stable windows where the men were rubbing down the farm horses, at four o'clock in the morning, he heard them talking one to another about " that Hiding-place!"

Yet, when in the church, the living voice breathes no spiritual inspiration, or when it gives an uncertain sound, and therefore few flock to hear it, and none at its call prepare for battle, the Liturgy of that Church still bears in its words the power of the soul-quickening truth. The hallowed Liturgy flows on like a sacred stream, from generation to generation, and those who observe the way by which God leads the most humble and lowly-hearted of the poor, will often find how they have drunk of its still waters and fed in its green pastures;—its supplications, adoration, and thanksgiving, it psalms, lessons, epistle, and gospel, combining an amount of Scripture truth, which, applied by the Holy Spirit, has, without any other teaching, trained many a meek spirit for the kingdom of Heaven. A poor woman, who had still worshipped only in the neglected church of her parish, lay dying, and Mabel went to see her. She could not read; she felt her own knowledge was small, her power to express it less, but still she had Hope. She listened with patient thankfulness to all that was said to her. She was still, as to her years, in the midst of her days, and leaving a young family, yet satisfied that God's will should be done: and when death drew near, and all that was then present faded from her eyes, and all that had but lately been said to her faded also perhaps, from her weakened memory, her spirit turned again to the only teaching it had known before in life, and with her remaining strength she uttered the familiar prayer of the Litany, "By Thine Agony and bloody Sweat, by Thy Cross and Passion, by Thy precious Death and Burial, Good Lord deliver ME!" She did not speak again, but with that last and life-long supplication, breathed her meek believing spirit into the bosom of her risen and ascended Lord.

CHAPTER XXIV.

"HAVE you heard of Matthew's visits to London?" Stephen asked of Mabel when she was again at the farm, after an absence of some months from her home.

"No; has he really been there?"

"Yes, but he cannot say much in praise of the treatment he met with!"

"I am sorry for that. Tell me what happened."

"Well, you see, the fame of our horse winning the prize against all England, as you may say, got talked about there, and one of the great horse-dealers thought, I suppose, that if there be such wonderful horses down here, he must have one up there. Matthew had not one at that time of the highest value, but still he must have one; so Matthew said he was welcome so to do if he pleased, and named his price, which the man appeared satisfied with, and Matthew was to take the horse up to London, and receive the money there. So Matthew took our man, and they went up with the horse. The dealer seemed very well satisfied, but said he must fix a later day for the payment; so Matthew found he could not get his money, and came home. Well, he went up again, and our man with him, for his money; but the dealer said the horse was still in his stables, and he could not as yet make good the payment. Matthew told him, that he did not consider what expense and trouble he was putting him to, contrary to the agreement; but it was of no use; so he and his servant came home again. Well, I said, they may not love honesty in London, but I cannot have you put off like this! You shall wait the set time, then go up again, and if you cannot get honest dealing, have no dispute with the man, but just step to the Temple, where Mr. Samuel now lodges, and name the particulars to him, and let them consider what they will say when they have heard a few words from him; I can promise them he will not say a great many!"

Mr. Samuel was one of the Rector's family on the Eastern hill. Stephen often said of him, "What he undertakes he will stand master of, and he certainly will always be much thought of by us." Stephen continued his history. "So, when the time came, Matthew went up again. The London dealer had grown insolent, and told him that he did not want his horse; he might go and look at him, and take him home if he pleased, but no money would be paid for him there. Matthew went to the stables, found the horse had taken a disease then prevalent, had been neglected, he thought; and looked almost worth nothing. This after illness he told the dealer could not alter the agreement. But the man offered the horse and refused the payment. So Matthew said no more, but found his way to the Temple, told Mr. Samuel the particulars, who, when he had heard them, said, 'I will come with you,' and so they went together. When Matthew came back again into the yard, he saw in a moment that he was thought quite another man now that he had Mr. Samuel with him. All the men turned an eye on Mr. Samuel as he passed, so they went into the office together. Then Mr. Samuel lays down Matthew's demand on the counter, and says, 'I request the payment of this debt for the gentleman with me.' The clerk was quite changed in behavior, and said, 'I will take it in, sir;' and Matthew saw pretty plainly they would now all be up to minding what they were after. Then one of the principals comes into the office in no time. He looks at Mr. Samuel, and says, 'There is a mistake in this business; the horse proves worthless; he can be returned, but the money cannot be paid.'

"But Mr. Samuel makes answer, 'That cannot be admitted, sir; you know the agreement, and you also know that you have given this gentleman a great deal of vexatious trouble. I have known him all my life, and can trust his every word, and will stand by him to the end; therefore, if you are prepared now, in my presence, to settle his just claim, all will be well; if not, I shall know what course at once to pursue: there is my card.' So the principal takes up the card, but he never speaks a word, only he steps back again where he came from, and in two minutes there comes back a clerk with a cheque for the whole sum of money! So Mr. Samuel takes the cheque, and says to Matthew, 'Now we will go to the bank;' and when he gets there, he asks Matthew if he would like to have the money all in new gold to take home with him? Matthew says he does not wish to be troublesome, but Mr. Samuel goes straight up and asks for it at once, and they shovel out their new gold, and he gives it to Matthew, who gets home here with all this new gold, which showed pretty clear what his success had then been! and so that trouble was ended with Mr. Samuel to stand by him; but it was no bad lesson for us country farmers not to trust to the word of those London dealers; but if they want a thing, let them pay for it here, before it leaves the place, and let them fetch it away for themselves; for if they have not a right principle, they are too much for us. And now the horse is their own, it is likely they will take better care of him."

The Rector of Stephen's parish being absent on a Sunday, engaged a clergyman to preach for him, who was reported to be, as Stephen said, "a very good man." Stephen looked forward to the Sunday, when, without offence to any, he might worship again, and all his household with him, in his own familiar church, and hear the same gospel of glad tidings there, which was fresh life to him every Sunday at the little church on the hill. Mabel entered into his hope, and rode over soon after the Sunday had passed, to hear if that hope had met its fulfilment. When she asked of the Sunday, Stephen's face did not brighten as it was wont to do at the very mention of that day, so she waited until more alone with him, and then said, "I am afraid you were disappointed on Sunday!"

"I was surprised!" Stephen replied, "and never more so in my life; nor can I ever think highly of that preacher again; they may say what they will, my mind is made up!"

It was evident that Stephen had been much displeased, and Mabel wondered what the offence could have been. It was not Stephen's wont to be hard on any good man · no one felt more strongly the slowness with which he had himself apprehended divine truth in its fulness; he well knew how long the true light may shine dimly; yet he had never seemed more hurt. She asked what the preacher had said. "Well, I should have been slow to believe it, if I had not been there; he preached his sermon upon that one fault that is recorded of that blessed servant of God, Moses. I wondered that he was not ashamed to stand up and set out in more words than could have been thought possible, that one fault of that servant of God, that the Bible tells in so few words! I felt ashamed to sit there and hear him. Could he think that a good man had to stand up and preach all his sermon, as you may say, on the fault of a better man than himself! is that true religion? And of Moses, too! Did he never take notice, I wonder, that God speaks of Moses as He speaks of none other, for He hardly ever so much as mentions his name without saying, 'My servant.' I think that must show pretty plain what thoughts we ought to dwell upon about him; and that if by any means we might attain that great honor, that God should say of us, 'My servant.' And then only see how many times that blessed man made intercession to God for that rebellious people, and prevailed: surely we must say there was no intercessor ever came so near to our Lord as he did, when he said, 'Blot me out of Thy book,' for their sake! And did he never sit down for a few moments and consider what a heavy displeasure God showed upon Aaron, the saint of the Lord, and upon Miriam, when they took in hand to speak in dishonor of His servant Moses? And then to bring it on to the very end of the Bible, and to see that out of all the servants and saints of the Lord, there is only one chosen to that highest honor, to be named with THE LAMB! for it says, 'They sing the song of Moses, the servant of God, and the song of the Lamb:' sure after so great an honor put upon him, we had need be very careful how we take in hand to make the most that we can of that one fault of him, whom God called 'the meekest of men!'" As Stephen proceeded in this, his own eloquent apostrophe on Moses, the servant of God, the shadow of the fault-magnifying sermon passed away from his expressive countenance, and as he ceased speaking, he looked bright in fellowship of spirit with the saint of whom he spoke. But he never forgot the sermon; and it was evident that his best hope for the preacher was forgiveness, and a low place at the feet of Moses in heaven. And ever after, when Mabel heard any sermon that held the magnifying glass to the faults of the saints of the Bible, she thought of Stephen's deeper wisdom, and clearer vision of truth.

In her intercourse with Stephen, she often wondered how it could be that in his busy life, he yet seemed to know every saint of revelation, as a most familiar friend. Whenever any passing allusion was made to them, he would, if alone with Mabel, take up the subject as he did with Moses, bringing out the peculiar position of each character, the distinct way in which the divine Spirit spoke of each, and points of interest and profit, which Mabel had never heard dwelt on before; so that when she thought of Stephen, she thought not of earthly characters as his most familiar associates, but of Moses and Elijah, of Daniel and Peter.

Peter was the character he most frequently dwelt on; it was evident, although he said it not, that he felt resemblances in the history of that disciple, to some of the vividly impressed facts of his own spiritual life.

"It used to be what I could not understand, that Peter should say, 'Depart from me, for I am a sinful man, O Lord.' But there came a time for me to see the meaning of that. Peter was overwhelmed with a sense of his own unworthiness, when the Lord showed him that great mercy in the miracle of fishes; so that we may say of him, "The goodness of God led him to repentance!

The blessed Saviour knew the spirit in which he made that mistaken prayer, 'Depart from me, for I am a sinful man, O Lord;' so He did not take him at his word. But when the wicked say unto God, 'Depart from us, for we desire not the knowledge of Thy ways,' He takes them at their word. But the poor trembling penitent He receives in His arms, and bids him abide with Him for ever. We see that, instead of then departing from Peter, the Lord from that time never suffered Peter to depart from Him! Then to come to that part where Peter must needs walk on the waves; he was very forward to go to his master, but he forgot his master's words, 'Without Me ye can do nothing!' and so he found there must be something more than he had naturally in himself, there must be a divine hand stretched out to save and uphold him. And so we must be brought to see that without the Holy Spirit, coming down into our hearts, we can do nothing that is pleasing in the sight of our Saviour.

"I think there is one truth that we see pretty plain in St. Peter, that no man living can stand praise! Let him be who he may, praise will be too much for him here: if he has praise, he will want some humbling to follow after it. I often thank God who set me out of the reach of praise. Only to look at St. Peter and there see what our poor human nature is, and how sure praise is to carry it wrong, because the heart is so fond of it! St. Peter could not even be humble enough to bear the commendation of the LORD! but the next thing we find is Peter rebuking his Master, and then the Lord was forced to say to him, 'Get thee behind me, Satan, for thou savorest not the things that be of God, but those that be of men.' Peter had to be shown his own heart, before he knew how it was for this world more than for the next!

"I have often wondered that, when our Lord told Peter to go to the sea, and that he should find a piece of money in the fish that first came up, Peter, being a fisherman, should not express any surprise at such a thing; but I see it is just as we are—taking all God's wonderful dealings for us as common mercies, without thinking like Jacob, 'how unworthy we are of the least of them!' Oh! how often I think of the words of that blessed man who preaches up there on the hill, when he said, 'If we would only sit down for half an hour and CONSIDER the dealings of God for us, what different men we should rise up at the end of it!' Yet I do hope I shall never think any thing against that blessed disciple, whom I pray to meet in heaven; but I do find the greatest instruction thinking over all he went through. And then to see how plainly it was THE PRAYER OF OUR SAVIOUR that carried St. Peter through all! and to see what that prayer was,— 'I have prayed for thee, THAT THY FAITH FAIL NOT;' and so we see how that after His resurrection, the blessed Saviour brought St. Peter to nothing but the faith of a little child, not to hold any longer by what he knew, or by what he could do; but to say, 'Lord, THOU knowest all things, THOU knowest that I love thee!' And when we come to that simple faith in Christ, without any trust in ourselves, then He will teach us, not before. And then to turn to St. Peter's Epistles, and see the effect of Christ's prayer in them; how St. Peter writes to them that have obtained 'LIKE PRECIOUS FAITH.' And so all along—in his tears, and his repentance, and his first sermon, and his sufferings, and his Epistles, and his death—we see nothing as we may say but the answer to that one short prayer of the blessed Saviour for him, 'I have prayed for thee, THAT THY FAITH FAIL NOT.' So he was truly saved IN THE LORD, with an everlasting salvation. And what can we think to do for ourselves, but to come to that blessed Saviour, and ask Him to intercede for us as He did for St. Peter. If He offer up but one short prayer for us, that will be seen in its answer through all our future life! And does He not even say that He liveth to make intercession for them that come unto God by Him? Let us ask Him, and sure He will not deny His own gracious word, upon which he has caused us to hope!"

None could puzzle or baffle Stephen in the Word of his God.

"Safe in my heart, and closely hid,
Thy Word, my treasure, lies."

Even in his retired home the cavils of the ungodly, and the oppositions of science—falsely so called—met him. A question being talked of before him as to whether the words or only the truths of the Bible were inspired, after quietly listening, he replied—"It is quite evident to me that they who raise such questions, don't yet know what depends on a word! or they would not stand in doubt about that. I can tell pretty well what to think upon that, seeing it was a single word, and that the shortest word that could be, which turned me from darkness to light. Do they think that all their learned arguments could persuade me, that it was man chose that word 'No,' in answer to the poor sinner's inquiry, 'Will He plead against me with His great power?' Man could never have asked the question, and much less given the answer, straight to the point, as it is done here; he would have had a different way of laying out such great things as they be. What they want is a little more experimental knowledge of what lies in a word! and that would settle the question for them better than all their great learning can do. Or let them come on to the New Testament; do they really suppose, that if a man had been left to choose how best to express the greatness of the love of God, that he would have done it all in a little word of two letters—that little word 'so'? 'God so loved the world.' I should think they read and hear enough of man's wisdom, to know it would not have been told in two letters if man had had the telling of that!"

Stephen rarely lost an opportunity of bringing before those who called in on business, the supreme claim of eternal things over temporal. And whatever their cavils might be, he was ready with his answer. It was not alone his knowledge of the Bible, but his constant meditation upon it, which armed him at all points, as a veteran who might be assailed, but could not be surprised or overthrown. One instance will show his readiness. A trader having finished his business, Stephen spoke of the necessity of looking beyond the things that are seen and passing, to those that are unseen and eternal. But the trader said he had enough to do in what lay before him; if he minded that, he must trust for the distant.

"But does not the Bible lie before you, as near as the mercy of God could put it? and is not your immortal soul as much with you as your body? Your excuse don't hold good. You are choosing the less, and neglecting the greater, when both lie alike near and before you."

"Oh, as for the Bible, I don't believe that God gave it."

"Why not?"

"Why, because the Old Testament finishes up with the word 'CURSE!' I will never believe a merciful God would have ended with a curse."

"Can you repeat the last verse in the Old Testament?" Stephen asked.

No, I cannot repeat it, but I know the last word is 'curse,' and that is enough for me."

"What, have you settled such a question, on which eternity depends, and yet cannot tell the one sentence that you have made up your mind upon? I advise you to open the Bible once more, and you will see how great a mistake you have made; for it is not that God will curse, but that He may not have to curse! "He shall turn the heart of the fathers to the children, and the heart of the children to their fathers, LEST I smite the earth with a curse.' Surely that is saving the earth from a curse, not bringing one upon it?"

"Well, now, I only looked at the last word, and so I took it quite different."

"Then, let me tell you the words of a blessed man, that have been the greatest use to me, and I pray God they may be to you. He said, "If we would only sit down one half-hour and CONSIDER, what different men we should be when we rose up again!' Now, you see, you had made a terrible mistake, and brought a false accusation against the Book—that certainly is the first and chiefest of all books, just because you did not consider what it really did say. And, surely, if there be but one Book in the world that can declare, 'THUS SAITH THE LORD,' and that not once, but hundreds of times! one half-hour, if it were every day, is not much to consider its words, when they be the only ones that can tell of Eternity."

One day, when conversing with Stephen, Mabel learned the secret of his knowledge of Holy Scripture, so remarkable in one whose business claims were incessant. He chanced to say playfully, speaking of early waking, "A cuckoo has called me all the spring-time. He perches on the tree at my window, and awakes me at the same hour every morning."

"At what hour?" Mabel asked.

Stephen waited a moment, then said, "At four o'clock."

"Do you rise at four o'clock?"

"Yes, I do; it is the secret of my life through the day—the blessed hours of the morning! In the summer-time I never stay within, but get out before any are stirring to a little shed in the pastures; that is my sanctuary! and there I have pretty nearly two hours alone with the Bible; and so I have lived, as you may say, with the blessed saints of the Lord, and that has enabled me to try and endure the contradiction of sinners, as my Lord and Master has taught me by His blessed example. I sit there while the world is sleeping, and there's none to disturb, and there I have meat to eat that the world knows not of."

Stephen had thought that none knew of his little lonely sanctuary, where, amidst the solitude of nature, and the sweet breathing of the morning on the hills, he drank of the Living Waters, and thirsted no more. But Matthew, long after, told Mabel of it, not knowing that she knew; saying that, wondering why his brother always came to breakfast from the pastures, he had secretly watched, and seen his early visits there. And he told her, what Stephen never spoke of even to her—that at evening-times they had often wondered why he left them an hour before he reached the church farm, and Matthew had watched, and seen him go evening by evening to a lonely pit in a distant field, that no pathway lay near, in the bottom of

which he kneeled, pouring forth his supplications to
Heaven. Then Mabel wondered not that his face sometimes shone like one beholding, as in a glass, the glory of
the Lord, changed into the same image, even as by the
Spirit of the Lord!

CHAPTER XXV.

THERE came at length an autumn that compelled the Rector of the Eastern hill to leave the high bleak lanes and open fields of his country parish, for the safety of a warmer church, and the sheltered streets of London. Then the little gleaners cried beside their gathered wheat in the harvest-fields; the village mothers wept within their cottage doors, and poor men's eyes overflowed with tears; for truly all felt that he, who now must leave them, had been gentle amongst them, even as a nurse that cherisheth her children. He could not take leave of them, his own deep feelings forbade a farewell: with the hope of many an after visit, he left them to one, no less able than himself, to teach them the things that belonged unto their peace. But around Mabel the poor people gathered, and still they asked, "When shall we see you again?"

"When the wild roses bloom!" Mabel answered for the sake of some reply; and so the winter passed away, and the spring deepened into summer; the villagers watched the hedgerows for the first wild rose: but deep anxiety was engaging Mabel's thoughts in the great city, and she had forgotten her words.

The spring-tide had passed, and summer was come in—loud sang the cuckoo in the fields of the farm, but Mabel had not seen the Blackthorn or the May. The first spring-time had passed away, in which she had traced no violet to its lowly bed, by the fragrance that it breathed;—she had seen the little purple flowers of spring in the great city's streets, held up for sale by hands of pale and woe-worn children, who for pity's sake begged her to buy their scentless violets. Oh! how unlike the sweeter world that she had known before, where rosy village childhood hunted the mossy banks, and came to her with laden hands of fragrant flowers, all given for love!

The spring was gone—and Mabel had heard the blackbirds' and the thrushes' song, only from wicker-cages in the narrow streets, where some of the great city's worst inhabitants offered for sale the prisoned songsters of the woods, and where the field-lark was ever stretching vainly his caged wings for flight. June had come in, and on the farm the band of mowers had cut down the scented grass; but Mabel only saw the sunshine fall on endless streets, where brick and mortar made a shadow, and the noisy life of men filled all the city's heavy air.

She was sitting in the parlor of her city home—the window open to let in the air of June, but with the air came in the din of the great city, so strange a sound to unaccustomed ears; so loud a din that you could not, with open windows, hear the voices in the room—but Mabel was alone. Then her brother entered, the friend of all her life, her preceptor in all heavenly and earthly truth; and sitting down by her he said, "I have seen the doctor, he says I cannot live! And such a longing comes to me to leave this city air, and see our own dear people, that I thought perhaps you would, for my sake, go to the forest farm to-day, that I might follow you to-morrow there. I am afraid to go in illness, and take them unprepared."

It was easy to venture anything for him—he who at any time would lay aside his cherished studies to attend her walks, always saying, "When I am here, I do not like that you should walk alone." And he was still here, but of this world no longer, for the sentence had been uttered, which, in a moment, snaps asunder the ties that bind to usages of earth;—the moment that makes that awful transition in the position that we fill, from the sense of being a living, to that of being a dying man!

In two hours more she was hastening to the haunts that all the records of her childhood, and her brother's, had made redolent of life and love. And the great city which had, with its endless windings of its chain of streets, and its countless throngs of careworn faces, pressed on her spirit like a prison—whose limits she had never seen, was left behind in the lengthening distance. It was evening when she reached the far-off country town, and a nine miles' drive still lay between her and the forest farm. On her way she passed through the villages most dear, crossed the Eastern hill, passed by its old church, and the homesteads of the poor. Some were already closed, the little lattice curtained with its white window-blind, and rest and sleep within. Some doors were open still, and here and there an old familiar face looked out, at the unusual sound of carriage wheels, but no one guessed who the lone traveller was in the late evening twilight: and Mabel was too sad in that evening's errand to venture on a single hurried greeting. In the hedges she saw the festoons of the wild rose, then remembered her promise, and wondered if other hearts had thought upon it also, and little knew how they had questioned and watched for that fair token. And she thought upon the strange foreshadowing often given to the words; her own vague promise, spoken in will rather than belief, fulfilled, and with attendant circumstances how unexpected!

She passed the lonelier lanes, and now she saw the Farm upon the hill; the evening hour was scarcely more than ten, and yet its white blinds were all drawn, and it was evident that night was resting there. She crossed the valley, climbed the steep hill slowly. Why did not the great watch-dog sound alarm? Could it really be that, in the still of the night he had heard her voice upon the hill at the farm-gate directing the driver, and was the first of all in her own land to know her, and, fierce and resentful as he was at strange wheels even by day, had only welcome for the unknown carriage horse, and man who brought his friend? Poor Gruff had died long before Mabel's birth; he soon followed his master to the grave; seeming to think it little worth his while to guard the place when he returned not. Another mastiff followed, and had his day and history; and now a huge and foreign dog, of long and shaggy hair, excelled all who went before him in intelligence, and it must be allowed in fierceness also. He was never let loose because of his tremendous power, and therefore his instinct became concentrated on the farmyards around him, and perfected itself for its place. As his masters sat within, they could tell from the different tones of his sonorous bark what was passing without; he had three distinct household alarms, apart from all the other modulations in which he occasionally proclaimed his presence and his power. One of these betokened a stranger's approach, another told without failure if any animal had got into a wrong place, and the third if there were any quarrelling amongst the cattle. Fierce as Bell was, he won universal respect and admiration. A new man came to the farm who boasted that he could approach any dog when he pleased, but Bell soon convinced him that he must make one exception. Every attempt at acquaintanceship failed; at last, relying on the dog's sagacity, the man one day carried him his own dinner, saying to his master, "He'll know 'tis my dinner I have given up to him! and 'tis worth the loss of it for one day to win his good-will!" Bell was supposed to understand the sacrifice, as he became friendly from that time. He was a generous dog, and allowed the fowls to share his bowl of barley-meal and milk; but the moment they began to quarrel about it, which they often did, he laid his huge paw on the back of the offender, and held it down, until the other got fairly away. The tones of Bell's bark, when any contention began amongst the farm animals, were interpreted by Stephen to be, "I am set here to keep watch over these yards; and I will not have any piece-of-work, either, one with another! if you do I shall interfere, I can tell you; so let me hear no more of that." His friendship for Mabel was so trustful, that he would stop his terrible alarum, even at the arrival of strangers, at the call of her voice; and on this night he barked not at the wheels, horse, or man, though he knew all the farm except himself was asleep.

At the garden-gate Mabel sent the carriage away, and then went to the door to waken its inmates; but she had not calculated upon the difficulty of doing this where bell and knocker were not. After some ineffectual attempts, she waited, again to enjoy the exquisite beauty of the night. She had returned into an older and a dearer world, in which she stood alone. After the city's tumult, the stillness of the earth—where every living thing seemed sleeping, was something indescribable; but while she listened to the voice of silence, a nightingale upon the hill woke up his carol to the stars, still pale in the blue sky above, and from the wood by Linstead's cottage another answered him; all the air was fragrant with the night dew on the meadows, where the hay lay strewn in swaths or standing in small heaps, and Elsie's flowers were blooming in the garden; such perfumes Mabel thought she had never known the air laden with before; she did not think how contrast quickens even the natural senses, making perception keener. She felt glad to be alone in the farm-garden, in her childhood's land, with all its waking memories, that, like the answering voices of the nightingales, seemed to echo one another in blessing on every side, songs in the night around her. The sentence of death, uttered on that day for one dear to her as her own life, had brought her nearer to the unseen world. And she was standing now where death had taught her childhood its deep lessons, standing where she had parted with the sister of her heart; with Margery also, her childhood's friend; and where around her in one large circle lay the scattered cottage homes, from which she had seen the poor of this world, rich in faith, departing to inherit the Kingdom prepared for them. Some of them lay sleeping in her sight, within the green churchyard above the valley of the farm. It was an hour of strange, sweet loneliness, amidst, a silent sleeping world around, and wakeful heaven above her; no voice but the nightingale's, no eye except the faithful watchdog's, and the stars in the blue sky still brightening as she looked at them.

But night deepened, and she grew weary. She shook the door, but no one answered. "Elsie," she called, but Elsie did not hear her voice. One sonorous alarm ton. Bell, the watchdog, and some one would have looked from the lattice windows, but friendship kept him silent; he was apt to give many a proof that he considered all must be right when Mabel stood beside him. Within the length of Bell's chain she was safe from any depredators of the night; but no robber by night or thief by day invaded that happy farm, so safe it lay beneath the eye of the Lord God of Israel, under whose wings it trusted. Even in that terrible time—when the evil spirit of incendiarism troubled the land, and night after night, as Mabel looked from her high chamber windows across the horizon, she saw the yellow flames glowing fiercely in the sky, from burning stacks and farm-buildings—Stephen would have no watch kept on their farm; "No," he said, "'It is better to trust in the Lord than to put confidence in man;' we have always laid us down and slept in peace, none making us afraid, and we will not be mistrustful now!" Many a farmer, in those evil days, set up his stacks separately in distant fields; but Margery's children still raised theirs where the farm stacks had always stood, close sheltering the western side of the buildings, and no evil came. Stephen had more earthly security than some, because he had never allowed a pipe on the farm. A pipe or a lucifer match being never seen there, one danger that many were liable to did not arise; if an evil spirit had tempted, there was no fire at hand; and men are less liable to temptation when the brain is not drugged by smoking, or any form of intemperance. Margery's sons themselves never smoked. Benjamin, their father, liked his evening pipe with a friend, but he had too much refinement ever to take it within doors; he built a close laurel arbor at the end of the grass-plat, and whenever he smoked alone, or with friends, it was always in that laurel arbor.

Mabel now thought this laurel arbor would be her best shelter for the night, and it was the nearest to the house; but it looked so dark and gloomy with its closely twisted boughs and small entrance that she rather chose to go on to her own seringa bower. As she was turning down the steps that led to it, the farm door opened, and Matthew looked out, but started back at sight of Mabel in the garden. None had seen her since she left for a home in London, and now to find her in the garden not an hour before midnight, no wonder if he thought it her angel! Matthew had had a misgiving there was something to be seen to, had thought he heard a call, and had come down to look. Then the welcome of the home awoke, and Mabel's tired head was soon at rest upon its childhood's pillow, and the farm reposing again until the dewy sunrise.

The next day brought her brother to the farm, and all was tenderly prepared for his welcome there. It seemed a mystery of heavenly love, that he whose childhood and whose youth had both been given to God, whose brilliant intellect had been a hallowed thing through life, whose heart was ready to pour forth its fulness to win the sinner to his Saviour, and build up the faithful in the holy Word, that he must pass from earth with every gift and grace to bless it, while within the near Rectory dwelt one, living on to advancing age, who darkened the hallowed courts he trod. Yet, "Even so, Father, for so it seemeth good in Thy sight!" We see only the personal preparation here, we see not the place for which each child of the covenant is preparing. Doubtless there is an appointed place for each heir of the Kingdom, and when the point is gained at which the divine work here is ready to pass into the divine work there, the call is heard, "Come up higher." "Delight thyself in the Lord, and He shall give thee thy heart's desire," was fulfilled unto him. One longing thought had guided all his childhood and his youth—to preach the everlasting gospel of the grace of God; that desire was granted him. For a few months he preached with a power never to be forgotten by those who heard; and God vouchsafed to own and bless his youthful servant's word. To the village people of his childhood's home he preached his last sermon; and then, having lifted his voice like a trumpet, passed from the Church militant to the Church triumphant, "made a king and a priest unto God, through Him who had loved him, and washed him from his sins in His own blood.

And so the farm still thought upon the children of the Eastern hill, as gathered with the youth of their own home in Paradise. And years after it was found that Stephen—who through life had never allowed anything to delay his home return upon the market-day, when the Rector's family were gone to London from the Eastern hill, would often stay after business on that day to visit the churchyard beyond the town, in which, for family reasons, had been made the grave of her who yielded her sweet life to God within the shelter of his home. He said, "When all the family were gone I thought there are none to visit and watch that grave, so when the market business was done I often used to say, 'I shall be back at such a time, you have all ready for me then.' And I used to walk and look where they had laid her, for I thought there should be some one still to watch that spot! And I often wished that, as it had pleased God that she should die amongst us here, that she had been buried here amongst us all as you may say, and I have often thought that I would have put up a palisading round the white tomb, and kept her grave a sacred place. For she can never be forgotten by any one of us—to see the sweetness that she showed in life, and the blessing God has made to follow from that hour, as you may say, in which we all received her here. I often sit and wonder, as I think on all the good and holy men, and all the blessed servants of God, from one place and another that He has sent to and fro to us, since the day she crossed the threshold of our home. When I think it over I often drop a tear, and say, 'Surely Thy servant is not worthy of the least of all Thy mercies, and yet Thou hast shown me this great kindness to bring so many of Thy blessed servants to visit here!' And to see how all followed from the day we took that sweet child to our home to die! Often when I think on these things, and on them that are gone, I say that psalm—

> 'Oh! render thanks to God above,
> The fountain of eternal love'—

and those lines of it that certainly will always make a prayer for me—

> 'Extend to me that favor, Lord,
> Thou to Thy chosen dost afford;
> When Thou return'st to set them free,
> Let thy salvation visit me!'"

CHAPTER XXVI.

ON one of Mabel's visits to the farm she persuaded Elsie to return with her for a week to London—Elsie, who had never slept from the maternal roof, never travelled in a stage-coach or covered vehicle of any description, and never seen a railway!—in truth, had "never been on the road behind any horse but their own." The first half of the journey was by coach, at which point it met the railway. Elsie looked grave on the eventful morning, a settled expression of countenance that in more than usual silence showed her determination to go through all. It was much to leave her home and its household duties for the first time in life, much to take a journey by such new and strange conveyances, and much to see London at the end; but with Mabel as her guide, she ventured. The coach, with its four horses, was standing ready in the market town. It happened to be the last day of the old stage-coach; on the next the railway was to be opened to the country town, the ostlers had hung streamers of black crape on the horses by the way of lament, which was no cheerful omen for a first journey, but Elsie only gave them a rather serious smile, and, seated by Mabel in the stage-coach, resigned herself to all that might follow. After three stages the travellers reached the railway station in safety. The train was ready to start, so Mabel drew Elsie's arm in hers, and led her on to the platform. The engine was up, puffing and steaming, and Elsie for a moment held back. Mabel waited, quite sure that her courage would rise to the occasion. "Do you see any great fear?" Elsie asked, as she looked at the tremendous leviathan that was to draw the long line of carriages. "No, I do not see anything to fear; suppose we get safely in here." Elsie silently obeyed, and seated herself in the large cushioned carriage opposite to Mabel, but it was quite evident that the whole arrangement of travelling by smoke instead of "a good horse on the road," was very mysterious, and would have been a doubtful propriety to Elsie, had she not been conducted by one whom she believed "would never be found to go very far wrong." Elsie knew that Stephen had already travelled by railway, having been constrained by courtesy to yield to the pressing requests of the gentleman who yearly visited the farm, to accompany him for a few days to his own estate beyond London. They travelled by coach to London, but there had to take the Harrow line. And Stephen assured Mabel "that no sooner were they seated in the train than the first thing it did was to shoot right away into darkness!" "Well, I thought," said Stephen, "if this be your pleasure in travelling I can tell you it is not mine, and if I once get safe out of the bowels of the earth, I will not go down any more into darkness below ground. I don't know who would, that had always travelled before above in the light!" Matthew also had once travelled by railway, and was unfortunately in a carriage alone, which, as he said, was a very uncomfortable thing, as it was impossible for him to tell whether they might not be going faster than they had any intention of doing, and, shut in there alone, he had no one to ask. But both journeys were safely performed, and now Elsie and Mabel had a carriage to themselves. Elsie shuddered, as might be expected, at the shriek of the engine, proclaiming its desperate intention of drawing them along, and evidently felt doubtful again of being absolutely right in such a situation, looked at Mabel, quieted all moral fears, and kept silence the whole way. She afterwards said that the fine old psalm tune, *Java*, that they so often played of an evening at the farm, made its solemn music in her ears all the way as they travelled, keeping out all her fears after they had once started.

As they completed their journey and entered the low suburbs of the metropolis, above some of its most wretched habitations, Mabel sighed, for she felt the oppressive atmosphere strike on her like the air of an infected chamber; she sighed for Nature passed away, with all its freshness of life and vigor, now again to fade for her into languor and suffering; sighed at thoughts of the throng of careworn faces that would soon people the pathway of the world around her. Elsie understood that sigh, and instantly responded to it by saying, "Don't think about those things that trouble, look up and see the sunset in the sky, how beautiful it is!" Mabel looked at the glory of the clouds over the great city, their gold, and rose and purple, all undimmed by earth, thought of all that might be won by looking up, of the Heaven for ever open above the thronging masses of toil, and want, and weariness, and woe; of the Eternal Eye that rested on each wanderer here; and these thoughts brought relief. Elsie was again silent; it was her wont to say the one thing wanted, and no more.

It was the ebb tide of the city, its throngs pressed on, hastening from the day's toil home.

Elsie, astonished at the mass of moving men, asked if they should not let the carriage stop a little while, until the crowd passed by, adding her expressive pity, "Sure such numbers cannot each one find a home!"

A week was spent by Elsie in London, of which each day became eventful; her grave attention and observation, her pointed and original remarks, her interest without any overpowering surprise, added a charm to "sight-seeing," that Mabel had never felt before. Amongst other sights was the Coliseum. The representation of the day was an earthquake by the seashore. Elsie sat through all the silence of the sea, and through the tossing of the waves, but when the more terrible representations began, she whispered to Mabel, "Do you not think we had better go now?"

Mabel took her out, and then inquired, "Did you feel any fear, that you wished to come away?"

"No, I knew it had no reality; but I think it would be better to leave the judgments of the Almighty alone, and not take in hand to imitate His terrors!"

So spoke the reverential piety of Margery's child, breathing the same dread and love of God's Divine majesty, whether one amidst millions, or alone in the solitary pastures of her home.

The chief hope in a visit to London was a possible sight of the Queen, and of England's royal children, of whom little colored prints hung amidst the birds of paradise on the parlor walls of the farm. And before the week ended, tidings came that the Queen was expected to leave London, from the terminus at Vauxhall. No escort could be obtained at that moment, so instead of venturing to the crowded terminus, Mabel took Elsie to stand upon the unfrequented bridge leading to it. Before reaching the bridge they alighted and walked to its centre, standing there alone; the great river rolling below them, and adown its sides the buildings that traffic with the world. A royal van passed with luggage: Elsie turned pale in her silent expectation: all the heart of England's loyalty beat strong within her breast. Mabel looked at her, thought how the coming moment fulfilled the waking dream of sweet lifetime, thought of Elsie's earliest childhood, when the farm had mourned the Princess Charlotte, thought of all the prayers on bended knees that Margery and her patriarchal children had offered up with fervent feeling for the royal maiden, so early called of God to wear her kingdom's crown. But a policeman with white gloves came hastening on. Mabel said, "The Queen is coming now." Then Elsie for the first time spoke, and answering said, "Oh! don't it make you turn all cold to think what it must be to see her passing by?" A rush of horses' feet from royal stables, a moment's smile on Mabel's lips, full brimming tears in Elsie's eyes, and England's Majesty was past and gone. The royal face was turned away, and the children's eyes were gazing up the river's bend, so Elsie saw them not; but still it was the Queen,—it was those royal children she had so often looked up to upon her parlor walls—that dream of deepest loyalty was real. For a little while she stood silent and motionless, then said to Mabel, "Now I know it is as they have always said, she is the sweetest lady in the land, and they the sweetest children that live upon the earth!" Dear, loyal-hearted child of England, you have believed nothing less since the hour that first breathed their cherished names over the fields, and in the chambers of your home. And had the Majesty of England known that you stood trembling there to see her pass, with all the gathered feeling of a lifetime, surely she would have blessed you with a royal smile.

The farm had received yearly the inspection of the same landed proprietor, whose sympathy and interest had been so warmly called forth on his first visit to Margery.

His strong feeling of friendship never changed, and his confidence was never disappointed. He had no anxiety for the welfare of the farm; but the farm had many anxious thoughts for him. Stephen saw him engrossed with the interests and cares of this world, but he often said, "You cannot put the thing to him, you can only plead it for him; for with all the pleasantness of his behavior as a gentleman, you never heard the word drop from him that tells beyond this world!" He was advancing far in life, and Stephen prayed yet more earnestly for him. One year when he came, all thought him looking ill. He would not stay the night as he usually did, said he felt unwell, and must hasten home. But on that same evening as they were retiring to rest he returned, and said to Elsie, "I fear I am seriously ill, I found I could not reach my home, and I dreaded an inn;—will you take me in?" How gladly the farm with all its kindness received him! Illness increased, and his life was in danger. Hour after hour through the long feverish nights, Philip knelt by him on one side, and Elsie on the other, while he grasped Philip's hand and would not let it go. At length he said to Elsie, "You must go to my portmanteau, you will find a book there that you know all about, and that I never travel without." Elsie went, and found there a volume of Prayers and Meditations, a most favorite book of Stephen's, which he often gave away, and continually used. Stephen had sent some of his best laborers to live on this gentleman's distant estate, who said, he must try and bring his farming up to something like Stephen's! And before they went, Stephen gave each of them this volume of meditations and prayers, called "The Pocket Prayer-book," published by the Philanthropic Society. Their new master had seen it in their cottage homes, had heard whose gift it was, and obtained one for himself. As Elsie brought it to him he said, "I need not tell you how I came by that book! but I may tell you that it is never away from me; I make it my constant companion." And truly Elsie said it appeared like it—to see how its pages were worn! So secretly had the prayers of the farm been answered by God, for him whose tears had once fallen for its widowed mistress.

The cleverest doctor was sent for, who said, "Nothing but the best nursing can save; my medicines can do nothing without that."

"That I have," said the sick man; "so do what you can."

A few anxious weeks and he lived again, and returned to his home, and the doctor, looking upon Elsie, said, "It was only such nursing as yours has been, that by God's blessing has restored him to life." So did this friend, in his hour of distress, prove even in this world, "Whatsoever a man soweth, that shall he also reap."

The Rector of Stephen's parish died; died, alas! so far as human report went, in gloom as hopeless and as dark as the state in which he had lived. It was Stephen's office as parish churchwarden, to supply the church through the short interval until his successor came. Great efforts were made that the time might, if possible, prove one of instruction and benefit to the parish. At length a clergyman from London brought his family to a little house in the village, that the opportunity might not be lost. He was a very plain, impressive preacher, and the poor people flocked to the church. He visited them from house to house, and this stamped reality on his teaching. That long-neglected village church was crowded by the poor, none were absent save the infirm. Stephen listened, and looked around with deepest interest. On the first Sunday that this minister spent amongst them, as they sang their Sabbath evening psalms as usual at the farm, he entered; they were intent upon their songs of praise, and did not see him until they heard his voice joining the melody. And then he took their Sabbath evening prayers. This much affected Stephen, "that at last, after a life of effort and of prayer, there should be that Sunday seen, in which the minister of their church should come and join with them in hymns of praise, and lead their Sabbath evening service!"

One evening Stephen sat silent and thoughtful for some time; at last he said, "I had a thing put to me last night, and I don't know what to say to it! As the minister was walking home with me, he said, 'I want you to tell me what advice you would give to one, who built a house with only half a roof over his head? I suppose you would say, "Get a whole roof as soon as you possibly can?" Well, I could not see much to differ in opinion upon that! Then he said to me, 'This seems to me something like your condition. I come down here, and I find you always have evening prayers in your household; but where are the household prayers of a morning? I can't see that to be better than half a roof instead of a whole one!" He put this to me, and I have been thinking upon it, but I do not see how we are to order it in such a way as we could most wish; all the business lies so early, and the men going and coming, I cannot see how it could be; and it does not do to take a thing in hand and fall under it."

"Never fear that," answered Elsie, with her tone of blessed assurance; "that's a thing that will order itself, and all else that comes with it, if we do but give it the opportunity! There is no reason why we should not make time for family prayers before breakfast, as well as for any worldly concern. I can see it clearly, and so will you when it is done."

"Yes," added Matthew, who never let a good word stand unsupported, "I should say, let us breakfast now one hour later, then we can get everything settled to its place well beforehand, and be as quiet as need be for the family service at seven o'clock, and sit down to breakfast in more comfort after it." So by the next morning it had all ordered itself, as Elsie said it would. At seven o'clock Philip was seated, with his brass spectacles, and the

Bible and book of prayer on a little round table before him, Stephen in his arm-chair, breakfast laid out in the centre of the room, and the family and household seated in chairs round the walls for the first morning prayers. When once begun, no one welcomed it more fervently than Stephen, though at first as a family difficulty it had worn a doubtful aspect to him. But ever after "it ordered itself," as Elsie said it would, and every one rejoiced in the change. So truly is it written, "He that hearkeneth unto counsel is wise."

It was the harvest-time, and the London clergyman took great interest in the ingathering of the grain. Heavy rains fell when the corn was standing in sheaves, and he was not a little troubled at the length of time which Stephen allowed for its drying. Morning after morning he would come from his lodging as far as the farm-gate, to look if the wagons were out for carrying it in. And as one fine day passed another, he urged Stephen not to delay. Stephen was amused at his earnestness. "It troubles our clergyman wonderfully to see our corn standing still in the field. I see he knows more about the minister's, than he does about the husbandman's faith! Why, I shall have to send him to the Bible, to read there how it is the husbandman's that is spoken of as '*long patience.*' I see it is longer than he can take the measure of! He would have me make SURE of injuring the good crop by gathering it in damp, for FEAR He who sent it should not give the opportunity for garnering it dry! He must have more practical faith than that to make him a good farmer! No; I can tell him the right time WILL COME. The question is, shall we have that 'right judgment' we have been so many years taught to pray for, so that we wait with patience until it comes, and act with diligence the moment it does come? Ever since I can remember I have heard it said, 'The season is so dry, there is not moisture for anything to spring;' or, 'the season is so wet, the seed will rot in the ground;' or, 'the weather is so uncertain we must not wait for fine;' or, 'so scorching, the grain will shell upon the ground.' And yet I have never seen but what seedtime and harvest have come, as yet, according to the promise; and I believe they will, and so I farm in trust. And certainly we have been wonderfully blessed, for many is the time when others have made too great hurry for fear, as they said, and spoiled what they gathered; or waited too long, because there was no fear, and so missed the opportunity, when we have been blessed to gather in the crops right. So I always say, take the thing the moment it is ready, but wait until that moment; wait in prayer and trust that He who blessed the springing, will bless the ingathering; but don't go after counsel from any man, for every man's judgment must come from the Lord!" The clouds withheld their rain, and a bountiful ingathering satisfied the anxious clergyman.

Mabel left the farm to stay for a time not far from it. But she was soon sent for again; Stephen had been taken suddenly ill, and begged to see her. She found him with a face of heavenly peace—"he knew not what his Master's will might be," he said, "whether he was now to die or live; and there was one thing he had thought to do that was not done, and he did not know how to put it to any one but her. The new Rector was coming, and it had been in his mind to give every poor man in the parish a good print prayer-book: we could not tell, he said, it might be for good every way! He had a little money to lay out for the parish, and what more was wanted could be added. There was nothing else on his mind; he only wished that God's will might be done for life or for death."

Stephen recovered, and the new Rector came—a Fellow of the College, far advanced in life—and hope died within every heart at his coming. When Mabel entered the cottages, the sick looked up with the earnest, touching anxiety of hope long delayed, and asked, "Have you seen our new minister?"

"Yes."

"Pray, is there any hope in him?"

"Our hope must be in God: Let us think of Him who loved us and gave Himself for us!—He will be our hope for the life that now is, and that which is to come."

Too well they understood the softened answer, and turned their weary eyes away in disappointment's sadness. Yet the Lord's hand was not shortened that it could not save, nor His ear heavy that it could not hear; and that His Name is near, His wondrous works declare.

CHAPTER XXVII.

THE lapse of years had changed the aspect of the Forest Farm; its sheltered lanes and hedge-rows had been laid open by the woodman's axe; one broad sweep of upland and of valley met the eye, where trees of lofty stature and wide-spreading foliage grew. And now a wood, which crowned the sloping hill, above the sweeping curve of a valley, adding exceeding beauty to the scene when the corn waved in the valley,—this wood was sentenced also, and sixty men were engaged, through one hard winter, to clear it for the plough. They did their work with greatest care, so that when for the first time the plough-share cut the woodland soil, not a single edge was turned. Stephen mixed lime in large quantities with the soil, which, mingling with the great amount of decayed vegetable matter already there, produced the richest crop of wheat the neighborhood had ever known. It stood so high as to conceal the reapers, and yet its ear was most abundant. John Wilton had for many years been woodman on the farm, and had felled many a tree within the grove—as this fair wood was called. He was living still in a very bright old age, having passed his ninetieth birthday. And as Stephen stood amongst his reapers in the field, admiring the rich harvest around him, he sent a lad to run to the village and bring John Wilton to him. The old man came, life in his kindling eye, and light in the bright smile that always lived upon his lips. "Come, John, I sent for you because this is a cornfield on the farm you never reaped before!"

"Yes, master, but I have, aye, scores of times, too, with my billhook!"

"Ah, that may be, the green boughs, but not the golden grain; and so I have a mind that the field should not be reaped without the sickle in your hand. Here, give old John the sharpest sickle that you have."

"Oh! master, I can't harvest now."

"Yes, but you can, John, and I say you shall; you take this sickle and put it to the corn, and you shall be reaper on your own account to-day; as many sheaves as you can cut and bind shall be your own. I give my promise; now let us see what skill can do to help out strength."

The old man took the sickle smiling, and all the harvest men as they still cut the corn looked up, with pleasure in their eyes, to see what he would do. Seven sheaves he cut and bound, then put the sickle in his master's hand, "There, sir, I have reaped again, so let none speak too certain against things that yet may be. Thanks be to God for all His goodness!"

"You are a farmer in your old age, John. You must

go home and get your thrashers, and lay up your corn, for those sheaves are yours!"

"No, master, no, 'twas never seen like that. I couldn't call them mine!"

"But I do, John. You send your laborers here to cart them home, but I shall have you carry one. There, I lay this upon your shoulder, and you go home and tell your mistress at the church farm how good a day's work you have done, and say you are come for Beever, and she is to give you a little of the old brown ale, and one of her good harvest cakes." So at ninety, the old laborer, who had worked all his lifetime on that farm, from the happy day when Margery engaged him as her dairy-boy, bore the sheaf, five feet in length, to the church farm, where Margaret gave him a smiling welcome, and hospitable harvest cheer; which the old man said made his old life feel young again. Then bearing through the village the trophy of the day, he sent to fetch the other six sheaves of his harvest, home. So well could Stephen as master both think upon and please the poor.

Everything made it probable that Stephen's would be a bright and vigorous old age; but he had yet to learn his childhood's lesson a third, and last time, "It is better to trust in the Lord than to put confidence in man." And that lesson could only be learned in the discipline of personal suffering.

Foreign missions had long engaged the warm and self-denying interest of the farm. Its whole family attended missionary meeting on the Eastern hill; and of late, Stephen had been driven over by one of his brothers, to a very large one held yearly in a distant parish. "I call it my holiday," he always said, "the day on which I go there, and as I take but one day in the year, I think I may be indulged with a choice upon that!" The day had come round again, and Stephen expressed a wish to go; but an indefinite dread hung over both Philip and Matthew, making them unwilling to drive him.

"But can you see any reason for being afraid?" Stephen asked.

"No," Matthew answered; "but certainly I never felt such a dread."

"If we be frightened at shadows, what good thing shall we hold to?" asked Stephen.

So it was decided to go; but Matthew being the stronger spirit of the two, said, "I cannot do it, I have that on my mind that I never had before, and I will not go against it."

So Philip went, and with the steady horse they then used, he drove Stephen over to the great missionary meeting.

Coming home it was dusk, and Philip kept close to his hedge, thinking other carriages might be following. But a little four-wheeled chaise met them, too near in the darkened lane, lifted up the gig-wheel and turned it over on the bank. Stephen was taken up and carried to a cottage; the clergyman of the parish where the meeting had been held, and where the accident happened, came in to see him, and a doctor set the shoulder which was dislocated. The night passed in intense suffering. At the farm, they watched all night: Matthew walking to and fro in the road in his anxious forebodings.

Towards dawn a man arrived on the horse bringing the tidings, and one of the farm carts with beds was sent to bring Stephen home. Week after week no relief was obtained in the almost intolerable pain. The shoulder had not been rightly set, but nothing could now be done. These were the days of darkness to Stephen! wearied with the exceeding suffering day and night, unable to sleep, seeing only the same anxious, careworn faces that tended him for weeks; expecting that visits of Christian sympathy would follow him from the scene of the accident, but this expectation failed; he had no one able to strengthen his heart in his God, no one with whom he could take "sweet counsel" in his heavy affliction; and he felt it deeply. He had never expected sympathy from the world: he had been content to stand alone while he contended with it; but had looked for it from Christian feeling; and with hope deferred, his heart grew sick. And many a soldier of the cross has had to pass through this same discipline—to learn even of Christian sympathy the "Cease ye from man." Some have suffered and yet not learned it, and so have borne a troubled spirit to the end: it was not so with Stephen; he suffered, but he learned by the things that he suffered. This seemed his last cloud, for when he entered the furnace again, the glory of the Lord shone on him as gold purified seven times in the fire.

Mabel came down to the farm as soon as she was able after Stephen's accident, but many weeks had passed, and he was able to walk out again. She did not arrive until the Saturday evening, seeing him then for a few minutes only; and when she saw him again in the church on Sunday, tears filled her eyes at the wreck of that manly form—the stoop of the upright figure, the withered arm that hung useless beside him and could never raise his flute again; the shrunken shoulder, the head that suffering had blanched whiter, and the downcast aspect of the whole man. But ancient Job congratulates him whom God correcteth, and this was Stephen's happy lot.

He now retired much from active life, though he still walked his farms, and gave his counsel to his brothers; but oftener sat in Margery's chair, placed for him half behind the shelter of the always open kitchen-door. Here he communed with his own heart and was still; and, having set his house in order, he sent his thoughts and affections over death's narrow ford before him, while he, like Jacob, stayed alone wrestling with God and prevailing.

Another cause of dissension had arisen in the parish to trouble him. The poor people, in despair of better days in their church, began to preach to one another. Men of much religious profession, but no practical piety, visited the parish, and encouraged the poor people to set up teachers for themselves; sad scenes of scandal followed, ungodly men professed to have the gift of prayer, and some of the most ignorant could preach. These evils weighed heavily on Stephen's soul, and he besought God to remember their low estate. A short period ended the unhappy and ungodly life of the Rector, and hope rose once more at the farm. Mabel was with them when again they all ascended the green hill to attend another Rector's first service in the church; the voice was earnest and impressive, and the words were the words of truth. Stephen's white head bowed low, he wept abundantly; and all returned home in tears and thanksgivings.

Then kindness and benevolence found a home in that parish Rectory again; and the sweet mirth of childhood, after a century had passed, rang again in its old rooms, and under its noble trees. The beautiful moat, which had been polluted and darkened, was cleansed, and lay deeper and purer than ever, and the poor drank its clear waters from a pump the new Rector raised for them, and the once desolate Rectory wore a bright aspect again; and Stephen thanked God and took courage. His own health was in some measure restored to him, that, by the divine wisdom with which he was yet to turn many to righteousness, he might shine as the firmament, and as the stars for ever and ever. In one or two of his later visits, in which all that passed became known, we may see the gentleness of this veteran in the spiritual field. It cannot be without interest and profit that we trace the foot prints of one who, through a long life, held a course so noble and high, one who, pressed by the business of this world, gave hours to the study of the Bible while its very ministers were sleeping, one who was valiant for the truth upon the earth, and yet stood as "the repairer of the breach, the restorer of paths to dwell in."

On one side of the Forest Farm, and next to its fields, lay another farm of very small size. It was rented by an old man of great stature, but not possessing any other great qualification. His fields were very few, and his skill in cultivating them very small. The old man had not been long in his little farm before he found out that he had kind-hearted neighbors, and he would come down with his great staff in his hand, sometimes to borrow seed for his field, sometimes to beg for a man and horse for one day to sow it. Stephen would say, "Well, poor man, he must get his land planted somehow, but I fancy the day of payment will not be a very near one." So Philip and Matthew would grant his requests. To do good and lend was a principle so woven into all the life of the farm that it flowed naturally from it, though it sometimes gave trouble and difficulty; but "that was got over," as Stephen would say, "the best way it could be; surely it is with such *sacrifices* that God is well pleased."

It was a leisure morning, and Stephen took advantage of it to go up and call on the little farmer of great stature. He did not go to remind him of debts that were due, but to talk with the old man of the love that passeth knowledge. He knew that he was ignorant and cold, and feared that he might be hardened, for his life gave every token of indifference and neglect; but Stephen had paved his own pathway to the old farmer with kindness and good-will—how freely then could he speak of the love of Him who is kind to the unthankful and the evil, who commendeth His love toward us in that while we were yet sinners Christ died for us!

"Well, sir, how is it with you to-day?" Stephen asked of the old man.

"No matters! the world drags so hard, and I can't tell how to ease it a bit; it gets worse, to my thinking, every day that it lasts."

"You find it a bad old world then, it seems?"

"Yes, yes; 'tis so bad that it scarce lets a body live."

"But I suppose, if we come to consider, we shall find that it is all our bad hearts put together that make the poor old world what it is?"

"Yes, yes; folks have bad hearts, some of them at least, and they press you so hard there's no getting along if you be not all as ready as them."

"Well, there's one thing makes me feel how bad this world must be whenever I think of it."

"What's that?" asked the old man, to whom the badness of the world seemed a very welcome theme.

"That He that made it shed tears over it!" answered Stephen.

"What, did He?" said the old man, taken by surprise, and the hard look of indifference passed away from his face at the telling of so touching a fact, which he had never heard of before.

"Yes, He wept over it, because it was so bad, and would not let Him make it better!"

"Well, that's touching to my feelings!" the old man said, and he wiped away the first tear that, perhaps, had ever risen in response from him to love divine.

"It often goes to my heart," Stephen said, "when I think of it. And surely it is for you and me to consider; if He that made us shed tears over our bad hearts, have we ever shed a tear for them ourselves? Now let us sit down for a few minutes, and we will read of the tears shed over us by Him who made us." Stephen read of our Lord's lament over Jerusalem, and the old farmer wept as he listened. From that day he would attend as a little child to Stephen's instruction; and though he left the village when his health failed soon after, who could but hope that he had come there to be made wise unto salvation! This was the simple and beautiful teaching from one village farmer to another. Surely for such is that Book of Remembrance written, "And they shall be mine, saith the Lord, in the day when I make up my jewels, and I will spare them as a man spareth his own son that serveth him."

On the other side the Forest Farm, beyond the wood by Linstead's cottage, lay another farm. The eldest daughter sickened in consumption, and Stephen finding her untaught, and ignorant of heavenly truth, made her an object of his constant care. He saw her days were numbered, and therefore he often spent his temporal strength in the effort to win celestial life for her; and his daily reading and explanation of the Bible by her bed became so precious to her, that if he were hindered any morning from going, she could not be satisfied until her father sent to ask, if it would not be possible for him to come. "The blessed things he teaches me, they are my daily food," she said; "I am always wanting more." Much that she expressed gave a strong hope that death unfolded the gates of endless life to her; and Stephen, her aged teacher, wrote the inscription for the stone that bore the record of her youthful years, and blessed hope of immortality.

Wherever sickness, or want, or sorrow, pined unvisited around the Forest Farm, there Stephen's step seemed sure to pass—as if the good Samaritan came by that way *because* there lay the wounded man. In a distant part of the parish, in a most wretched cottage, lived two old people. It was a rich man's cottage, but he left it in a ruined state, unfit for human life, yet the old people paid the same rent for it yearly, and did not leave it; it would not have been easy to find a vacant dwelling-place; and they loved the old home, so long they had lived together there. Mabel knew them well; they were amongst the circle of her friends. On a visit at this time to the farm, she heard that the old man had died suddenly, and she went to sympathize with his poor widow.

"Oh dear! bless God, now you be come, that's comfort-like, it is! I never thought to see you here again. All troubles that ever came before, were nothing like the loss of my old man to me. I and he had lived together more than fifty years, and never had a hard word one with the other, never! and they came all on a sudden and told me he was dead! It struck like death to me, for he but just before had gone out well! such a feeling came into my head as if my senses must have left me! and they buried him, and that bad feeling kept on still, and I did really think my reason would all leave me. I could not fret, I only felt that senselessness come over me, and the neighbors talked, and said I should be taken to the asylum; and I believed that it must come to that, for I got no rest, and no ease, from that bad feeling in my head. Well, I was sitting here, and I thought all comfort was clean gone for me in my poor husband's grave; and I to be taken right away, as I heard the neighbors say. So there came a knock upon the door, and I heard the footstep of a man, and I never lifted up my head, I could not, I only said, 'You are come, I know, to take me to the asylum!'" Then I heard Mr. Stephen's voice, and he made answer, 'No, woman, no; you are not wanted there, the asylum is no place for you! put all such fancies out, and I will sit down here and let you know a little about where you really are going, and what you must be minding too, and getting ready for it!' Then he takes my Testament—I had not read a word so long; my poor head could not read, and never one had been to read a word to me; and he sits upon that stool, and he begins with the Saviour's own dear words, 'Let not your heart be troubled!' Oh, I thought no sound did ever fall like that; and then I wept. Oh, how I cried! and he still read about those many mansions, and the dear Lord preparing one for me: and I did cry; and then he knelt down there and prayed for me as if he knew all that I could never tell. Oh, how I blessed him! And so I do whenever I sit and think upon it, aye, twenty times a day, for I was not like the same creature when he went away. I am sure he lifted up my poor dead heart to heaven; and there was comfort in them tears I shed. And he was not long before he came again; and so he held on till he cheered me up to life again—and now, thank God, I've got the turn, and so I hope, by His dear mercy, I shall keep on until I be, I trust, made ready for that Heavenly Place." Surely this was to be a son of consolation!

Stephen made his visits in other places beside the cottages; he would find his men at their separate tasks, and had his way of meeting each. There were two of them who knew the Scriptures well, and thought themselves in earnest for eternal life, and yet never drew near unto the table of the Lord. Stephen found them alone, working in a ditch. His men were used to see the master come and stand a little while beside them. This day, when he had done so, he said, "I suppose if I were to ask you two to do a thing at my request, you would not do it?"

"Not do it, sir? that we would, let it be what it might."

"What, do you say that I have only to ask, and you would certainly do it for me?"

"Yes, sir; try us!"

"Well, then, I do say here is a strange thing, and you greatly surprise me. If I ask you a thing, you will certainly do it. I, a poor sinful mortal like yourself! and yet you have no heart to do that thing that was the last request of Him who is your God, you say, and even died for you. Now I advise you to consider what a situation your own words show you to be in. You say you will certainly obey my word, while yet you have continued to disobey the word of God! Now, must you not be deceiving yourselves when you think that the Lord is your God? Know ye not that he is your master to whom ye yield yourselves servants to obey? Now, I did but put a simple question, yet that is enough to show you your true situation. What, I ask you, can your religion be, if you put a poor sinful man up so high; and your blessed Saviour so low that you can turn aside and disregard even His dying request? So I can only say, May God, of His infinite mercy, give you and me the Holy Spirit, without which there can be no doing the will of God from the heart, whatever we may think of our knowledge of Him." Stephen would say, "They want teaching put to them in a plain, simple way, and sometimes to be put in such a way that they cannot tell always what is coming; that they may be more apt to see the thing in its true light, when perhaps if they thought what was coming they would set their minds against it."

When Stephen thought a personal address might be doubtful, he would take up his pen and write to his men, though this was a much greater effort. Thinking one of his younger laborers not kind as a husband, he wrote to him in all gentleness and truth, setting before him, from the Bible, the sin and the misery of such a course, and the blessing of family affection and heavenly love. The young wife found a change in her husband for the better, but did not know the cause, until some time after she accidentally saw the letter, and told Mabel of it with tears.

Stephen would say, "Sometimes, if you must give reproof, the hasty spirit is less apt to rise against written words than spoken ones, and has more time to consider; and perhaps you too are safer, not so likely to speak too sharply or in anger. So we must consider all ways, and do what is best."

"The fruit of righteousness is sown in peace, of them that make peace!"

CHAPTER XXVIII.

THREE years had passed away since Stephen's accident, and Mabel was again at the farm. They had good tidings to tell. The Rector of a market town some few miles distant, had consented to have a missionary meeting held there, and to preside over it himself. "Now there was hope," Stephen said, "for whenever the cause of the heathen abroad was taken up, he had seen that a blessing was not withholden at home!" It was beautiful to look upon the joy of the farm as it hailed this first ray across a long darkened horizon. All were going who could possibly arrange to do so. Three different carriages were fitted with horses from the farm, and only Mabel and Stephen and the maid left, with Bell the watchdog, as evening guardians of the home. It was the first and last evening that Mabel ever spent alone with Stephen; the joy of this awakening of missionary interest had brightened his aspect above its now usually chastened tone; the cause lay so near his own heart, he "expected so much to follow after it, so little without it! It was the very spirit of Christianity, and must rise or fall with that spirit, 'The love of Christ constraineth me,' because we thus judge that 'if one died for all then were all dead, that henceforth they which live should not live unto themselves, but unto Him that died for them;' and how was that to be ordered, but by fulfilling the law of Christ—to love our neighbor as ourselves; and He had Himself shown us who He considered our neighbor to be!"

When Nathaniel, the miller, was taken to his rest, Stephen had said, "I should not like my poor brother's offering for the work of missions to end with his life; I would have his subscription carried on the same. I know his name must be let drop, but the money can be added unto mine, and that will always be paid all in one!" Whenever Stephen saw an effort made privately or publicly for missions, he put forth his hand to strengthen it. "If we think—or if we know it to be the Lord's work, why then we must encourage them that have the heart to undertake it!"

The evening passed on, and Stephen drew many a retrospect in humble thanksgiving to God, and turned to the ever brightening future—as faith alone can turn, beholding it all in the light of the promises of God, which are Yea and Amen in Jesus Christ. The fire was made up with faggots of wood, which blazed and lighted up the quaint walls of the kitchen, the shutter was left down that the window might prove a beacon light of welcome along the distant road, for it was a rare thing for any one of the farm to be absent through an evening, and still more for all but one to be away. The supper table was set ready. Stephen often stepped to the door to listen, and at last his quick ear caught the sounds. It might have been thought they had been absent for months, from the beaming expression of Stephen's face as he looked on them, each one in their safe return; his own shattered frame and chastened aspect still telling what one such evening return had cost him. And also his forgotten vest of blue, for since that accident had shattered him he had worn only black, as if indifferent what his garb might be. They smiled at their home welcome, but no pleasure sat on their faces.

"Was it a good meeting?" Stephen inquired.

"I should say any thing but good!" Matthew answered, with decided displeasure.

"Not good?" asked Stephen; "how came that about?"

"There was more laughing there," said Elsie, "than might have been thought belonged to such things as they had to tell."

"Laughing!" exclaimed Stephen, in his severest tone of surprise.

"Yes," said Philip, kindly, "it would all have been well enough, but the deputation from London seemed to think he stood there to entertain all the people; so he told of the heathen and their doings, in that curious way that turned it too much to mirth for so solemn a thing. And though we knew they were no gods but false idols as you may say, yet he could not rid the laugh quick enough when he came to the true God.

"I think he might have learned a lesson for life," Matthew said, "if he had been where I stood, at the lower end of the room, where all the farm lads were gathered together, and young women there also, and after he had once set them laughing there was no more seriousness there, but only a look out for what mirth might come next. He might think he came there to do good, but I can tell him he did a very different kind of work."

"I am very sorry," said Mabel; "I don't know how it is, but sometimes good men think they must do what they can to enliven a meeting."

"I can not think much of his being a good man!" replied Matthew; "if he were, he would surely know better what are fit occasions for entertainment. I would not say that he could not be what he ought for a smile, I am sure; but to keep it on like that, I do say it, and if he goes about to make mirth at the heathen's idolatry, I think the money he gets will scarce pay for the harm."

"Sure, he must have sometimes considered that text," said Stephen, "where God says of idolatry, 'Oh, do not this abominable thing that I hate!' Let him make his discourse in that spirit, and it will not bring laughter, unless it be the laughter of fools."

Mabel could but silently feel, "Would that this village criticism could reach many an ear!" The deputations of societies sometimes little think what they do when to enliven a meeting they violate the deepest solemnities of the subject before them. Good angels may wonder and evil spirits rejoice, when every opportunity for a comic turn is embraced, in order to enliven an audience who ought to be humbled and solemnized, at fresh tidings of the degradation of their fallen humanity. The speaker's feeling may be deep enough to recover its true tone, but it is often not so with the hearers; and the village laborer turns away to think of the curse of idolatry as a child's play, the hearing of which amused him like the tale of a pantomime. Surely these things never ought so to be!

It was striking and beautiful to observe the change in Stephen's silent hours. In years gone by he might be daily seen, sitting long lost in thought, and it was evident to a close observer's eye that his mind was actively engaged in Meditation. Now his chastened aspect told another tale; many a silent hour he passed in the day seated in his arm-chair, half concealed and shaded by the room's open door, always as erect as his now stooping form could be, with one hand folded in the other; but as you looked upon his face you felt the spirit's active work of Meditation had passed into the more passive but not less blessed one of Contemplation. It is only the soul that has accustomed itself to active meditation on divine things, which can ever in any high degree attain the true and heavenly grace of Contemplation. It may surely be said that if the first act of the divine life be a looking unto Jesus, its last is a contemplation of Him. All the active conflict with the world with Stephen was over;

clad in the whole armor of God, every part of which had been put to the proof through his long and energetic life, he now waited at the threshold of the eternal Kingdom; looking back in humble thanksgiving, looking forward in adoration, and "the full assurance of hope unto the end." Sometimes as he sat, absent in spirit, though present in person, a smile would pass across his face, of which his outward man seemed as unconscious as the still lake of the sunbeam that lights up its surface; but the sunbeam on his face was no passing glory caught by reflection from the outer world, it was a spirit-smile from the hidden life within. It was seldom noticed in words by others, he was generally at such times left undisturbed in the silent sanctuary of his own thoughts, but at times Mabel would ask, "What was it made you smile?" And beautiful the answer always was, if answer came; for it might be that he would only say, with a more conscious smile, "I can not always undertake to give account of all my thoughts!" or he would tell the passing vision, "Well, I was then looking back through this generation and them that went before it, and I was thinking, surely it was a blessed thing that I could say with Job, that 'I have not eaten my morsel myself alone, but the poor hath eaten it with me; that I have not seen the poor without covering, but they have been warmed with the fleece of my flock;' and I hope I may say that 'the fatherless have been brought up with me, and that I have guided the widow from my youth!'" Here his voice faltered, and his white head bowed lower, and none could wonder, for touching as blessed must the retrospect of life have been to him.

Or again, another day, "I was thinking upon that fourth chapter of the Revelations, that has been greatly dwelling in my mind of late; that open door into heaven, and that trumpet calling, 'Come up hither!' I have often been thinking lately, Shall I see that open door, and hear that blessed call? I, who am not worthy of the least of all His mercies, how unworthy then must I be of the greatest! And so that dwelt greatly upon my mind, until I had a dream, and in my dream I thought I saw that open door, and heard that sweetest music blown— that trumpet calling me. I thought I looked in at the door, and saw the angels in their glory, and all the Hosts of Heaven. Then I felt, I dare not go in there! But as I looked I saw One at the further end, seated on a throne, His raiment so dazzling white I could not look upon Him, but He spoke and called me by my name, and said, 'Be not afraid, but come to Me!' then I thought that I could venture, and I went; but as I went, I woke; so I suppose I woke with joy! And I must believe such dreams are sent to them who give their hearts unto these things.

"Another time I was thinking how many preachers the country is blessed with now, men of great power. It is a wonderful thing to have such a change in my day; and tracts written so plain! Yet I must still say that for my part I shall never think any can get before that 'still small voice,' that used to teach me in that little church upon the hill! They that have all this power, I don't say but what it is a great and good gift, still they do need the more to remember that it is 'not by might, nor by power, but by My Spirit, saith the Lord.' And I think sometimes when they put it as if they were determined to thrust the truth upon you, that don't do so well as when it comes in that 'still small voice.' Oh, what great instruction there is to be seen in the visit of that holy man Elijah to the cave at Horeb! and if it was only in 'that still small voice' that the Lord drew near, that must learn us how attentive we had need be to His gentle teaching, not to wait for some great thing! for we see when that great thing comes, the Lord may not be with it. He says, 'My words shall drop as the rain, My speech shall distil as the dew, as the small rain upon the tender herb;' it is that tender heart we want, and then a small thing will do it; and without that, a great thing will not succeed. So I shall think none the less of my 'Zoar,' as it used to be, even though I might say of it, 'Is it not a little one? and my soul shall flee there that it may live!'"

Mabel was at the farm the last time that its oldest laborer, John Wilton, came to visit it, in his ninety-second year. His masters sometimes sent a little cart to fetch him up, to cheer his aged eyes with the sight of all most dear to him on earth. On this day one brought word that old John Wilton was come. Philip hastened out to lead him in, and as the day was cold, a chair was put for him upon the hearth-rug before the great wood fire. He stood a moment at the doorway, and smiled with more than earthly love on all before him; his countenance was radiant, as if already celestial joy and tenderness illumined that aged face. Seated before the fire, the old man looked down upon the hearth-rug, then lifted a bright glance of pleasure and surprise to Elsie, for in the centre of the rug he recognized the picture of the prize horse of the farm. Elsie always made the large hearth-rug; when one was worn out, she made another of small shreds of cloth, knitted in with twine. In the centre she wrought the prize horse, in scarlet cloth, so true to life, with his long tail, that old John Wilton knew him; he stood on smallest strips of green cloth, with an atmosphere of dark shreds around; and on either side of him two other horses, in the shade of a respectful distance, one of drab and one of grey shreds. The whole rug looked very imposing, and the old man's innocent surprise and pleasure were certainly flattering. The aged laborer was now so deaf, that only Philip's tones could penetrate his ear. Deafness seemed a benediction on him, for, living with his most ungodly children, he was, by his deafness, "hid secretly as in a tabernacle, from the strife of tongues." His soul was full to overflowing of words divine, words of peace and love, of praise and blessing; he did not need a single earthly voice to breathe hope, or prayer, or assurance for him. He had always "a song in the night, and gladness of heart, as when a holy solemnity is kept."

He spent his time between his own solitary communion with God, and exhorting others to seek the same Saviour—the light of whose countenance all saw irradiating him. His retirement was a certain lonely hedge, where he spent hours with his Bible; and whenever he met any by the roadside or the field, or on the wayside-settle of the village inn, he still accosted them with words that truth and love made eloquent. All knew his blameless life, his meek endurance of the ill conduct of his children—a sorrow sowed by his own earlier Sabbath neglect of them; and all knew the care and kindness of the farm for him. His earthly hope had been fulfilled—he had never received the parish pay; the farm kept all his wants supplied, with the assistance of the gentleman who yearly visited the estate.

Philip kneeled on one knee beside him, shouting into his deafened ear—

"Well, John, so you have come to see us all again!"

"Yes, to be sure I have! What sight upon earth can be like this to me? Why, did not I carry our master Stephen a babe in my arms; and did not I know each one from its birth? I say there can be nothing like it to me upon earth! And I can tell you something else: I have carried away heaps of money too; fifteen hundred pounds I have carried away in my service and my family's from this house. And I took care of it, too, when I had got it! I have had a large family, and never a penny from the parish; and my master Stephen says if I live to a hundred, I never shall!"

"No, NEVER!" said Stephen with his resolved smile.

"Why, I have worked seventy-six years on this farm. God bless ye all! And now I am ninety-two years of age, and the Lord hath not left me, no, nor ever will! But I read that in the last days perilous time shall come, and I can see they are come. The Lord help us to look up to Him; to see how He laid His bright robes of glory away to save sinners! and if we have been loiterers in the Lord's vineyard, we must be so no more."

"Then do you think the last times are come?"

"I can't answer to that, sir, because I can't see into those deep things; but I think they are drawing on." Then raising his face, **radiant as if** Heaven beamed upon it, he said in his loud, joyous tones, "I think MY last days are come! and I pray that the Gospel may cover the earth as the waters the channels of the great deep; that Thy glorious Name may fill all the earth. Amen and amen!"

Then the smile of his whole countenance passed into an expression of deepest adoration, as lifting his hands he prayed, "O say unto my soul, I am thy salvation!" He rose to go, and with an old man's courtesy bowed low to Mabel, whom he had known from her childhood. He could not hear her voice, but he took her offered hand in both of his, and grasping it said, "Dear lady! I don't think my God will ever forsake me! I have a SURE HOPE, a STEADFAST HOPE, and I trust it will prove a TRIUMPHANT HOPE!" And so they parted from the radiant old man, who looked back from the doorway, leaning on Philip, to shed one smile more upon all; it was his parting benediction. A few days afterwards he returned from his hedge in the fields, laid down to sleep, and awoke no more. That bright smile and those joyous tones were gone from the roadside and the field, lost to the traveller and the friend; but of his death it might be truly said, "Lord, if he sleep he shall do well."

It was not alone the village poor whom the farm welcomed as its guests; genius, and intellect, and high station, and eminent piety all found there a pleasant atmosphere. Occasionally a heart of lower tone would come, as companion or associate of some familiar guest, and it was not without its interest to observe that, while every courtesy was shown, the farm distinguished, and never made over to one unworthy of it, the freehold of its friendship; and sometimes when Mabel talked of other friends who might be coming, Elsie would answer, "Let any come who will do us the favor, if only you come at the head of them!"

And many thoughts the farm sent to where, beneath an Indian sky, the eldest daughter of the eastern Rector, with her husband, was gone to dwell. He had turned to the work of educating the degenerate intellect of India's heathen people, that they might be aided mentally, as well as morally, to receive the truth that maketh free. There, loved by Hindoo and Mohammedan, as he had been before by Christian undergraduates here, his highest aim was still to show them that, from generation to generation the Lord is God! Reveringly the farm thought of him, and tenderly of her; while she, beneath a foreign sky, was welcoming each missionary step, and every Christian worker; able to understand how intellect and human genius may have its work for God—converging rays from every point meeting in a circle of grace and glory around the cross of Jesus Christ.—Remembering that St. Paul, who magnified his office as the Apostle of the Gentiles, called in the aid of earlier truth, that their own poets taught them, and while obeying the divine command—"TELL IT OUT AMONG THE HEATHEN THAT THE LORD IS GOD"—strengthened and confirmed that testimony unto them, by the yet echoing voice of their own departed wisdom.

The farm still asked, "When shall we see them home again?" until a brother of the absent said, "What would you say if your own laborers left their work at noonday?" This question was a final answer, and silence sealed the longing hope the farm still entertained.

CHAPTER XXIX.

"I CANNOT think it to be right that you should now always come down in our dullest time of year, when the November fogs are here, and never see your own country, as we may say, in its pleasant spring-time!" said Stephen in an expostulating tone to Mabel.

"I will come if I can another year, as you say, in the pleasant spring-time."

"Suppose, then, you set a time, if it please God to grant it; for I consider when you have a settled time you can better tell how to conform your work to meet it. I should say, let it be the month of May, and so take all the spring-time as it follows."

So it was settled for the month of May; and when Mabel left the farm, all veiled in damp November fog, Stephen said, "We shall look brighter for you when you come back in May!" And Mabel said to Elsie, "You will look for me in May?" but Elsie answered, "I cannot look far forward. Day by day, is all I ever dare to reckon on or undertake with. But let your coming be when it will, you must be welcome, be it at midnight, or at the crowing of the cock, or in the morning!"

"Day by day," was Elsie's maxim, and the secret of

her calm untired cheer. She would say, "He who knew what the mind could bear, did condescend to teach us that! and sure we don't ought to drag down on ourselves a bigger burden than He saw good to lay! I never will engage, nor even look beyond the day, for I am sure His wisdom lies far above mine, and what He pleases to bring upon me He will enable me to bear, but how could I expect Him to undertake for what He never laid out for me to stand under?" So Elsie would not speak of May, yet made her own refined allusion to Mabel's evening surprise of the sleeping farm, to assure, if assurances were needed, that the welcome of a lifetime would never be wanting there. Stephen had also his household maxim; it was, "He hath set one thing over against another." When trial or difficulty arose, Stephen looked out for its opposite cheer, and was sure to discover it; for the spiritual eye, unlike the natural, weakens not by much using, but strengthens continually more and more, until it gains power to penetrate all clouds and mists, that to a less exercised vision obscure the objects of faith; or if the darkness impenetrably conceals them, it has its yet higher triumph, and enables the spirit to endure as seeing that which is invisible.

The London winter passed away. April poured its tide of life into the great city, and Mabel thought of the spring-time at the farm; but May had come and almost gone, and she had fixed no day for going there. To save her promise she would write, and fix the last day of the month, but before her letter went, one came to her, bearing few words—"Our brother is, we fear, departing; the doctor says that twenty-four hours must see all over." Mabel lost no time, but hastened down that day, if possible, to see her friend. The cottagers came out as she drew near the farm, and said, "He is living still, though at the worst, they say!" No one stood at the garden gate, none came stepping down the white stone steps to welcome her. Mabel entered the deserted kitchen, where the fire burned low and dim, and all was silent. Then she heard voices in the parlor, and Philip came and said they had laid him there, that they might all be better able to watch around him. They feared to tell him who was come, but they had no need to fear; he had long ceased to lean on any earthly friend; that lesson had been learned before; and Stephen's was a spirit that went from strength to strength, never needing that any should teach him again the first principles of the oracles of God. The meeting was peaceful, as of those who side by side have, ever as they met on earth, looked onward in faith and hope into the bright depths of Eternity. Stephen laid his hand in hers, and faintly said, "I am so thankful you are come! now I have all I want; with them around, and you in the midst, there must be a blessing!" He had been very ill for weeks, but it was not the habit of the farm to write unless immediate danger threatened, always hoping for better days. The night watchers took their place before Mabel left the room, always three in number, because of the distressing nature of the illness, and one of these was always Linstead, the reaper king. Mabel saw him stepping in without his shoes, his face so grave and sad as he looked upon his master—and without a sound seated his stalwart figure on a little stool behind his master's chair. For six weeks Stephen had not laid down; severe pain, a sense of suffocation, and continually returning faintness, weakening his once most vigorous frame. Sometimes no rest could be obtained, except by lifting him off his feet in a standing posture upon their shoulders, where they held him until themselves exhausted, while he, unconscious of their effort, would still exclaim, "O hold me up a little longer; it is mercy, it is relief, it is almost ease!" Yet Elsie and Philip added, "You could never think the place his sick-room is, unless you were to see. When he revives he is more cheery than in all his life before, and, what is more, he will have you be cheerful also. Not but what the tears do come, but he will make the smile to follow quicker than could be thought upon them. His heavy burdens seem so lightsome-like to him!"

"Will you let them call you, if I should depart before the morning? I should wish to see you stand beside me, if it might be, then."

Mabel answered, "Yes; let them call me any hour, and I will come."

All believed that death stood at the threshold, and any moment might enter in. Already its shadow seemed to have fallen on the changed countenance, and suffering and disease contended fiercely with the mortal life. The doctor left the next day, saying, that half an hour, he thought, must be the limit of existence here. He estimated the strength of disease, but not the strength of that manly frame. Naturally vigorous and healthy, a life in fields and woods, and, above all, those early mornings, when, at the breaking of the day, Stephen arose and went abroad with all the freshness of nature round him, to drink the living waters of eternal truth—those early mornings had so invigorated every natural function, that now disease had come, it seemed almost in vain that it battered and besieged the castle of his earthly life. Yet the doctor still said he must die, and that it would be in a moment when it came. All believed it; Stephen longed for it, and smiled at death, while all around him wept. It was under this constant strain of expectation of the final issue, that all had been watching for weeks and were watching still. Yet painful as it was to witness sufferings beyond the power of earthly aid to alleviate, never could the chamber of sickness have been more cheered. No need for Margery's western window to illuminate that little parlor with the radiance of the setting sun, when light from Heaven was pouring down its bright effulgence there! A retentive memory enabled Mabel to write down Stephen's words, at eventime, when she had left him for the night, without any change of expression; and it cannot be without its interest and its profit to follow this veteran soldier of the Cross, through the days when in each passing moment heart and flesh were failing him, and God alone the realized strength of his soul and his portion for ever.

On the morning after her arrival, as Mabel looked at his changed and suffering countenance, he marked her saddened face, and smiling said, "Well, but we don't want to take a care on her minds, do we, if He cares for us? Yet that was a true word which you once told me, that I should find a passive life harder than an active one; harder to suffer, than to go and do! But HE says, My grace is sufficient for thee; my strength is made perfect in weakness." After another most suffering struggle, instead of faith being weakened by it, it only triumphed higher, as with a smile of tender soothing on all who watched his meek endurance, he said, "Well, I suppose we must all go on our way rejoicing, like the Eunuch; for by what I can feel it will not be long before a change will come, and then to seek that open door and hear that trumpet call to Heaven!"

"What is the time?" he asked, when better; then called his orphan niece to him, who with Elsie, her aunt, was still his constant nurse, and said to Mabel, "When my illness came first upon me I said to her, 'Now, child, you shall be my minister, and mind you do what I tell you in all respects. Every morning and evening you shall read to me the Confession, some of the prayers, and the Psalms; in times past they have done me the greatest good!" I was often so distracted with suffering, that I was ready to say to every one, 'Go out of my presence.' 'Now, child, lock the door; I don't care who may be there, no one shall come in.' Well, then I had those prayers, and those Psalms, and then I seemed like a new creature. 'Come in; I can see any of you now!' That will show what PRAYER can do! I do say nothing can come nearer to the spirit of the Scriptures than those Church prayers; and for their brevity and comprehensiveness what can be like them! What is wanted is that we should go into the spirit of them more ourselves, and carry them out in our life, and set the spirit (not the mere words of them) before others!"

In the evening Philip, sitting beside him, told him of one of the transactions of the day, in which he had been obliged to meet "the wrongful doings of man." Stephen listened, and when he had heard all, he said feebly but firmly, as one counselling not only for the present moment, but for the future, "Don't be in a hurry to act against such men, nor even to speak! No, wait, and leave them in the Hand of God. I have watched the course of many such unprincipled men, and then have had to say, what hath God wrought!" Then after silence, in which the shadows of sad memories seemed to cross his countenance, he said, "I and my family have been much spoken against, I know! but they said of my blessed Saviour, 'He hath a devil, and is mad,' and they cannot say worse than that of me." And ever as he named his Saviour, he seemed to run into that high tower—the Name of the Lord, and feel safe, and with that heavenly safety the shadows passed away, and he added, "Has not God said that He will make all His servants' bed in their sickness? And so, though all through my life there has been so much to disturb and try, now, by God's great mercy, there seems not anything!" It was most affecting to hear this utterance of 'nothing to try him,' notwithstanding the extremity of his illness and distress. It did but testify to the blessed fact, that

> "Jesus can make a dying-bed
> Feel soft as downy pillows are,
> While on His breast I lean my head,
> And breathe my life out sweetly there."

The retrospects of life uttered by him, responsively to some passing word or circumstance, were beautiful; and heard as they were in presence of his suffering and unrest, they often filled the listeners' eyes with tears.

"I took those opening verses of the twenty-sixth chapter of Isaiah in my youth; I took my stand by them. 'There,' I said, 'is my part laid out—"to keep the truth"—and that other is God's part! "Thou wilt keep him in perfect peace whose mind is stayed on Thee;" God will do that!' So I settled myself there; and I had afflictions and trials, but I went through them, as you may say, by that word!"

His affections lingered in fond memories on his young brother, Edward. He would say, "Read me my young brother's psalm"—the twenty-fifth; and then in thankful calm recall the days, when, before he hastened to the claims of business, he always sat down beside the dying boy, and read that favourite psalm to him.

After a long conflict with the difficulty of breathing, when he could speak again, he said, "There was a thought that came to comfort me in that long struggle. When I was in my health and strength, there was an old man on the farm, who had worked on until his breath distressed him greatly, but still he would work on, and not give in to parish pay. So one day, when he came for orders, I said, 'Legget, you shall work no more!'

"'What, sir, will you force me on the parish?'

"'No, you shall not work again, but neither shall you go upon the parish!' So there was soon a settling of that: and now, when I was labouring so for breath, I thought of that old man, and how hard it would lie on my thoughts, if I had let him labour on!"

Two little orphan children came from a distance to see Mabel—their mother had been trained in the school upon the Eastern hill, and her children were brought by their grandmother, to see their mother's friend. Knowing Stephen's love for children, and that he had now an interval of partial rest, she led them in, and set them at his knee, as he sat in his arm-chair, in which he was never able to lean back, unsupported—except at times by a friendly arm. It was many weeks since Stephen had seen the face of a child—the sight so familiar, and always dear to him in all his busy life. He often said, with a glad look upon his harvest fields, "All this was planted by the hands of little children; and I shall always say there is no planting, for the wheat-fields, to equal theirs. Those little labourers in our fields, I often reckon to be our best!" When Stephen saw the little stranger children at his knee, he smiled most tenderly upon them, and said, "What, can you say to me some text from the Holy Bible?" The children lisped the twenty-third psalm to him, and most beautiful the picture would have been, could an artist's eye have caught it, of Stephen's drooping frame, his aged and suffering—yet beaming countenance, as it looked so tenderly upon the little orphans at his knee, who, with blue eyes uplifted, with their rosy lips repeated the words that were earth's sweetest music unto him. Mabel, seeing that it pleased him well, fetched in her gifts for them—a shepherd's coat for the little boy, and for the little girl a frock; the children were very young, and both delighted with their presents: but Stephen was not so well satisfied; he weighed the relative value of the little winter coat, and the small-print frock; and when the children were gone out with Mabel, he said to Elsie, who, through their visit, stooped on one knee beside his chair, "What, Elsie, can you not find up something more for the little girl? I never saw Miss Mabel do the thing so uneven before! She seems to me not to have thought enough of that poor little girl: do go and bring her portion up to her little brother's. Sure you can find something? It is more than I can stand, to see her come off so short!"

When his justice was satisfied, he thought on them with unmingled pleasure: "Poor little boy, he had a smile for everything; he will not look so happy when he is a man!" On through the day his musings were of children, and when he spoke aloud it was still of children—of Joseph—then of the sweet child in their own parish Rectory, for whom his daily prayer had been offered up since his infant life began; he charged Elsie to send him a favourite picture of the infant Samuel, from the walls of the guest-chamber, and to say with his parting love, that his daily prayer had been for that dear child, that he might be like Samuel, that God by His Holy Spirit might early speak to him, and that he might answer, "Speak, Lord, for thy servant heareth!" "There was a person to whom I once showed a little book, and when he returned it, he said, 'It might do very well for children.' 'For children!' I asked, 'why, I have read in the Bible that out of the mouth of babes and sucklings, God has PERFECTED praise! Be sure it comes purer from their lips, than from yours or mine! And I have read, that of such is the Kingdom of Heaven; and that, except we become like little children, we shall never enter there. How then are we going to order, if we cannot learn as a little child?'"

It was the calm of Saturday evening at the farm, and well Stephen knew the time. He called his watchers round him and said, "Now let us pray! we have need to pray for all who watch beside the sick, that their short sleep may be doubly blessed to them, so that they may be refreshed and able to read God's Word, and pray to-morrow. Even if we cannot go unto the house of God to-morrow, we can have a church in our own house: St. Paul had, so certainly we may." It could not but be most endearing to all around him, to hear the only special direction he gave was, that the watchers by the sick might be remembered in prayer. Through all his most suffering illness, his spirit, by its thoughtful tenderness and heavenly tone, gave a constant freshness to all around him. One said to him, "Yours must, I think, be the most cheerful sick room ever seen!" "That is what I wish," he replied, "and not only what I wish, but what I intend it should be: no one but the patient can ever make the sick room cheerful! When I found what an affliction was coming upon me, I thought to myself, 'Now here will be a long sorrow for them all,' (not sorrow one way, for they have made the waiting upon me only a pleasure,) but I thought to myself, 'Now I must do what I can, that it may not be too trying for them. I must try and make it so that they shall feel, each one, the wish to be with me;' and so I think it has been!"

Both were touching and beautiful—the unmurmuring patience with which he bore the exceeding distress of his bodily affliction, and the playfulness with which in every interval of relief, he brightened for others the oppression of the chamber of suffering. Elsie knelt for hours beside him day and night, and he would still win a smile amidst her falling tears. Once, with deepest tenderness, he said, "You will not have to weep so many tears, when this is over, as you do now! But our Lord has said He does take notice of His servants' tears—they are not lost! And that is a blessed word of His for His dear servants to think upon, 'Inasmuch as ye have done it unto one of the least of these, my brethren, ye have done it unto ME.' You see, He says, all these folks that you think you have been doing all these things for, it's not them, it's ME ye have done it unto!"

To Mabel he said, "It is a most singular thing that all my illness I have had a most distressing nervous feeling, so strong that I hardly knew how to bear it; as if there were always another person ill in this same room, and all done for me I had to do for this person. I had them carry me out; but still I could not get away from this person. But now, to-day, Matthew has shown me how it is; he tells me, what is true enough, that all my life long I have had more concern and more to think of for other people than myself; so that in my illness I have thought there was another for me to see after! Ever since I was a boy, as you may say, I went in and out and had no teacher. But the Lord was my Teacher, and there are two texts of Scripture that have been food to me all my life long, 'Inasmuch as ye have done it unto one of the least of these, my brethren, ye have done it unto ME;' and 'Pure religion and undefiled, before God and the Father, is this, to visit the fatherless and widows in their affliction, and to keep himself unspotted from the world.'"

"Now, let us pray!"—this he would often say, as though it were his very life. "You see, I have nothing to disturb me; all goes on without me just as well as when I was about. And do you consider that I am to sit here eating a little food, and taking a little physic, and then a little more food, and then creep into a corner like a snail for the night, as if that were all! No: I want prayer! I want to pray! Now, put me on my knees, and let us pray!"

"Do not fear; I wish to show that, as long as it is possible, I approach my God in the humblest manner; and what if Death does come, you will not be alarmed. The ending of all my prayers has always been, 'Be with me this day, and in the day of my death,' and having prayed that once, yes, three or four times, every day, I KNOW it will be answered!" Every attempt to dissuade him from kneeling failed. He who from his youth had knelt so reverently in the sanctuary of his God, he who evening after evening knelt in the lonely pit for prayer, he who had kneeled so often by the bedside of the dying, could not yield that posture of adoration. "What if death should come? I am not afraid of death! Don't I know that I must meet my God some way, and I would rather meet him on my knees than any other way!" Sometimes his head drooped on Elsie's, yet still he faintly murmured the petitions loved so long, and which had moulded all his life into the likeness of his Lord. Sometimes he could not in exhaustion kneel, and his weary eyes would close in restless sleep while all around him prayed. On recollection coming back, he would say afterwards, "Oh, I am so vexed; nature seemed gone and I was forced to go! but you must not allow it at such times; I tell you you must not!"

"But," one asked, "don't you know it is written in the Bible, 'God giveth His beloved sleep.' Now, if God gives you a little sleep sometimes, to rest and soothe you in your weakness, are we to say you shall not have it, and keep it from you?" He turned his face directly with that joyous look, that through life always kindled upon it when he was answered or refuted from the Divine word, and said, "No; you are right, quite right; that Word must be the beginning and finish of every thing."

Then came a long, agonizing struggle, but life lingered still, and the tide of suffering ebbed again from the exhausted frame. He smiled as he looked back from the shore he had so nearly won, and said, "Well, there will come a time when the spirit will get the better and leave the poor body behind it, and a voice will be heard, saying, 'Arise, and depart, for this is not your rest.' No, this NEVER has been my rest, BECAUSE it is polluted!"

"If we could but support your head a little in any way!"

"Yes; but you see you cannot, so that must be borne. Ah! at the beginning of my affliction I said I know it is all ordered in love. Yes; but do I feel the same now, that it has come twice as heavy as I ever expected it! Do my actions show that I feel it to be so? Words are very little indeed; what do the actions prove, that is the point? Have I that resignation, that patience, that shows that I do still believe it to be in LOVE?"

CHAPTER XXX.

JUNE, the loveliest month at the farm, had brightened upon it; the season was one of more than usual perfection; no later frosts, or nipping winds, or blight, had marred the natural beauty of the spot; the garden and the fields, every bank and hedgerow, and every tree around the place, reminded of the most descriptive words ever uttered of nature's loveliness—"Solomon, in all his glory, was not arrayed like one of these." All the young life of the farm sported around it, the playful foals in one near field beside their mothers, a little herd of young calves in the green orchard in the valley beside the stream, and the lambs upon the nearer hills; the fruit-trees laden with blossom, and the air filled with the song of the birds—one joyous circle of life and beauty all around. But what so beautiful as that white head within the home—bowed low in suffering, yet pouring forth its song of victory? What so beautiful as the circle of tearful tenderest care that ever visibly surrounded it?—What, save the unseen angel's presences who ministered in joyful exultation. Oh! Christian faith, and hope, and charity, can any see you shining and not believe your source to be divine? " If multitudes die joyless, and disappear from the upper air as if sinking in a stagnant pool, it is not the effect of Christianity."

Stephen loved to feel the odorous balmy air blow on him; it would wave his long white hair, and cool his calm decided furrowed brow. He smiling said to Mabel, "You have come to see the pleasant spring at last. But I shall never go out into it more; my next path must be an ASCENDING one!" Then he paused, his smile had passed into a look of deep solemnity, and when he spoke again it was to repeat the two first verses of his Sabbath psalm—

"As the heart panteth after the water-brooks, so panteth my soul after Thee, O God.

"My soul thirsteth for God, for the living God; when shall I come and appear before God?"

"Don't I know now a little what the poor thirsty animal feels when he pants after natural water? and if I have no such feeling in going to God, what can I expect?"

The thought of his earthly home, the home of all his life, seemed constantly to refresh him like a beautifully-pictured scene, to which his words were continually referring.

"God has blessed us with family union. I think there are none that can say to the contrary of that. We have had one mind and one heart, so there has been no feeling I am master, and you are not; but each one to mention what we think, and then if you don't approve it I will not say it again. Such union is not a common thing, I think?"

"It is heavenly grace above earthly feeling," Mabel replied; and then, as she sat on her childhood's crimson stool beside his arm-chair, she repeated the one hundred and thirty-third psalm—"Behold, how good and how pleasant, for brethren to dwell together in unity." No response ever delighted Stephen like a seal to his own words from the Bible; his countenance brightened as he listened, and when the last clause came, "for there the Lord commanded the blessing—life for evermore," he said, with all the emphasis he could command, "Well, it could not go further than that."

Their strong natural sympathies, and unselfish feeling, made all Margery's children most skilful as nurses. Few could equal Elsie in tenderest devotion to the sick, and Philip and Matthew stood beside her in this. Never once was a noise made by any inadvertence, though every wind of heaven had always entered the home at will, and now waited, as usual, to lay a boisterous hand upon doors whose wont it was to stand always open. You scarcely heard a footfall, though the parlor boards were uncarpeted. And the watchers through the night, always three in number, denied themselves sleep in his room, "Lest," as Matthew said, "it should trouble him to see us get that so easy, which no help of man can bring him." And in Stephen there was none of that unconscious receiving, that dims the glow of self-devotion. The smile that lit his eye, the tones of blessing that faintly fell, and the instant cheer when a little respite came, these kept that long and most unusually arduous nursing, bright, tender, and strong. The outward sternness of aspect and tone that was, at times, natural to his character, never showed itself in his illness. He was not now contending with the world, or with what he felt to be contrary to the thing that was right; he had around him only the truth and piety that blessed his home, and he was as one who laid aside his armour, meekly to endure, and tenderly to respond. "He is like nothing but a lamb!" said Elsie, as she wept apart; and as Mabel stood near, unseen, she heard him say to his family, "I may express a wish, but you must know whether it is to be attended to or not. That must be left to you now; I consider you must now know best. I think my knowledge but as one shade to three compared to your's." Then adding with his questioning smile, "I don't know that I can lie lower than that!"

Exhaustion, and the difficulty of taking food, were alike painful. Elsie had pressed him to try more than his usual spoonfuls, and the agonizing distress came on. When it had passed, Mabel went in, and instead of finding him cast down, he said to her, "I have been overdone with loving-kindness! Since you were here, Elsie thought she had a little dinner all for me; done very nice, and that was very nice; and I was to eat it, and get the advantage of you all, having my dinner first!

But that would not do: no, 'tis no use; only may God do whatever pleaseth Him, I know it will be all in love! Only may He give me grace to submit to His will in all things."

Finding them linger around him, after his revival from so terrible a struggle, he added, "Now go and take your dinner, and God bless your food to your soul's health, for Jesus Christ's sake!" Seeing unwilling faces, he put his finger, with his look of playful decision, upon the hand-bell beside him, "What! do you think that staying here you can be nearer to me than that bell-handle?"

Such words as these, which constantly fell from him, may appear, when recorded, light as the spray of the fountain, but yet they kept verdant the circle around him, as that spray does the grass — however scorching the summer. And they sparkled as the drops in which the light is seen shining, testifying no less truly to the depth and purity of his piety, than did the "greater things" of his more active life. And those who can look back on times of personal suffering, are happy if they have learned to endure with like patience and love. It is not so easy a task, as that any need think it unworthy attention. And it is a Christianity that conforms to the image of Him who, through His last conflict with the sufferings of nature, still watched over the comforts of those who attended Him. Stephen had disciplined his spirit by the divine precepts of his God, and also by his filial reverence, in years when the impetuous fire of youth was kindling his native energy. And now, when mortal diseases carried on so fierce and long a conflict with his mortal life, he disciplined his spirit to submit itself, not in patience merely, but in love, and so to rise a conqueror still, through Him that loved him.

Yet he had his times of depression — not times of doubt, for never one unbelieving thought seemed to pass between his spirit and his God; but times in which his whole soul was humbled in repentance and confession. They had all been sitting silent, while he they watched appeared absorbed in thought and prayer, yet with an unwonted sadness on his face. Weariness was alone sufficient to account for his aspect — unable even to lean back in his chair night or day, unable even to bear the slight relief of a cushion under his feet — any change from the one erect posture giving increase of distress. Slowly and faintly, with laboured respiration, he at length said, "You see I have NO STRENGTH, but He has said His everlasting arms shall be my strength; He says they are underneath me, and they shall bear and carry me, and what can I want more? Ah! but He tells us in Isaiah, that we won't take hold of His strength; and we know very well what His strength is — it is the Lord Jesus Christ Himself! and He says, let him take hold of my strength! but He says we won't! there is none, He says, that stirreth up himself to take hold! I know my own want of faith!" He had tried to rise, as he was wont to do, in the current of Divine truth, but his exhausted body weighed down his aspiring spirit, and bursting into tears he said—thinking of his early struggles after a righteousness of his own, "O that I could write my past sin and folly out so plain that he that runs might read it! I speak of myself, but we must each one apply it. God speaks to all of us, yes all; He says, there is none that stirreth up himself to take hold of ME! and He must know! And what then shall we do when we have to pass over the swellings of Jordan? do we think we can pass over them alone? Ah, but we cannot! Blessed be my Saviour, He has made all my sins to stand up on a heap by the side, so that I have nothing to do but to walk over; He is with me, and His rod and His staff they comfort me!"

Then pondering, he added, "I hope you won't think that because I speak from the Scripture that therefore I feel my knowledge of it to be great. No, I feel that knowledge to be nothing, but as a drop to the ocean!"

"I should have been glad to speak once more to the poor men, but I cannot. He who taught me is willing to teach them. I send them to Him!" then adding with a smile, "and I KNOW He never turned a bad scholar out of His school!"

Stephen's tears were always an affecting sight, because of his naturally firm and intrepid character. They had often flowed unseen by man, but now, when never left, others beheld him weep. Elsie, thinking it exhaustion, would bring him some smallest quantity of liquid, such as might be possible for him to take, but though at other times he tried to take all that was offered, he would never receive anything to stay his tears; he seemed to consider them the tribute of his heart to God. "No; it is not wine I want. My strength is not rivetted by this world's things! God says, 'My strength shall be made perfect in weakness!' Wait awhile, and He will revive me!" "What, did our Saviour never weep? and may not I?" Then after a while he said, "Well, perhaps there never was one entered Heaven without getting a slip as he went in, that he might be like the poor Publican, and only say, 'God be merciful to me a sinner!' I know that I have no good, nothing but sin!" After this confession so earnestly made, the same bright calm gradually encircled him again.

He had walked through life in such constant communion with the Word of his God, that he never seemed to have need of other counsellors. Whatever state he was in you had but to leave him a little time, sitting silent beside him, and the deep well-springs of comfort were sure to spring up within his own soul. Beautiful these uttered musings were, when after being cast down he reasoned aloud with himself, "But is not that fountain open to cleanse from ALL sin? And is there not my Saviour's righteousness—the righteousness of Christ for me? And is there not that Holy Spirit to sanctify?"

"Is it not written as plain as possible, 'Our God is a consuming fire?" I not only cannot go to Him in myself, I cannot so much as look to Him, only in and through my

Saviour; washed in His blood, clothed in His righteousness, and sanctified by His Spirit. Oh, that He may sprinkle me with His atoning blood! I do not find that faith in me that I want. I consider one of the **greatest** instances of faith to be that poor Syro-phœnician woman, to think how all things went against **her,** and that even the Blessed Saviour should check her! **Yes**; but it was He who **gave** her that strong faith; and He did it for our sakes who come after her; and then to hear Him turn and say, 'O woman, great is thy faith!'"

"LOOKING UNTO JESUS! Sure that is no hard requirement; it is a thing simple and easy to be understood. He will take me in His arms, and carry me unto the Father. None but he could do it; for He says, 'No man cometh unto the Father but by Me.'"

His weakness increasing, Philip said, "I will not give in but what something might be done;" and fetching his carpenter's saw, he sawed off the lower legs of the small **bed, at** which the sufferer had only looked for so many **weeks,** sometimes with a silent **weary** longing that was **more touching** than uttered words. He had never breathed **the** wish that he could feel its refreshment. His mother's principle was his even in this extremity, "When you cannot speak good of God's dealings, hold your peace until you can." Once, worn with fatigue and **his** continual cough, he gently said, "Oh, if I could but get rid of this cough!" but then added, with his patient smile, "I suppose if any of us were suffering, we should

17

like to have it our own way! I want to feel so that I may say, Thy will be done as in heaven so on earth." So deep and universal were the lessons his simple language breathed.

The bedstead was now made a slope, on which Philip thought it possible that suffering frame might find rest. They lifted him in their arms, wrapped in his militia cloak, and laid him down. Each aching muscle sank into repose; he closed his eyes, and looked as if sleep or death would instantly enfold him in its rest. The scene was striking and strange; the inclined plane on which he lay, raised like a bank, his long white hair above his soldier's cloak, with the face of death more strongly marked than Mabel—so familiar with its aspect—had ever seen it before; the anxious manly forms that stood around, with Elsie's face, who, as she wiped her tears, cast on him looks of such devoted love! and nature's landscape through the open window; nothing looked like the chamber of sickness, rather did he seem

"like a warrior taking his rest,
With his martial cloak around him."

All were silently rejoicing in realized success, but in a few minutes incessant cough came on, and he had again to be raised and seated in his chair. Mabel uttered a lamentation, hers the only voice that spoke, but he at intervals, as the cough allowed him, gently answered, "So many things meet together in my illness, that I cannot get rest.

But then if it had not been so it might have held me all the longer, but by these all meeting together so at once, it may be that it is to make the shorter work for me; so I suppose I must still say of Him that ordered it for me, 'He hath done all things well!'" and he raised his inquiring smile, unable to look up for more than a moment, for Mabel to echo his trust. He waited a little while in silence, then, with the smile of God's peace upon his lips, he said, "Well, I suppose that sleep will never come again, so I must work on by degrees, and wait until I am perfected in Zion!" Mabel had laid his Bible on her lap, and seeing him looking towards it, she said, "You know what this Book is?" On which he smiling answered, "That is the master of all books!" And then expecting her to read, and as if wishing to say something by way of comfort to his brothers, who had seen their effort fail to give him rest, he said, "Philip and Matthew are always happy when they think I am well attended to, in the Scriptures and prayer, even though they be away; and when they think I am not well attended to in that way, they are not happy!" So gently did he bring their sad thoughts back to the blessed fact, that "Man liveth not by bread (or rest) alone, but by every word that proceedeth out of the mouth of the Lord, doth man truly live."

"I want you to read to me and talk to me; and though I don't take any notice, don't you think that I do not hear, because I do, and understand it too. God has promised to give me the hearing ear, and the understanding heart, and I think he has in some measure done that for me."

"You are a little better now?"

"Yes; you see you have been all taking care of me, and reading to me, and that quieted me. Surely no one can be so well off as I am!"

"How great must the fulfilment of that promise have been, 'My God shall supply all your need,' which could enable one under such circumstances, with all truth of feeling, to cheer those around him by saying, 'Surely no one can be so well off as I am!'"

"There is one thing I am afraid of, and I don't know how to come at the knowledge of it, whether I may not at times have had a complaining, murmuring spirit? It was not my wish, but Satan is busy with his devices."

"It seems to me as if I could not hold long; but I don't know, and I don't want to know. Oh, I think it a great mercy that the Lord has taken from me all SELF-KNOW-LEDGE. I have none, no more than a little child, and I don't want, for into Thy Hand I have commended my spirit, O Lord, Thou God of Truth! And I hope my blessed Saviour will make intercession for me, and say, 'Deliver him from going down to the pit, I have found a ransom.' He has promised that He will, and hath He said, and shall He not do it? hath He spoken, and shall He not bring it to pass? so that how can I fear what any may say against me, when He says I have found a ransom!"

"But you need not be troubled when you think I am dying. There will be nothing to be seen then (alluding to the great distress of his present attacks). I shall only fall asleep like a little child—nothing harder than that—somewhere, where you lay me down, nothing more than that!"

This prophetic word was not at this time to be fulfilled. A great apparent aggravation of illness came on, in another form of disease, but though temporal hope was dead, life was not, and the very aggravation proved a step to partial restoration. Stephen revived; again laid down and slept, and his sleep was sweet to him; again joined the social circle; again visited the sick and dying—who blessed his footstep as they heard it fall upon their threshold stone. His glory and joy was to be yet fuller and deeper, at the appearing of our Lord Jesus Christ. Then suddenly a gentle stupor came over him, they carried him to the favourite great chamber, laid him in that place of blessed memories, watched beside him day and night. He could not speak, and Elsie said that "it was well he could not, for his good words would have made it more than they could have stood up under!" He lay in utterable prayer, calm, peaceful, and adoring. Then from the spot on which, fifty years before, he had wrestled with God for a blessing for his young dying brother, wrestled and prevailed, and won also a personal, a household, an eternal blessing—from that very spot in the earliest morning of December 31st, 1860, like a child in its slumber, his spirit passed to eternal rest. Faith had made him a threefold conqueror; over the world, over himself, and over death. Thanks be to God which giveth us the VICTORY through our Lord JESUS CHRIST! So beautiful he looked in death, "as if corruption were already passed!" He had chosen his own place of rest beyond the chancel window, for the long line of household graves beside his parents' had all been filled from his own home. Ten of his labourers bore him up that green hill side; and many mourners followed him—for whom unnumbered tears still fall. The chancel window rose in full view from the maternal home; and only the churchyard hedge divided his grassy bed from the garden of the church farm. "I never step in or out," his sister said, "but I turn a look upon it!" There amidst the home of all his life, and the sleeping forms of many led by him to a Saviour's feet, he sleeps in joyful hope of the resurrection of the just.

www.ingramcontent.com/pod-product-compliance
Lightning Source LLC
Chambersburg PA
CBHW032017220426
43664CB00006B/275